WHOREDOM
IN KIMMAGE

Books by Rosemary Mahoney

The Early Arrival of Dreams

Whoredom in Kimmage

WHOREDOM IN KIMMAGE

Irish Women Coming of Age

ROSEMARY MAHONEY

Anchor Books
DOUBLEDAY
New York London Toronto Sydney Auckland

AN ANCHOR BOOK

PUBLISHED BY DOUBLEDAY

a division of Bantam Doubleday Dell Publishing Group, Inc.
1540 Broadway, New York, New York 10036

ANCHOR BOOKS, DOUBLEDAY, and the portrayal of an anchor are trademarks of
Doubleday, a division of Bantam Doubleday Dell Publishing Group, Inc.

Whoredom in Kimmage was originally published in hardcover by Houghton Mifflin
Company in 1993. The Anchor Books edition is published by arrangement with
Houghton Mifflin Company.

Library of Congress Cataloging-in-Publication Data
Mahoney, Rosemary.
Whoredom in Kimmage : Irish women coming of age / Rosemary
Mahoney.—1st Anchor Books ed.
p. cm.
1. Women—Ireland—Social conditions—Case studies. 2. Ireland—
Social conditions—Case studies. I. Title.
HQ1600.3.M32   1994
305.42'09417—dc20   94-11848
CIP

ISBN 0-385-47450-4
Copyright © 1993 by Rosemary Mahoney
All Rights Reserved
Printed in the United States of America
First Anchor Books Edition: September 1994

3   5   7   9   10   8   6   4   2

AUTHOR'S NOTE

To protect the privacy of individuals, I have changed the names used in this book with
the exception of Jean O'Brien and public figures.

For Nona Rohan Mahoney,
my mother

ACKNOWLEDGMENTS

I am grateful to Franklin Curley, M. B. Whitaker, and Cray Stein for their kind assistance, to Peg Anderson for refining the text, to Estela Abosch for her insights and many forbearances, and to Betsy Lerner, my editor, who gave her wit, enthusiasm, and intelligence so generously to this book.

Contents

Preface xi

Preface

WHEN I WAS SEVENTEEN I spent the summer on Martha's Vineyard working as domestic factotum to the playwright Lillian Hellman. I was as ornery at seventeen as Lillian Hellman was at seventy-three. We argued our way through that summer, argued about everything from the rules of the road to the temperature of the day to herbs and vegetables. ("*You* obviously didn't grow up in the country, Rosemary." "How is that obvious, Miss Hellman?" "You don't seem to be able to recognize vegetables." "What haven't I recognized?" "Mint, for one." "I grew up in the country. Mint isn't a vegetable.") Once, when I returned from the market with the wrong jar of pickles, Lillian sucked on her cigarette, boosted her formidable nose into the air, and said, "You're smart, Rosemary, but you should learn to write things down."

I *was* writing things down. Every night when released from the scullery, I went to my room and wrote things down. I was unhappy and exhausted, and I charted my woes with a pencil and pad. *She's stingy. She buys Jim's vodka, the cheapest there is, and makes me funnel it into a Smirnoff bottle to trick her guests.*

And then one evening I overheard Lillian saying to her friend William Styron, "I see the little Irish girl has set out the wrong dinner plates again."

The remark—which amounted to an epithet—conjured images of a feckless, carrot-topped rustic with a camel's long lashes and a blush that traveled from throat to freckled hairline, awash in a sea of plates the likes of which she had never had the privilege to be confused by before. And in spite of Lillian's ire, the remark delighted me. At fifteen I had, by dint of my Irish grandparents, requested and acquired Irish citizenship. Though I was born in Boston and grew up there, Irish was always the way I thought of myself and the way I wanted others to think of me. I *was* an Irish girl—Lillian Hellman got that right.

❖

MY GREAT-AUNT Elizabeth Fraher had a long, expressive face, was tall, never married, and wore black dresses and a wide-brimmed hat. Like her sister, my grandmother, who died when I was an infant, Lizzie had come to Boston from Ireland in her early thirties. She was a bewitching storyteller who could walk into a room and, without undue effort, win the attention of every person in it. Though my six older siblings and I vied for Lizzie's attention, she managed to make each of us feel like the only child in the world. She would slip you something forbidden and desirable—a dime, say, or a piece of chocolate—while the others weren't looking, and suborn you in a whisper of exaggerated severity to "tell no one about this." She was the most exciting person we knew. But, though she was famous for her warmth and her sense of humor, I have yet to see, among hundreds of photographs of her, a single one in which she is smiling. In every photograph she looks slightly pained. As a child I was not aware of this. I knew only that Lizzie was to be trusted as my own mother was trusted.

Lizzie's house was the safest place on earth. It was filled with Irish information: two Irish flags crossed above a mirror in her hallway, an Irish doll named Pegeen lying in a wooden cradle, holy water in a dish by the door, an alleged piece of the true cross in a pyx, a portrait of Pope John XXIII, a German shepherd named Bran after Finn Mac-Cool's Irish wolfhound, rounds of soda bread with crosses slashed into their faces, and a damask tablecloth that had a shamrock pattern woven subtly into it—you could see the shamrocks only when the light struck the cloth from the right angle. The first thing you saw when you walked through the door was a series of framed portraits of the Irish revolutionaries—Joseph Mary Plunkett, Eamonn Ceannt, Thomas MacDonagh, Sean MacBride, James Connolly, and Padraig Pearse—and a framed copy of *Poblacht na hEireann*, the Irish Republican Proclamation of 1916. Lizzie and my grandmother were staunch republicans and friends of the revolutionaries. Lizzie had harbored various escaped Irish revolutionaries in her home, among them Liam Mellows, the editor of the Proclamation, who was later executed in Dublin. It was Mellows who had planted the hedges in front of Lizzie's house.

Lizzie told us about Ballylanders, the Limerick village she and her ten siblings had left behind. We heard how Lizzie skipped school and caught trout in a stream with her bare hands and how she shaped a hideout for herself in a thick hedge. We heard about her donkey, the priest, the Galty Mountains, Limerick City, the Golden Vale, Miss Condon the schoolteacher, and the village idiot. We heard about fairies and banshees and triple rainbows. We heard ghost stories told in speech scattered with modified Irish words and phrases. (If a child cried wildly, she cried "gafook" [*ag fuachas*], a too-generous person was "flahool" [*flaithiuil*], and when you got a shock, you got a "croost" [*crusta*]. There were always parties in progress at Lizzie's house, with a lot of Irish people singing sad Irish songs. If you stayed long enough, you began to think you could hear a donkey's little hooves clip-clopping up Nahant Avenue.

Because I loved Lizzie, I loved Ireland. It was a place I was deeply aware of but knew nothing about, something I possessed but couldn't grasp. In our own house we had a shelf of Irish books that had belonged to my grandfather. Some were written in Irish, a strange script like Cyrillic. I stared at the books until I understood them; that I couldn't read them was irrelevant.

�※�

ONE NIGHT IN 1968, I sat with Lizzie in her house watching a TV movie about the *Titanic*. I was seven years old; Lizzie was eighty-six. On the black-and-white screen the sinking ship tipped at a forty-five-degree angle, and a grand piano careered across the ship's dance floor and crashed against a wall. That was, of course, terribly funny. I guffawed at the screen, and before I knew what was happening Lizzie reached out and slapped the backs of my hands with stunning force. I looked at her, astonished. Lizzie had never hit me before. She had never so much as raised her voice at me. I pressed the backs of my stinging hands to the O of my mouth and cried.

" 'Tis nothing to laugh at," Lizzie said. "People died."

I didn't know anything about people dying and didn't care; I was ashamed only that I had angered the person I loved. Later, when I asked my mother why Lizzie had slapped me, she told me that Lizzie had planned to sail from Ireland on that ship, but a chance event had delayed her a week. The last people to climb aboard the *Titanic* at Cobh Harbor were people Lizzie knew.

❈

I PASSED my miserable seventeenth summer with Lillian Hellman, daydreaming about Ireland. Faced with a dreaded final year at boarding school, I had contrived to spend the school year in Ireland studying Irish Gaelic. I wanted to escape familiar things that had grown alien, to surround myself with alien things that had been familiar for years. I often felt that with Lizzie's death, when I was eight, I had been robbed of what belonged to me. At that time it was fixed in my mind that Ireland was the one place where I would feel comfortable.

And I was right. When I arrived in Ireland I felt as at home as I had in Lizzie's house, and this had as much to do with the pretty distortions that had trickled down to me on Nahant Avenue as with the reality of the country itself. I listened to Irish people talking, and I understood them; I understood what lay beneath their words, what humor, what rancor, what frustration, vibrance, begrudgery, intelligence, and fear. I felt I was among people I knew. In Irish faces I saw faces I knew and was related to. In a Dublin tearoom one afternoon I saw a woman who looked so much like my mother that I followed her into the street. I studied the Irish language — a particularly strange and difficult one — and it sounded familiar to me. It was an eerie thrill to come across the stray Irish words that Lizzie used to utter and to recognize them. In finding things out about Ireland, I was finding things out about myself.

I was particularly fascinated by the way Irish women talked to each other. They seemed to have a secret among themselves, to know everything there was to know about each other. They had a habit of whispering, as though everything they said was scandalous and private. And they were contradictory. They colluded, then criticized each other. They helped and hindered each other. They were soft and strong at once. They liked men yet were separate from them. They were subordinate in the society, and yet they had remarkable power and control. They were disrespected but feared, fearful but frightening.

※

IN 1991 I returned to Ireland. I wanted to learn more about the women and to write about them. I saw Sinead O'Connor's face on the covers of American magazines and thought to myself, This is unlikely. Mary Robinson had been elected as the first woman president of Ireland, and that seemed twice as unlikely. Something in Ireland that was directly related to women was changing, and I wanted to know what it was. I spent six months in Dublin and four months in the village of Corofin in West Clare, and I talked to the people I met. I met Irish women from all walks of life. I had lunch with the Irish Housewives Association, sunbathed naked with the women on Dublin's Bull Wall, talked with Dublin fortunetellers, nuns, abortion activists, poets, students, lesbians, Jews, street venders, and schoolgirls. I talked with Irish poet Eavan Boland and President Mary Robinson.

In my conversations and travels I learned that a book about Irish women would also have to be a book about Irish men, for a large part of the tale of Irish women lies in their absences. Women have been virtually absent from politics, the church, business, the courts of justice, and the pubs, the central point of Irish social life. In learning about Irish women I was also learning about Irish men, for the women often seemed to be engaged in a response to men. As separate as men and women are in Ireland, it is difficult to separate them.

The stories in this book combine to tell the tale of women in contemporary Irish society and, by association, the tale of the society itself. As Mary Robinson said at Trinity College, "In a society where the rights and potential of women are constrained, no man can be truly free. He may have power, but he will not have freedom."

In Ireland, the rights and potential of women *are* still constrained, and the men are *not* truly free, and that's what this book is about.

PART

I

The Animal Show

WHEN I ENTERED Dillon's Pub late one rainy October afternoon, the publican, Francis MacNamara, began drawing a pint of Guinness before I could ask for it. He was pleased to see me—I could read that in his eyes—yet he remained expressionless, stared into the glass in his hand as he waited for the stout to settle, and did not speak. His large false teeth seemed to be hurting him, and he ground them gently, as if to ease the pain.

The pub was dark that Saturday afternoon, lit only by the dim window light and by the coal fire in the hearth across the room. Four middle-aged men, two of whom I had seen before, sat silently at the bar in their Wellington boots, woolen jackets, and caps; their faces were obscured by shadow. In this small rural village of five hundred people the odds were excellent that these four men were related by blood. Certainly they had known each other since childhood. They looked tired and bored and mildly self-conscious. They smoked their filterless cigarettes wearily, squinting with each inhalation, as though smoking sickened them. They drank their Guinness in a lunging fashion, opening their mouths wide, fitting in as much of the lip of the glass as the mouth would hold, tipping their heads back, and swallowing hugely. They made drinking seem more an obligation than a pleasure.

The village butcher sat at the end of the bar, drinking an expensive bottled beer. He wore a black leather ski glove on his right hand—the hand he lifted his glass with—and from that glove its mate dangled annoyingly, attached at the wrist by a metal clip. Each time the butcher lifted his arm to drink, the loose glove flopped against his chest like a dead fish. When he pushed his empty glass across the counter, the glove dragged lamely after it. When he straightened the cap on his head, the glove struck him in the face. The butcher didn't seem to notice. Drink seemed to have dulled his intelligence. He had a sleepy, molish face and enormous heavy-lidded eyes that seemed on the verge of closing. His tiny mouth twisted weirdly off toward his right ear and lent him an amused, abashed expression. From what I had witnessed in the two weeks I'd been here in Corofin, the butcher spent more time in this pub than in his shop. His name, I knew, was Eamon. He was reputed to be swimming in money.

The butcher smiled moonily at me from his end of the bar, baring two exceedingly long front teeth, and said something in a West Clare accent so knotted and spicy and steeped in beer that it was thoroughly unintelligible. I gathered he was addressing me and asked him to repeat himself. His second utterance was more muddled than the first. I turned to the man beside me and with considerable embarrassment asked, "What did he say?"

The fat-faced man looked startled, then deeply pleased to have been spoken to. "He only said, miss, that he passed you out this afternoon on the road to Rath."

I said "Oh" and waved affably to the butcher. His face opened up into a sheepish and delighted smile. He ducked his head and waved uncertainly back at me, the loose glove slapping against his forearm.

The room smelled not unpleasantly of stale beer and coal smoke. Francis put my pint on the counter and murmured softly, "Now, miss." I counted out one pound sixty-eight from a fistful of coins and slid the money across the counter to him. He stared for a second at the coins, then, turning his sallow face slightly away from me, he pushed them discreetly back to me and walked away. I must have looked puzzled, for the man beside me gave me an encouraging nudge with his elbow and nodded coyly at the coins as if to say, *Take them back again before he changes his mind!*

I had been in Ireland for six months, living mostly in Dublin, and I knew the unspoken rules of the Irish pub well enough to know that I was breaking most of them. I was a woman and I was alone. I was drinking stout instead of lager, a pint instead of a half pint. I was trying to pay for my own drink and, since there was no real lounge in this pub, I had no choice but to sit with the men. These were things a woman, traditionally, should not do, but I had a strong sense that in Ireland most rules had been created precisely that they might be broken, and here in Corofin no one had yet objected either to my presence in the pub or to my behavior, least of all Francis MacNamara.

I sat near the fire in one of two large wooden armchairs and turned the chair just enough that I could watch the men at the bar out of the corner of my eye. In the other armchair a very old man sat drinking a glass of ale. He blinked his watery eyes at me, valiantly trying to clear his clouded head, unsure perhaps of what he was seeing. He sipped from his glass, then tried to put it down on the stone floor by his feet, but repeatedly he miscalculated the distance to the floor, expecting the glass to touch bottom long before it actually did, which caused him to lower the glass in slow, comical stages.

Walking with a stiffness beyond his years, Francis MacNamara came out from behind the bar and sat near me on a low stool. He sighed, raised his hands to the fire, and without looking up from his feet he asked shyly, "How are you since? Everything all right over?"

He meant over in Ballyportry Castle, where I was living. The castle was a fifteenth-century keep of Norman design and Irish construction, a five-story, ten-room fortified stone tower taller than anything in the area and visible from a great distance. It stood a mile outside Corofin, within view of two small cottages, and for most of the year it was unoccupied. The castle belonged to friends of mine to whom it had been willed several years before, and it worried Francis that I was staying there alone. When I first met him, two weeks earlier, and told him I'd be living in the castle for a few months, he had said with bald authority, "You certainly will not be," as though he knew something I didn't. Simply, he didn't believe me. When I finally persuaded him that I would in fact be living in Ballyportry alone, he said almost irritably, "But would you not be frightened in a place like that all by yourself?"

"No, " I said, "I wouldn't really be frightened."

"But I mean *frightened*," Francis said. "*Frightened*. Would you not be *frightened*," as though perhaps I had misunderstood the meaning of the word.

"Frightened of what?"

Francis considered what. I could see he wasn't sure. The very idea of Ballyportry Castle frightened him. I asked him if he was thinking perhaps of ghosts. He said, "Well . . . I guess ghosts is what I do mean. Ghosts, like. Or ghosts. Or I don't know what."

Francis MacNamara was fifty-eight years old and, like an alarming number of men in rural Ireland, had never married. He was small, with the graceful slenderness of a young woman. His strong, angular features held elements of sadness and skepticism. He had large, slightly popped brown eyes, and he combed his oiled, graying hair straight back from his forehead. His speech was slow and drawling, and there was a great sense of confidentiality in everything he said, for he spoke with his head inclined toward his listener, and often, when shifting the direction of his ideas, he said softly and urgently, "But come here to me," which was the Irish way of saying, "Listen carefully and keep this between us." Francis sighed heavily when he spoke, as though he had been too long deprived of fresh air. He had a gentle manner, was serious and curious, and his mind worked in a ruminating, solving way. He had myriad questions and few answers, and he often began a conversation by saying, "Now, I been thinking . . ."

Francis engaged in unending speculation on the most improbable subjects. His favorite topic was the Ice Age, inspired by the fact that the village of Corofin sat at the edge of the Burren, 250 square kilometers of exposed limestone and one of Ireland's eeriest and most beautiful geological wonders. On my first visit to Dillon's Pub Francis had said thoughtfully to me, "You see, miss, it is known that the Ice Age was up in Mullaghmore, and Ireland was all under water at one time, and they reckon it will be again."

Mullaghmore, a weirdly pretty limestone mountain ten miles north of Corofin, was at that moment the focus of a bitter controversy between conservationists concerned for the delicate balance of the strange ecological forces at work there and local business people who wanted to build a tourist center on it.

Francis had a theory, based on "authoritative reports," that when the ocean came in and covered Ireland again, it would come in first over Willbrook, an area only a mile or two from Corofin. He spoke as though this would be happening soon, and I could never tell whether he thought this was Corofin's good fortune or bad.

At the age of nineteen Francis had left Corofin for England, and for thirty-four years he had worked in the foundry of British Leyland Motorworks. In 1985, when he was laid off from his job, he returned to Corofin for a visit and stayed, taking on, somewhat by accident, the management of Dillon's Pub, which belonged to his nephew. Francis lived in rooms above the pub. He confessed that he still felt unsettled here in Corofin, felt he was only here on an extended visit. There were remnants of British mannerisms in his accent.

Like many Irish people, Francis had a sharply honed awareness of—and concern for—the flaws and shortcomings of his own race. In one of our earlier conversations he had told me plaintively that he believed the Irish living in England were more generous and industrious than the Irish who had stayed in Ireland. "They were more helpful towards each other across in England," he had said, "more considerate towards each other, and no one would see anyone down. But here everyone is out to do you. We are a bad race of people. You see these Asian people? They help one another in business, and the Indians. But the Irish begrudge each other. They do. I didn't realize it until I came back home. I went away when I was barely eighteen, and I didn't have any views. When you're eighteen you're only interested in a job. We had no money for drink back then. We were never in a pub before we left home. We had no money. You'd be lucky to get a packet of fags at that time. But I became very aware of it when I came back. The Irish here. They really are out to do you as much as they can. You won't get a fair day's work for a fair day's pay."

With this Francis held his hand up, thumbnail pressed into the first crease in the index finger, an Irish gesture that indicates pettiness and parsimony, an illustration of just how *little* has been offered. He carried on in his slow, confiding fashion, "A fair day's work is gone. How is it they work so hard in England but they won't do here? If they worked half as hard here as they do in England, we'd be one of the best countries in the world. Do you know what a story in the *Irish Press* said here one time? And I believe it was true: if the Dutch were in Ireland, they'd own half of Europe, and if the Irish were in Holland, they'd drown. Honest to God, 'tis true. They'd drown. If the Dutch did have Ireland, they would be controlling half Europe. Everything we have here in Ireland is imported. We have no real factories. Think of what we could do with a factory."

At one time there was a small factory just behind Dillon's Pub along the river Fergus, a diamond factory, whose stone building had since been converted into a private home, owned by a South African businessman. The same man also owned the mansion house next to the factory, the biggest and most beautiful house in the village.

※

I NEVER HEARD Francis use the word "alcoholic" to describe himself, but it was clear that he believed his desire for drink was, no matter how he tried to overcome it, uncontrollable. He had raised the subject with me one day by remarking matter-of-factly and in response to nothing, "I'm off the drink just now." He explained that if he took even one sip of beer, he wouldn't be able to stop. "In no time I'd be up to the top shelf," he said, rolling his eyes up toward the shelf of rum and whiskey bottles above the back of the bar. "And when I'd be on the drink, I'd be giving away free drinks hither and thither. I'd be tossing the customers the key to the storeroom, the key to the kingdom."

Francis had been drinking off and on for years. Once he'd stopped for sixteen months. Another time he planned to stop for twelve, succeeded, and extended it to thirteen, "just to prove my point." The time he'd managed to stop for sixteen months he was delighted with himself, but one day he drew a pint for a customer, and as soon as the man sat down and sipped from the glass, Francis picked up another glass and poured himself one. "If you had told me ten minutes before that I'd be drinking a pint ten minutes later, I'd of told you you were cracked," he said.

A pub seemed like a trying place for a self-policing drinker to be working, but Francis said that when his mind was made up, it made no difference to him to be surrounded by alcohol, and when he was not drinking he could keep an eye on his patrons' excesses. Francis often sat by the fire, and the men had to call him out of his seat when they wanted another drink. He displayed little interest in the pub; in fact, he claimed he hated it. He complained that the flagstone floor was too cold, the room was too small, and that women never liked to come into a place like this.

I, for one, thought Dillon's was one of the prettiest and most welcoming pubs I had been in anywhere in Ireland. It was the oldest pub on Corofin's one street, a short, narrow lane dominated by eight other pubs, several tiny houses, a post office, a credit union, and three or four shops. The pub occupied the ground floor of an old stone house that had been roughly plastered and whitewashed — its ancient double-hung windows stood crooked in their warped frames. Inside, the walls of the pub were maroon and turquoise with green trim. Dark wooden beams ran across the low, whitewashed ceiling, which was tinted sepia from years of cigarette smoke. The fireplace was small and shallow, with a vertical grate across its front that kept the coal pressed hard against the bricks at the back of the hearth. Francis's nephew, an antiques dealer in Ennis, had filled the pub with rare furniture and strange artifacts from his shop. The graceful gray marble mantelpiece over the hearth had come from an old mansion house. The wooden armchairs by the fire, caned in a checkerboard pattern of red and white hemp, were more than a hundred years old. On the walls hung numerous framed political cartoons from *Punch*, most of them to do with the grinding relationship between Ireland and England; in these cartoons the Irishmen were always depicted as protohuman, with jutting brows, huge jaws, and dripping fangs. There was a stuffed pheasant under glass on the wall, a mounted fox head over the bathroom door, a stuffed woodcock, and various other novelties displayed about the pub in a ceremonious manner. Behind the mahogany bar was a large green cabinet built into the wall; its many tiny doors opened into compartments, like a Chinese medicinal herb cabinet.

Francis mentioned the antiques only to say that they were altogether too good for the place. He seemed bored, like a man in a state of perpetual waiting. He was dissatisfied, but his many years in the factory had inured him to tedium.

That rainy afternoon Francis raised the subject of ghosts with me again, and I sensed the men at the bar straining to hear our conversation. It was October, and at this time of year strangers were uncommon in Corofin; a newcomer, however dull, was a point of burning interest. The men did not turn their heads to look at us, but they were listening; their faces betrayed their concentration. It was impossible not to eavesdrop in this small, low-ceilinged room.

I explained to Francis that I was not afraid of ghosts, which I believed was true. So far I hadn't been truly frightened by anything that had happened in the castle. I slept easily, though at night I heard a fabulous parade of noises: the wind pushed screaming voices through the windows, doors rattled mightily on their wood and stone hinges, the timber floors spoke as they settled, and at dawn and twilight, when the temperature of the building changed, there came a soft booming noise, like that of ice shifting on a lake—a dull, resonant sound that surrounded me and seemed to have no exact origin. In bed at night I sometimes heard the velvety flap of bats' wings overhead, and in the morning the gently thumping footsteps of jackdaws hopping across the wooden floor of the vaulted garret above me. I was often awakened in the dead of night by the sudden distressed roaring of cattle in my courtyard, a murderous beseeching so loud the beasts seemed to be in the room with me. I could hear the weird mating whistles of foxes at night and the melancholy songs of night-crying birds. But these noises I knew by heart, and it was only when a new one arrived that I felt frightened.

I did not confess to Francis MacNamara that on my first night in the castle, when I had allowed my mind to indulge in spectral fantasies and unbridled conjecture on the opportunities for ghosts in such a place, I had become paralyzed with fear, a fear so primal and powerful that I sat in a chair for an hour and a half, unable to move, breathing shallowly, afraid I might draw attention to myself. I was certain that if I looked toward the dark east window I would see a leering, disfigured face, beclawed and bloodied hands scraping at the windowpane, a headless woman.

A tattered Irish tricolor hung from the wooden balcony in the room I used most often, and on the tip of its flagstaff were printed the ominous words, "Be Prepared." That scared me. It seemed like portentous advice aimed directly at me. When I first arrived I was afraid to use the radio in case it might drown out the sounds of impending danger, and I found myself doing everything very quietly so as not to attract notice. The wooden doors on the stairway shrieked wickedly when I opened them, and that terrified me, though it was only I pushing them. I hated the dark windows at night and quickly found some wooden boards to shutter them with. In time I learned to block my dark thoughts out. I blocked them out so thoroughly that eventually I couldn't conjure them when I tried, and so it became true that I rarely felt afraid in the castle.

"Well, all right," Francis said, drawing a pouch of tobacco out of his breast pocket, "but I been thinking. Would you not be afraid of people then? I'd be maybe more afraid of people than ghosts. Maybe somebody would try to get into that castle while you were there. That's a dark place out there at night, and not a soul around. And, miss, if you don't mind me saying, you are only one small person."

I had considered the possibility of human intruders. Castles like the one I was living in had been built to keep people out. The walls were five feet thick at the ground level. The lower windows were a mere seven inches wide and set into wide internal embrasures; only an arm or a very small child could fit through one. The wooden door was three inches thick and so heavy I had to use both hands and all my weight to pull it open. Just above the door was the traditional "murder hole," a vertical slit of a window through which the inhabitant could peer down on the visitor and skewer him with a long, sharp sword if necessary. Around the steeply pitched slate roof was a parapet walk with a machicolation extending out above the door. The outer stone wall that surrounded the castle was six or seven feet high and had iron gates and flanking circular turrets. I believed that when I was inside it, the castle was virtually impenetrable. But more than any of its real and calculated defenses, the castle's greatest defense was the terrible effect it had on the imagination. It was dark and oppressive. It was secretive. During a storm it looked thoroughly malevolent. I never thought anyone would have the nerve to approach the place at night with the intention of breaking in. There were no outside lights, and only two houses nearby. Coming upon the looming silhouette of that castle on a dark night was a truly daunting experience, and that was the only time my heart still quickened in fear. In the moments when I stood in the dark, unlocking the door, I fully expected to feel a cold, bony hand seize me by the throat, and I was amused and embarrassed to catch myself affecting an air of confidence and boredom—whistling and yawning like a simpleton—when I returned to the castle at night and walked up the dark dirt pathway to the outer gate. I was not confident and I was never bored.

When I had come to know the place, however, my overriding feeling was that Ballyportry Castle was remarkably peaceful and benign. It had the buoyant self-containment of a ship. Though it was impenetrable, it was not hermetic, and it had a yielding and responsive relationship to the forces of nature. I felt at times as though I were living comfortably out of doors, for whatever was happening outside the castle also seemed to be happening inside it. On heavy, humid days the stairs and walls became damp and slick, as if in imitation of the air. The temperature in the castle changed with startling rapidity. In the upper garret large green weeds and ferns grew in the crevices of the floor-level window ledges, in dirt that had over the centuries gathered there somehow, seventy feet above the ground. Radiant clover grew in the cracks between the large stones of the kitchen wall. Ivy had covered some of the windows and managed to work its way under the panes of glass, into the rooms, and up the walls. When the wind blew hard in a certain direction it capped the enormous chimney and forced smoke down into the rooms. In a storm, rain seeped through the walls, bucketed down the chimney, and gathered in pools on the stone floors. And when the storm was exceptionally heavy, a river of rainwater spun fast down the ninety-three steps of the spiral staircase. Scores of mosquitoes came to life in the kitchen but were sluggish with cold and uninterested in me; they were interested only in light and heat — clouds of them gathered around the light bulbs or lit on the stones of the fireplace. Enormous flies flung themselves crazily against the windowpanes or buzzed up into the vaulted ceilings to bask in whatever warmth had risen there. There were grayling butterflies and brilliant orange and black burnet moths that lay still on the windowsills and came to life only when the morning sun massaged their backs. I often found these butterflies on the floor of the upper living room or on the kitchen counter or on my desk, shredded into tiny bits like brilliant confetti, as though they had exploded in midflight. Bats, drawn to water, perched all night on the toilet seats. Spiders wove magnificent webs across the windows and up into the cathedral ceiling at the top of the castle. Wands of sunlight shot through the narrow windows and split the dusty air, revealing another galaxy of minute activity. Sparrows entered the castle through the chimneys and through a broken window in one of the upper rooms, and they flew down the spiral staircase and back and forth over my head as I worked.

These small things that made their way into the castle were dwarfed by the brutal size of its rooms, and they were welcome; they made me feel that I was not completely alone. When I tried—in vain—to explain that feeling to Francis, a man sitting at the middle of the bar in a yellowish canvas smock like a doctor's coat suddenly spun around on his stool to look at me. He knocked the brim of his cap far back on his head, revealing a high forehead pierced by a sharp widow's peak. His strikingly handsome face was half hidden behind large, heavy-rimmed eyeglasses. He leaned back against the bar, resting his elbows casually on its edge. He was solid and muscular, and his slightly protruding stomach pushed at the front of his sweater. He radiated energy, and it was obvious he had been itching to speak. He pointed a finger at me.

"Miss!" he said loudly, "I know what you are talking about!" the tone of which sounded remarkably like, I know what *I* am talking about. "You like it there in Ballyportry, and you're dead right. May I say 'twas I who did all the plumbing and wiring in that castle?" The man shifted his pointing finger away from me and back toward himself, waiting expectantly for my reply.

Francis MacNamara sighed deeply and immediately got up and returned to his dreaded place behind the bar. He put the radio on loud and switched the ceiling lights on, bathing us all in a soft yellow light.

The man in the cap talked eagerly over the noise of the radio. "'Twas I that got the water to travel all the way up them pipes to the top floor of the castle. That is a hell of a long way to travel, a hell of a hundred feet I don't mind pointing out, miss, to you, and that is how strong I got that water pressure to be. I got it so strong that if you turned the water on in the sink on the top floor and put a mug under it, the water would snap the mug clean off, and you'd be left standing with nothing in your fist but the handle!"

The man interrupted himself long enough to take an athletic slug of his Guinness, then hurried on. "Not only did I do the plumbing and wiring, but it was also I who managed to get that stone bathtub inside in there. Miss, may I ask are you acquainted with the tub I mean?"

I was well acquainted with the tub he meant; it was the largest bathtub I had ever seen—nearly as wide across as a conventional bathtub is long. When I sat in it I could barely see over the edge of it. I could almost lie flat in it with my legs outstretched. A single bed could have fitted inside it. It was straight-sided, solid limestone, and it must have weighed one ton.

The man said, "Miss, that tub came out of an abandoned house over in Rath. The minute Bob Brown saw that tub he had his heart set on it. 'Twas I that got that tub in there for Bob."

Bob Brown was the American architect who had bought the castle in the late fifties, when it was in a state of dereliction, and lived in it for thirty-five years while he carefully restored it. In 1986, when the renovation was nearly complete, Brown died. He had been a friend of my aunt's, and years before, when I was seventeen and a student in Ireland, I had visited him there.

The man in the cap told me that Brown had found a crane company in Cork City that would have charged him five hundred pounds to lift the tub into the castle through the roof, but when the company came to Corofin to study the situation they discovered that it wouldn't be possible to bring the crane close enough to the castle to do the job. "That castle is built on a very little hill—I don't know if you noticed—and they just could not bring the crane close enough."

I had noticed the hill. It looked man-made to me, deliberately constructed to elevate the structure of the castle.

The man shook his head vigorously, remembering. "Ah, God, Bob Brown was stone disappointed when they told him they couldn't get that tub in. He came to me that time and said, 'Conor, if you can find a way to get that tub into the castle, I will pay you one hundred, and I will make you and all your friends drunk down at the pub in Mrs. Mac's.' So, all right, I said, I do not mind if I try it! So what did I do? I got a winch. And I built a steel cage for the tub, and I lifted that sucker up inch by inch, and, Jesus, was I scared the whole feckin' thing would come crashing down upon the lot of us."

Conor's accent was heavy and, in the western Irish manner, he pronounced the *s* in front of a consonant as though it were *sh*, a remnant of Irish Gaelic: the word "stop" became *sh*top and "scattered" became *sh*cattered. Like most polite Irish men within earshot of a woman, Conor transformed "fuck" and "shit" into "feck" and "shite," presumably diluting their vulgarity. He spoke with a constant breathlessness, as though he had just come sprinting into the room, and there was something squashed about his words, as if he were unable to open his mouth wide enough.

The old man who had been blinking steadily at me from the other side of the fire suddenly leaned forward in his armchair and shouted at the top of his voice, "Miss, welcome to Ireland!" He reached over with surprising celerity, grabbed my hand in his, and shouted, "Ah, God, you are welcome to Ireland, dear miss." His grip was so sincere it was crushing. He nearly pulled me out of my seat. He had tremendous strength for such a small man. He said, "I am called by the name of Denny Leary. Come here to me, miss. I want to talk to you." And then he began to sing "Galway Bay" slowly and loudly, his face not three inches from mine, his breath hot on my forehead. He yanked my hand hard against his chest and covered it with his two arthritic ones. He closed his eyes and smiled rapturously as he sang, displaying the toothlessness of an infant. His singing was slow and suffered great gaps where he had forgotten the lyrics. He was dressed in the uniform of the older village men: a rough-cut suit of thick dark wool with short and extremely wide-legged trousers, a white cotton dress shirt buttoned up to the throat, a tweed cap, and heavy brown boots laced up to the shins. The suit was several sizes too large for him and made him look even tinier. When he'd finished his song he said with dazzling depth and sobriety, "Does the unbaptized baby go to limbo? And if so, where is that? Where do we go when we die? God did not create us!"

This sort of apostatic pronouncement was common in rural Ireland. Everywhere and always the Irish are portrayed as exceptionally devout, but I witnessed more blasphemy and disbelief, more light-hearted disregard for the Church here than I had ever seen anywhere else. The Irish country people possessed elements of lawlessness and superstition that were like remnants of Celtic paganism; some of them appeared to believe in ghosts more than they believed in Jesus Christ, and it is possibly only the people's acute awareness of the Church and the way it pervades every aspect of Irish life that the world mistakes for true devotion and piety.

Denny Leary's eyes were tiny and helpless. His little face was lit up by the firelight. "God save us, you are a lovely girl," he said.

Inspired by Denny's familiarity, an ursine farmer slid off his barstool and lumbered across the room to hover over me. He had a huge head and enormous red hands. He peered at me through inch-thick glasses and said in an incongruously soft voice, "Miss, you are

welcome to Ireland. I once won the All-Ireland Drama Festival. Do
you believe me?"

The man knocked on my shoulder with his knuckles, prompting
my approval, and he looked down at me with the spellbound expression of a child peering at a strange and tiny insect.

"Anyhow!" shouted Conor, impatient with these interruptions and
eager to return to his story. "When I was setting up that winch I nearly shlipped off the damn roof, one hundred feet above the ground,
and just as I felt meself shlipping I grabbed onto a pipe that just so
happened to be there, and ended up hanging on by my little finger,
four feet beyond the castle wall!" He held up the little finger as evidence. "And you can ask my brother, miss, if you think that isn't so."

"Who's your brother?" I said.

Conor jerked his thumb over his shoulder to indicate Francis
behind him. Reluctantly Francis said to me, "This is my brother,
Conor MacNamara."

The faces of the men at the bar turned wry and knowing, and they
glanced collusively at each other. Conor removed his cap, dropped it
heavily onto the bar, and talked on, smiling cheerfully. With a faintly
put-upon air Francis picked up the cap and pointedly hung it on a nail
on the wall.

Conor said it was also he who had laid the pipe into the castle for
the Electricity Supply Board. He had had to blast through the outer
wall with dynamite. "I blasted through stone and stone and, Jesus, I
never so much as broke one of them precious old stones in the castle
itself."

I asked Conor why there were no lights outside the castle.

"Miss, Bob never liked lights outside. He never liked that kind of
crack at all."

"Crack," from *craic*, the Irish word for chatty conversation or a
crazy person, had evolved into the Hiberno-English slang word for
fun. Conor continued in his galloping way, "I told Bob he should put
spotlights outside, but he never would. And he would never allow
any radiators to be showing in the rooms. Instead he wanted me to
set up a mess of heating vents in the floors. I had to hide the electri-
cal wires in between the stones, and that's what he was like. Everything had to be like the original. And, miss, did you see the key to the
door?"

The key was six inches long, a thin metal skeleton key with a delicate locking mechanism.

"And did you see the lock on the door? I searched the countryside looking for a big old lock for that door, and I finally found it. The door is four or five inches thick."

It was not. It was three inches at most.

"I had to cut the key and weld three more inches onto it so it would fit the door. I thought that key wouldn't last a week, but it hasn't broken since. That was almost twenty-five years ago. You may have noticed."

Conor was so caught up in his tale that he had begun to speak as though he were still working on the castle. "The black toilets we have in there? They come all the way from America. You couldn't get a black toilet in Ireland at that time. Bob wants them black so they won't stand out too much. And I have all the heating done with hot air from the water heater, and I have thermostats in every room. Jesus save us, them fireplaces is so big you could walk straight into them. You'd want to be burning whole trees in them."

The three other men at the bar looked expressionlessly into their Guinnesses, heads in their hands: they had heard it all before. A young, black-haired man came swiftly through the door and began helping Francis behind the bar. He looked no more than twenty-two. When he heard Conor talking, he raised his eyes heavenward for the benefit of the other men. The butcher lowered his head and smirked goofily into his glove, delighted by the conspiracy against Conor MacNamara.

The more Conor talked, the more animated he became. Although I could see that he irritated his peers, he boasted beautifully, and I found his manner thoroughly engaging. He was girlishly histrionic. He punctuated his story with wide gestures of his arms, wiggling his fingers airily. He bounced on his barstool, excited by his own success. He was as interested in his story as if it were happening for the first time. He had a perfect Roman nose and fine white hair that he brushed straight back from his forehead and kept all one length just below his ears. His widow's peak was deep, and from time to time he curled locks of his hair delicately behind his ears with his index fingers in an effort to keep it from hanging in his eyes; the mannerism struck me as delightfully effeminate in a man of such self-conscious virility. His two eyeteeth were missing, and when he laughed, which he did often, he tried to keep his upper lip pulled over his teeth to hide the gaps, or he put his fingers up to his mouth. His vanity was revealed in subtle ways, and beneath his brash outward show I sensed a gentleness and sensitivity, which further endeared him to me.

"All them wooden beams in that castle had wooden dowels in them for nails, and it was the custom in those times to leave a bit of the dowel showing, sticking out like, like a peg. And guess what the mortar is made of in that castle?"

I couldn't guess.

"Of course you cannot guess!" Conor brayed agreeably. "I knew that I was going to have to tell you! Bull's blood, bull's hair, sand, and water! And that mortar is as strong today as it was five hundred years ago."

That explained the hair I had seen stuck to some of the walls in the castle. I had first noticed the hair as I was brushing my teeth, staring at the stones of the bathroom wall. There, stuck in the mortar, were a lot of coarse red hairs. It looked as though someone had shaved his beard off with a straight-edge razor and wiped the razor on the wall or, worse, as though a short-haired person had had his head dashed violently against the stones. Most of the hairs were red, and some were gold. In certain spots there was a reddish hue to the mortar, reminiscent of dried blood. The sight had struck me as bizarre and ugly, and almost as ominous as the words on the flagstaff, and I was relieved now to be told what it was.

"And there was an escape tunnel where we found old bottles of porter. In that castle you will notice the walls are five feet thick at the bottom and only three feet thick at the top. Therefore. Didn't I get that tub up the side of it and fit it right through the roof?

"And there was a big hooley Bob threw when he first started restoring the place. He had two hundred candles lighting the place because of no electricity yet, and a bonfire, and the fiddlers were there, and Mary the Somebody fell head first into the fire and Mike Menahan pulled her out again. Mary the Somebody fell head first and burned her hair. Jesus did that woman burn the feck out of her hair!"

Conor shoveled in some more Guinness, laughed, said, "Holy Jesus," and called to Francis for another pint for himself and one for me. When I declined the second pint, Conor waved his hand at me in violent dismissal and said in exactly the admonishing tone Francis had used to tell me I would not be living in the castle, "You'll drink it and that's final." When I protested, he clamped his eyes shut, grimaced, batted the air at me, and carried on. "And there was another party where we all had to dress in costumes and I came in as Superman."

"*That* suited you," snapped the dark-haired boy behind the bar.

Conor hunched up his shoulders and turned a sweet, pleading smile on the boy.

A long silence followed, in which we heard the judicious voice of Don Coburn, the Raidió Teilifís Eireann newscaster, reading the six o'clock news. The news these days was mostly bad. The Irish government was caught up in a seemingly unending series of scandals, and the various political parties were in constant battle for possession of the moral high ground. That day John Bruton, the leader of Fine Gael, had blasted the Fianna Fail government, saying, "It is rotten to the core and must go!"

As if reminded by Coburn's voice, Conor MacNamara said, "And I built a pirate radio station some years back. I built it out of bits and pieces and was broadcasting out of my garage to a thirty-mile radius!"

Unlike Francis, Conor raced from one subject to the next, inspired by whatever was before him or whatever grazed his mind, and unlike Francis he had no questions. Little of what he said required a reply; his listener could be anyone.

"What were you broadcasting?" I asked.

"Music mostly. I got musicians to come into my garage and play live over the air, or I taped some music myself and put that on. Sometimes I talked. I was popular. I used to get a lot of letters. One day I got two hundred and seventy letters from around Clare in response to this one show I did. The postmistress was steamed at me for that. Jesus, she tore strips off me. But then I had to close the show down. They made me close it because it was highly, highly illegal. But 'twas a great crack!"

The dark-haired young man came out from behind the bar to retrieve some empty glasses and wipe the tables. He was tall and slim and moved with lissome efficiency. His manner was all business. He said to me, "You shouldn't believe him, you know," and there was admonishment in his voice, as though I were somehow in league with Conor MacNamara.

Conor giggled and shrugged, his fingers held up to hide his teeth. "Ah, God, miss, don't mind that one there. He's only my youngest son, Michael."

"Jesus, I am not his son," said the young man.

Conor looked at him adoringly. "God, he's a cheeky little thing, and he's my son all right. I had thirteen children. When they were little, Bob Brown used to love to come to my house and line them all up like steps and see if I could name them all. I never got past the eighth. Bob got a bang out of that."

Weeks later, when Conor was trying to tell me about one of his children, he said, "My daughter . . . you know the one I'm talking about . . . my next-to-eldest daughter . . . ah, Christ save us, what do you *call* her?"

As he swung past me, rag in hand, Michael sneered, "After three or four more pints he'll be telling you about the submarine he built."

Conor sat up straight on his stool, electrified by the thought of the submarine. He fortified himself with a drink from his glass and a deep inhalation and shouted, "Correct! I have built a submarine. Miss, this is going back some years. I made it out of barrels of lubricant oil that came over from America. Those biggy barrels that are black?"

Michael threw up his hands and disappeared into the back room, but I couldn't wait to hear the story.

"And then the BBC came over from England and made an award-winning documentary film about it. After I got the thing built, I realized the lake wasn't deep enough to test it when the BBC came to make the award-winning film, so I asked Francis Cahill to dig a hole in the bottom of the lake. Therefore, he dug the hole with a backhoe."

This was starting to sound positively mythological, like a passage out of the Irish epic *Tain Bo Cuailnge*, or *The Cattle Raid of Cooley*, the pre-Christian saga of Cuchulain and the warring kings of Ireland, in which preposterous feats of skill and power are described in fantastic detail.

Conor carried on. "And from down at the lake I got on the short-wave radio and called my daughter Sile who was minding my garage and told her to get on the air and broadcast the news of the submarine all over West Clare, and the next thing all the local farmers were arriving at the lake. Jesus, I don't know where did they all come out of at all. There were *rakes* of 'em. They were like a herd of ants coming down the hill and across the lake in boats, all to see me test my submarine. Half of them came swimming across the lake, but more of them was in boats or whatever way. And they were crowding up agin' me so thick you could not see the shoreline. And when the BBC fella saw all these people arriving at once, he says to me, 'What did you ever do at all to summon this lot of people here?' "

Conor spoke so freely and with such assurance that I found it difficult to disbelieve him. While Conor was in the bathroom, Michael and the other men at the bar ridiculed him with a humorless directness that surprised me. While the Irish have a genius for scorn, most often they choose to express it in a glancingly witty and satirical fashion that precludes any real expression of anger, renders them inculpable, and soothes their dread of confrontation. An outright personal attack is uncommon, but the men in Dillon's Pub were unanimous in the view that everything Conor MacNamara said was invented or exaggerated. I thought there was too much specificity of detail for these stories to be made up. They were far-fetched, that much was so, but could Conor's imagination really be that good? What he said was so large that I wanted to believe it, and it charmed me enough that I could persuade myself to believe it.

When Conor returned from the bathroom, I moved up to the bar and sat next to him to keep him from shouting across the room. Sitting close to him I noticed two small and identical scars transecting his upper lip in perfect symmetry, as though long ago the missing eyeteeth had been forced clean through the lip by some terrible blow.

Conor told me that not long before he had been living in Africa, working as an engineer on a gold-mining project, and he claimed he had another family in Sierra Leone. He said the Africans were lonely people out in the bush. They never heard the radio or saw the television. They were so poor, the Irish were rich compared to them. He ate snake there.

"We used to run over them snakes with the tractor, and the blackies would get so mad because they liked to make steaks out of the snake meat. It tasted like salmon, honest to God. I was often out in the bush, and I seen a girl of fourteen giving birth to a baby, and I often tried to stop and help, for I had a small bit of experience in bringing a baby into the world."

Conor said he had assisted many a baby and saved many a mother, and that if he won the national lottery tonight, he'd return to Africa and build a thousand small nurseries there. He also told me he owned a fishing boat that he kept in Ballyvaughan, a harbor town in North

Clare, on the way to Galway. In summer he slept on the boat several nights a week, and when he was not fishing or bringing other people out fishing, he worked as a mechanic in his own garage.

"I love the water," he said gamely. "Do you love the water? Because I do."

Eagerly Conor told me about the things he loved. He loved brown bread and a cup of tea with it. He loved to fly and he loved being a mechanic. He loved Halloween. He loved electricity, he loved to dance, and he loved nature shows and animal shows on television; he loved the way a camera could get pictures of animals doing amazing things. "In a minute now that animal show will come on the TV, and you and I can go in the other room and watch it. All right, miss?"

It pleased me that he was inviting me.

At seven o'clock we went into the pub's second room to watch the animal show on a color television that hung from the ceiling. Conor had two pints of Guinness on the table for himself, and he ordered another for me, even though I hadn't touched the first one he had bought me. The room contained a pool table, a fireplace, a dangling circular lampshade with a saucy red fringe, and several long couches. The room had been empty of people, but the moment we sat down on a couch to look at the television, six teenagers in leather jackets came in to play pool.

Conor said to me, "Ah, Jesus, as soon as I want to watch my animal show those pups have to come in and start playing pool, and not one feckin' fella in the place until now."

The boys, most of them sprouting mustaches, wore jeans and boots. The one or two who were old enough to drink bought several pints of beer and shared them with the rest. They smoked and jeered and cursed at each other, their voices breaking. They were insolent, tugged at their crotches, whispered to each other, and snickered derisively. They were the youth of Ireland, and in a few years, like most who had come before them, they would leave Corofin for England or America.

The animal show concerned internal compasses and maps. We learned how animals find their way against impossible odds: how turtles find the same beach they were born on to lay their eggs, how hummingbirds find the right flower to drink from, and how desert ants, after a day's wandering for miles across the monotone landscape, are able to find again the microscopic hole they call home. We saw honeybees flying from Africa to Europe along the same route they had taken the year before. An elephant shrew ran along an elaborate network of jungle paths at breakneck speed. Before our eyes a marmoset peed on his prehensile hands and rubbed them on a tree to identify it as his own. With similar intent a hyena rubbed his rear end on a plant. We saw swiftlets and caterpillars and bats, eels demonstrating their electric echolocation, and lobsters parading in a militaristic line across the ocean floor. When one hapless lobster got his legs chewed off by a fish, Conor gasped in fright and covered his mouth with his hand. "Jesus," he whispered, eyes trained on the television, "I love lobster. And I love crabs. I hunt for them when I'm out in my boat. Miss, would you by any chance love lobster?"

The animal show was so fascinating and strange that one by one the teenagers turned from the pool table and wandered over to sit before the television. They stared, and their mouths fell open. Their pool cues fell to their feet. Mesmerized by the long-snouted elephant shrew, they were stripped of their studied indifference. We were all reduced to a hypnotic, childlike state, utterly defenseless and trusting. Michael, Conor's son, threw himself down in the seat next to me, all the disdain gone out of his face, and Francis appeared in the doorway, staring, an unlit cigarette dangling from his lip.

When the show was over and the boys had gone back to their pool game, Francis turned the television off and went out again. Conor watched him go, then said, "I don't know what that brother of mine is about. He never enjoys anything. He never laughs. I think he's still a virgin. I'd say he never went to a woman at all."

With a show of great contempt Michael sneered, "How would *you* know?" and walked away into the other room.

Conor said proudly, "You see, miss, that is my youngest child, Michael."

Conor's first child, a son, had died at eleven months. Conor called him a "blue baby," and with the first trace of sadness I had witnessed in him said, "These days they could save a baby like that. But forty years ago they couldn't do nothing for him. That was our first baby. We had to bury him in a little coffin."

Conor's wife had been dead only a year, but he told me this with little emotion and just as quickly said, "I love them little Italian apples

Tom Hogan is selling in his shop. I bought a bunch tomorrow week as you go back."

Conor and I moved back into the barroom, which was filling up now with men coming in from the Saturday evening Mass. They stood lined up at the bar and some of them sat in the seats near the fire. Conor ordered one man at the bar to give up his stool for me, and the man did so willingly and courteously, saying, "God, I would be honored."

Most of the men coming in now were wearing their best clothes, not for the Mass but for the Saturday night dance in Daly's Pub across the street. Daly's was considered posh, not the sort of place one could walk into on a Saturday night dressed in work clothes. How that rule had been established I never found out, but it was related to the fact that Daly's was one of the two pubs in the village that women frequented. Daly's was modern by Corofin's standards; it had a linoleum floor, an enormous television, a carpeted lounge, a gas fire in the hearth instead of a real one, and ugly Danish chairs. It appealed to the women because it was said to be more like the sort of bar one would find in America. Too, the men felt that whenever there was the possibility of dancing, they had to be clean. The older men wore clothes left over from the forties and fifties — well-made clothes of excellent quality — and the younger men dressed in the freewheeling style of the mid-seventies, with flared polyester trousers, pastel colors, and wide lapels. Saturday nights in Corofin found the men self-conscious, proud, uncertain, and boyish. Their sartorial struggles were apparent, but still they looked faintly soiled and rumpled, as though their clothes had been stuffed in a peat creel since the previous Saturday. They all wore their hair slightly too long.

A man wearing a white tennis sweater and checkered pants stood at the bar near Conor. His clothes, stiff and powerfully oversized, looked as though they had belonged to his dead father, but his hair was combed and his necktie was neatly knotted. Conor turned to him and said, "You're all Gillette tonight, Finn." This meant Finn looked as though he'd been touched by the razor. Finn said wryly, "I never saw you in Mass tonight, Conor."

"That's right," Conor said loudly and somewhat drunkenly, "because there is no maker! There is no maker big enough to make this!" He thumped himself on the chest.

Micky Nolan, a cool, ironical man who had once given me a lift on his tractor, jumped into the conversation with a statement that was somehow a defense of God. "Sure, wasn't it man that made the television?"

Nolan was dressed in a gray suit, an oatmeal sweater, a tie, and a dress shirt. The sweater had a large stain on its front. His hair was combed so tightly against his head he looked nearly suave. He had long sideburns and dense lines of hair across the tops of his cheekbones, hair he'd missed shaving, possibly intentionally—the hair had the effect of making him look masked.

Before long there was a circle of men around me, dominated by Conor MacNamara, Paddy O'Brien, Micky Nolan, and a younger drunken fellow who kept saying suggestively to me, "Don't you remember me? We were up in the creamery together making butter." This man reminded me of a starving coyote. He had greasy, straw-colored hair that stuck up wildly in tufts all over his head and was matted flat in the back, like long wet grass that had been flattened by an ox. He had a narrow face, a sunken mouth, eyes too close together. I had been in a different pub a few days earlier, and he had begged me to play darts with him, which I declined to do.

Most of the men at the bar were unmarried and over forty; a number of them still lived with their mothers. They fought over who would buy me drinks, and so bitterly that at one point in the evening I counted five glasses of Guinness before me. They offered me cigarettes relentlessly. They called me Miss, and some of them called me Mrs., and one of them called me Good Lady.

Conor MacNamara controlled the conversation, changing its subject wildly from one thing to the next. During a lull he asked the company in general, sounding oddly like his brother Francis, "If the icebergs in the North Pole melted, would we all be drowned?"

Micky Nolan made mocking faces behind Conor's back, completing the circle of contempt.

Paddy O'Brien said little to Conor. O'Brien was a serious man, perhaps the most serious of all the men I had met. He was known as the Badger because of the way he combed his woolly white hair across his balding head. His hair was like upholstery stuffing, and his heavy, yellowish lips were dry and shiny in a way that reminded me of plastic wrapping. He had little cuts in his ears and several cuts on his simian face. His skin was pocked and sere, sensitive and irritable. He had remarkably short, blunt fingers and tiny little teeth, like a child's, with gaps between them. He looked very worried, like a man stuck wondering whether he had left the oven on at home. He lisped. And he was so gentlemanly and courtly that I forgot how ugly he was. He hated Conor MacNamara's bad language and what he perceived as the village people's provinciality and foolishness. He was embarrassed by the men in the pub and tried to apologize to me for them.

When Conor announced to the men that I was living in Ballyportry Castle, they immediately began arguing about castles. They argued over whether or not the best stone from the Burren was used in Bunratty Castle. Micky Nolan believed it was, for it was his father who had carried the stone the forty miles to Bunratty in a pony cart with some other men. Conor MacNamara denied him with characteristic directness. "'Tis not the best stone."

"'Tis," Nolan insisted.

Wildly, as if defying all in the room with this sudden change in subject, Conor shouted, "Corofin is the gateway to the Burren!"

The starving coyote, steadying himself with one hand slapped flat on the bar, howled that the hill he lived on was the gateway to the Burren. He was soundly ignored. The argument switched from the Burren back to castles and finally to whether the nicotine on the pub's ceiling would wash off and whether it was a health hazard. The conversational competition was fierce and reached far beyond that evening. It was a matter of intellectual hierarchy, who fit where, who was sharpest and most knowledgeable, and who, therefore, deserved the greatest share of attention.

Paddy O'Brien asked me again and again if I wouldn't be afraid to walk home at night along the dark Gort Road to the castle. Wouldn't I be afraid that a man would try to force me into a car? He asked this so many times that I began to wonder if perhaps he wasn't precisely the sort of man who would try to force a woman into his car. I told him repeatedly that I was not afraid. On a back road in Vermont I would be afraid, but in rural Ireland I was rarely afraid. There were fewer guns here, fewer knives, fewer drugs, and a less violent ethos. There was, I thought, an inherent gentility in the Irish. Or perhaps it was simply timidity. Whatever the case, the Irish seemed so unanimously gentle and unassuming that I could not persuade myself to be wary enough to satisfy Paddy O'Brien.

The men agreed that they would all be entirely too afraid to walk out to the castle alone at midnight, let alone sleep in it. I found this hard to believe, but I knew their eminent regard for ghosts was at the root of their fears.

Conor pressed another drink upon me. When he wouldn't hear my protestations, Paddy O'Brien growled at him, "If the miss doesn't want it, she doesn't want it."

The entire pub was listening now to one conversation, with each man throwing in his two cents. Everyone got equal time, but Conor MacNamara repeatedly stole more than his share. The conversation returned to God and mortality. Micky Nolan said mischievously to Conor, "I'll be shouldering you into the cemetery someday, Conor."

With a venom greater than any that had come before, Conor roared, "The hell you will! I'll not be buried in any coffin by any fuckin' priests."

Francis MacNamara winced at his brother's profanity.

Conor's face had gone scarlet. "I'll be cre*mated* and have my ashes scattered in Galway Bay, where I spent half my life fishing. That's what I want and that's what I'll have." He was adamant about his plan and infuriated by the thought of the Church involving itself in his disposal. Micky Nolan provoked him further by insisting that Conor would have no choice in the matter, that he must welcome the traditions and rituals of the Church. Nolan said with malicious glee, "I'll be shouldering you, Conor, into Cill Vaidaun cemetery, and I'll be lowering you into the ground, and the priest will be shouting out the Hail Mary, and you'll be going lower and lower into the ground and nearer and nearer to God, whether you like it or no."

Conor was tormented. His eyes were wild behind his glasses. He writhed on his barstool, waved his arms in the air, curled his hair behind his ears, and straightened his cap on his head all in one sweeping gesture. At the top of his lungs he roared, "Ah, for fuck's sake go away to hell, you'll not be shouldering me anyplace, Micky Nolan, and I'll not be having any fuckin' cunt of a priest over my body! You wait and see how I take care of myself! I'll be buried at sea in Galway Bay, as God is my witness!"

Quietly, Paddy O'Brien said, "I thought you said you didn't believe in God."

At a loss for a smart reply, Conor turned to the drunken, innocently blinking coyote and snapped, "Fuck off, ya fucker."

Francis MacNamara turned his pained face away from the room. With his hands on his slender hips he stared at a calendar above the sink. When he spoke, his gentle voice wavered and seemed close to tears. "*Stop* it," he pleaded. "A lady is here."

I was exhausted. I had come into this pub planning to spend an hour, and six hours had passed. I had had no dinner and had missed a telephone call I had promised to be home for. Paddy O'Brien looked hard at me. "How can you stand listening to these fools?" he said.

And then Micky Nolan began telling a story that the whole pubful of bachelors fell silent listening to: a bank manager known to all of them had bought an engagement ring for a woman and presented it to her with a proposal of marriage. The man was simple, economical, and plain. He never used a plate when he had his evening tea; instead he spread a piece of newspaper on the table, put the teacup and the loaf of bread down upon it, and cut himself a few slices of bread. When he was through with the little meal, he would roll the newspaper up and throw it away, leaving nothing but the one teacup to wash. (The men in the pub nodded approvingly at this reasonable method.)

Eventually the woman in question came to see her suitor about the marriage, and when she saw the humble cottage he lived in with its sparse furnishings, she said, "But if we're to be married, you'll have to build us a proper house and buy proper furniture and plates, and we'll have to be entertaining your bank manager friends and so forth." The manager responded, "Ah, God, I wouldn't want any crack like that. I would want no such thing as entertaining anyone. And if you insist upon it, it will have to be the end of our match."

So the woman returned the ring, and the manager sold the ring back to the jeweler, and they never spoke of it again, and neither one of them ever married, and the last time he heard from her they were seventy years old, and that was the end of the story.

In the long silence that followed, there was a palpable sadness in the room. Paddy O'Brien seemed to have fallen into abject depression listening to it. He looked disgusted by its meaning and sick of the smallness of his own people, and perhaps of himself. He squinted at Micky Nolan. I thought he would strike him.

It was midnight by the clock above Francis's head. According to law the pub should have closed an hour before. Soon Francis would begin encouraging the men to leave before Sergeant Kavanagh came by to do it for him. Every night all across Ireland there was a cat-and-mouse game between the people and the police over the closing of the pubs. The people wanted so badly to stay and, like children, needed to be told when to go home to bed. Sergeant Kavanagh was like a nanny, a person needed and respected and feared and lied to. In the cities enforcement of the law was strict, and customers and publicans alike were forced to pay fines if they were caught open after closing time.

When Francis saw that I was preparing to leave, he passed a book over the bar to me, a history of County Clare. Shyly he said, "You can borrow this, Rose, if you like."

Conor stared at him. "That is *my* book, Francis," he said. "I lent you that book. You know I lent you that book." Conor snatched the book out of Francis's hand and turned it over to me. "Here, miss," he said. "I am lending you this book."

Francis smiled sadly and shrugged and began gathering empty glasses.

Bridie O'Daly

I HAD BEEN IN COROFIN several weeks before I spoke to my nearest neighbor, a woman known in the village as Mrs. Bridie O'Daly. The road Bridie O'Daly and I lived on, approximately a quarter of a mile from each other, was not as wide as a New York sidewalk, and like most small roads in rural Ireland it was walled on either side by a dense hedge that rose several feet over my head. In some places, walking this road was like walking the dark corridor of a maze. The hedge was a treacherous wall of blackberry bushes, thistle, holly, whitethorn, blackthorn, and the occasional rowan tree with thorns as fine and long as sewing needles.

I had passed Mrs. O'Daly's farm countless times on my way in and out of the village and had seen her busy at chores in her yard. She was short, stout, bowlegged, big-bottomed, and toothless. She walked in a lumbering way. And she was shy. The one time I waved to her, she turned slightly away from me, showing me her profile, and acknowledged me by raising a stick held in her hand. It was a half-salute that looked suspiciously like a gesture of dismissal. I was curious about this woman's life, but few people seemed to know her, and I rarely saw her in the village. Sometimes I glimpsed her figure beyond the hedge, not more than three feet from me, solid as a mailbox, peering with a cow's patient gaze through a gap in the hedge, hoping to see who was passing. Her motionlessness was calculated; she didn't want to attract my attention. She was acutely aware of me, and I of her, and though we had seen each other many times, neither one of us had spoken, as if under a spell we dared not break with our own voices.

If the wind was blowing in the right direction, I could smell Bridie O'Daly's farm before I could see it. The smell was both acrid and sweet, a mix of fermenting silage and slurry, cow dung and peat smoke. Everything about the farm looked makeshift and improvised, rigged up out of whatever materials she happened to have on hand. An open-fronted barn of red corrugated iron housed hundreds of bales of yellow hay, and in the muddy barnyard was an enormous pile of scrap timber and fence poles that looked like the remains of a collapsed house. There were four long-haired, yellow-eyed goats who, despite their tight hobbles, managed to wander around Bridie's muddy yard, through a hole in the stone wall, and across the road to the apple trees and the small patch of cabbages and turnips. The vegetable patch was ill defended from the goats by an improbable fence of old automobile doors strung together with wire. Someone had tied colorful plastic shopping bags to the branches of the apple trees, and the bags rustled and flapped in the wind—an ingenious variation on the scarecrow concept. The gnarled trees looked sinister and spooky. Even Bridie's sheepdog was slightly bizarre, with his lame foreleg tied up in a sling devised from a piece of string knotted around his ankle, then pulled up short and tied around his neck. The dog looked slightly ridiculous, posed in this perpetually waving posture. Only Bridie's cottage, painted a blinding Caribbean white, was solid and straightforward.

I spent a great deal of my time in Corofin walking around the countryside. One Saturday morning late in October I set out walking to Ennistymon, a market town fifteen miles to the west. The morning was cool and bright, and the sky was scattered with sloppy white clouds that drifted languidly and wiped the face of the sun. Flies whined angrily in the hedge like electric machinery, and swollen blackberries the size of grapes caused the arms of the hedges to bend and droop.

As I neared Bridie O'Daly's farm, I looked for her in her yard. She moved quietly, like an animal, and sometimes I missed her entirely, though she might be standing only a few feet from me. That morning I saw smoke rising from her chimney and saw the sheepdog waving from the open doorway of the cottage, but there was no sign of Bridie and I was disappointed.

I carried on past the turnoff to Tubber, past Tom Cahill's farm, past the graveyard hill, and through the village, and at the entrance to the alley next to Connolly's Pub I saw, out of the corner of my eye, a thing that aroused a primitive fear and embarrassment in me even before I knew what I was seeing: it was a dead fox lying on the cobbles, legs outstretched in a leaping posture. When I saw the animal, my hands flew up instinctively to protect my face, though I knew very well the fox was dead. I moved closer. The fox's mouth hung slightly open, and his tongue, drying in the sun, was like a sliver of beef jerky held gently between the tiny white thorns of his teeth. His fluffy coat glistened with mist. It seemed if I put my hand on him, my fingers would sink deep into the thick fur and disappear. He had long black whiskers like a cat's, brown ears, and soft brown feet. He was fat and perfect but for a small bullet hole in his face just beneath one eye. It was startling to see this shy, pretty animal exposed in such an undignified way in the middle of the village. He seemed to be smiling at me.

I went into Connolly's Pub. Rory O'Malley, a slow, staring, gray-faced man, was behind the bar. I had never seen Rory look anything but torpid and depressed. I had hoped to find his wife, Veronica, who was infinitely easier to talk to. I said, "Rory, there's a fox in your alley."

He leaned on the bar and stared at me with his big head propped up in his hands. "I know it," he said dryly.

"Whose is he?" I said and was surprised by the excitement in my own voice.

An old man drinking at the bar said, "He's yours, if you want him."

"What would *I* do with him?" I said.

Without lifting his gaze from the surface of the bar, Rory said, "Make a mink of him."

A clock ticked mockingly on the wall.

"I could make a hat," I said.

With the weary conviction of a husband, Rory said, "*You* never wear a hat."

Rory was right, I never wore a hat, but how did he know that? I had come into Connolly's Pub only once or twice before. "How do you know I never wear a hat?" I said.

Rory sat upright on his stool and smiled at me, and then he began to laugh loudly, and he banged his hand down on the counter in amusement. The sight of him laughing was rare and strange. He had big teeth, like a horse's, and a big meaty tongue. His wife came out of the back room in her wire-rim glasses to see what was making him laugh. When he saw her in the doorway he said, "The Yank wants to know how I know she never wears a hat."

Veronica smiled. She was handsome and wry. She said, "Do you think you go unnoticed in this village?"

The old man drinking at the bar sighed resignedly. "In a place like this, miss, nobody goes unnoticed."

Veronica picked up the man's empty glass and began refilling it. "You won't need to tell us about yourself, Rose," she said, "for we already know you."

<hr>

THE MOST DIRECT ROAD to Ennistymon was small, more like a paved path than like a road, and not much traveled. The houses on it were few and far between. Near the station house I was beset by three black-and-white collies who bristled and barked ferociously at the sight of me. They stood with their feet set hard against the pavement, knees locked, heads down, teeth bared. It was clear they planned to bite me. One was missing a hind leg, and another had a patch over his eye. There were a lot of dogs like this in Corofin: one-eyed, three-legged, hairless, crippled, deaf, blind, and otherwise maimed, which only increased their viciousness and their quickness. I turned to look for a stick, and as I did I saw a muzzled collie come sailing over a four-foot fence and fly down the road at me. He ran so fast that he skidded past me on his rear end, then turned, nails scrabbling on the macadam, and butted his muzzled nose against my legs, trying to bite me. He had a plaster cast on his tail. I could see his fangs and his mottled pink gums through the vents of the muzzle. "Nice dog," I said, and when he persisted in harassing me I gave him a mighty kick in the chin and heard his teeth clack together inside the muzzle. He scurried off, with his friends close behind.

I passed the old station house, which had been turned into a pub, now closed. Through the window I could see the long oak bar, the mirrors behind it, the barstools and tables covered in sheets and cob-webs—the place looked haunted and sad.

A few miles farther along, at a fork in the road, I saw two figures standing by a car shadowed by the large chestnut trees that banked the road. It was Mike Menahan and a heavy, red-haired man I often saw around the village. The man leaned patiently on his car door and smoked while Mike talked at him.

I had met Mike Menahan a few nights before at the dance in Daly's Pub. That night, without introducing himself, Mike had approached me and asked, "Will you be singing a song later in the evening?" He had an odd, distressed voice that sounded like air forced between two wet reeds. Standing, the top of his head was level with my mouth. He had a wide wet smile and pinched little features, and he kept pulling off his cap and putting it on again as he talked. He said, "I play the flute. I love music." When I asked him if he knew the song "Father Halpin's Old Coat," he said, "No, but Halpin is a local name. There's a Halpin here in Corofin."

I learned quickly that Mike Menahan was giddy with useless infor-mation about Corofin. He found a way to bring everything back to the subject of the village and its people. He told me the name of each person in the pub that night and how they were related to each other. He asked if I was on holiday. I told him I was living here for a little while. "And where were you from before this?" he said.

I said, "Boston."

He looked surprised. He tipped his head at me abruptly. The arthritis in his twisted fingers forced him to hold his glass of ale in a dainty, effeminate way. "Boston! How is it I never saw you before this?"

I looked at him, and it dawned on me that he was talking about a spot on the road to Carron, a tiny cluster of houses called Boston. I said, "Not that Boston. Boston in America."

Mike gasped and pressed his hand to his heart. He was startled by everything I said. "But where were you from originally?"

I had no idea what he was getting at. "Originally?" I said.

"What part of the country were you from?"

"Boston. That's where I came from."

He looked confused. "So how is it I wouldn't know you?" His voice squeaked as though his vocal chords had been smashed. Something had made him think I was Irish.

"I'm American," I said. "I came originally from Boston in America."

"You don't sound American to me!" he said doubtfully.

Irish people often told me I didn't sound American, and when I asked them what an American sounded like, without fail they imitated something Texan.

"What's your name?" Mike said. I told him, and his hands flew up in triumph. "Mahoney!" he cried. "'Tis a local name! Tommy Mahoney, Patrick Mahoney, Eileen Mahoney, Terence and Theresa Mahoney, all belonging to Paddy Mahoney. Mahoney is a very local name."

Ireland was the world to Mike Menahan, and Corofin was its heart; everything presented to him had to fit into that picture one way or another. When the band appeared and began playing, Mike told me their names and who their fathers were. I noticed as he talked that he stomped his right foot every now and then in a wildly uncontrolled way, as if trying to shake a hornet out of his pants leg.

I asked him what he did for work. "I never worked," he said. "I had an accident when I was a boy, and I could never finish school or work in a real way."

The barmaid passed our table, and Mike tried to ask her a question, addressing her as Miss O'Connor. She made an aggressive swipe at the table with a wet rag and without looking up at him said irritably, "What's wrong with you, Mr. Menahan?" which in Ireland means, What can I do for you? In this particular case, however, it sounded distinctly as though the barmaid was asking Mike what was the matter with his mind.

I remembered Mike Menahan and now, on the road to Ennistymon, I said hello to him. He looked startled and stared at me with intense pleasure at having been spoken to. I could see that few people bothered to speak to this man. Without taking his eyes off me, he said to his fat companion, "I met her in Daly's. She has the singing voice of a bird."

Mike Menahan had never heard my singing voice.

The companion said nothing, only raised one red eyebrow to show he had taken in this bit of information.

I asked Mike if he remembered my name. He stomped his foot. "Mahoney," he said. "'Tis local."

That day Mike wore an overcoat and he carried a walking stick, a large white envelope, and a plastic shopping bag weighted down with something very heavy. He held the stick around its middle, like a crosier, and punctuated his statements by jabbing the air with it. His coat was tattered and stained. He was clean-shaven but for a missed area beneath his chin, and a tuft of white hair stuck out at the throat of his shirt like a piece of cotton wadding. Mike asked me if I had walked all the way from Corofin, and when I told him I had walked most of the way but had gotten a short lift, his fat acquaintance stared at me in disbelief and said, "But where are you going on this road at all?"

"Ennistymon," I said.

"Christ, you'll never get there," said the man. His voice was high and loud, like a baby's. "That's eight miles yet."

I told the man the truth: I would walk eight miles for fun, then turn around and walk the same miles back again. The man began to cough in a horrible rattling uproar. His yellow eyes went red, and during this graphic seizure he stared off into the distance above Mike's head. He coughed a long time and without taking a breath. I thought he would vomit.

Mike said eagerly, "Miss, how is it that you remembered my face?"

He had an unforgettable face: epicene features, triangular ears like tortilla chips tipped away from the side of his head, smooth, hollowed cheeks, false teeth too large for his mouth, and tiny eyes.

The fat man, seeing his opportunity for escape now that I was here to distract Mike, cried, "Good-bye!" fitted himself into his little car, and drove off in the direction of Corofin. Mike and I set off together toward Ennistymon.

"I am just after coming from the village myself. I was in picking up me fire," Mike said. He hoisted the plastic bag for me to see. "'Tis in here."

I couldn't image what he meant by "fire," but whatever it was it looked heavy. I guessed it was an electric heater. In Ireland senior citizens are entitled to free electricity, and many of them switch from solid fuel to electric to save money. "And I got a letter from my sister in San Francisco as well," he said, displaying the envelope. There were spots of fresh blood smeared all over the front of it. I pointed that out to Mike, and he studied the envelope, then studied his hands, which were also stained with blood. "Must have cut me finger," he said.

I looked at his finger; a large flap of skin was missing from above one knuckle. "How did you do that?" I said.

"I guess I fell down on the road a bit earlier," he said sheepishly, sucking his finger. "I'm not steady on me feet like I used to be." He grinned, and the blood was on his tongue now and coating his teeth.

"How do you usually get into the village?" I asked.

"I thumb a lift sometimes. Or walk."

It was far for a man his age to walk. I realized how frail he was. He looked tired, and older than he had the first time I met him, and I noticed what I hadn't before in the pub: a hairline scar traversing his forehead. The skin beneath his eyes was a deep violet color and tight, like the skin of a plum. He walked slowly, stopping frequently to talk and to gesture with his stick, and every now and then his leg would come down hard in that weird stomping motion.

"Your problem, miss, the reason you have got no proper lifts, is that you have come out during the dinner hour. There'll be no lifts on this road this time of day. Who was it that gave you the lift you mentioned?"

"I didn't ask his name," I said.

"Well, did you come by the station or over the bridge?"

"Station."

"Was it a red fella?"

"Red-haired, you mean?"

"That must be Paddy O'Malley," he said.

"But he *wasn't* red-haired," I said.

"Was he not? What was he, then?"

"Dark."

Mike pressed the shiny knob of his walking stick to his nostrils, then pressed it to his mouth, deep in thought. He seemed to be smelling the wood, as though it were fragrant and sweet. His foot swung out and stomped down into a puddle, shattering the clouds and the blue of the sky reflected in the puddle's surface. He moved the stick back and forth from mouth to nose trying to think of the dark-haired men he knew. Most of the village was dark-haired. I said, "All I know is that there were two brown dogs outside his house."

"Big or little?" he said.

"The house?"

"The dogs."

"Big."

"Had they yellow eyes?"

They had striking yellow eyes. "Yes."

"Mick Fitz. His sister was buried last month, God rest her. He has two big sons married in America."

Mike was delighted to have fitted that piece of the puzzle into place.

He was determined to sort out all the members of the village. I said, "Well, it probably wasn't Mick Fitz, because this man was too young to have grown sons."

Mike was off like a hound again. The stick flew up to his lips. "Had the fella blue eyes?"

He had beautiful blue eyes and amazingly long lashes.

"Peadar Garvey!" Mike was grinning now; this was high drama for him, more work than he'd had in a year.

I had heard there was to be a funeral that day in Corofin, and I asked Mike who it was that had died.

"A young woman. Only forty-seven years old. Jean McGarry."

"Will you go to the funeral?"

"I will, of course."

"Was she a friend of yours?"

"Well, I knew her, like, but you couldn't say we were friends."

I was certain that this was Mike Menahan's relationship to most of the people in Corofin. He knew everyone but was friendless. But everyone in the village went to everyone else's funeral, whether friendship was involved or not. It was simply something they did, like going to a parade. They went to remind themselves of their own mortality and to feel relieved that it wasn't them.

As we walked, Mike told me who lived in what house and who was related to whom. He told me the names of all the people buried in the last five years and the names of all the babies born. The farther we traveled, the fewer and farther between were the houses, and then Mike began pointing out various fields and gates and telling me whom they belonged to. Alongside one gate he stopped in the middle of the road and said, "Now, miss, that"—he pointed his stick toward the east—"is the diocese of Killaloe we were just in! The diocese of Killaloe, parish of Corofin! And this"—he spun on his heel and pointed to the west—"is the diocese of Galway we have just stepped into. Would you believe that?!"

He put down his fire and drew an imaginary line across the road with his beloved stick. "This is the line here by this very gate! I would not make a thing like that up."

He was delighted with this distinction, delighted to have sorted out yet another thing. And then his face changed, and I saw him peering off into the distant hills of the diocese of Galway. "There's a farmer—Kevin Higgins, I believe it is—going after his cattle, bring-ing them down off that mountain."

I turned my eyes to where Mike was looking and saw nothing but a vibrant green hill far off among a lot of other green hills and fields. The fields stretched across to the horizon like crushed velvet. They looked important and wise and were inspiring in their depth, but I saw no peo-ple and no cows. I saw no movement at all. The countryside was glori-ously empty of human life. I stared a long time, and finally at the top of the hill I saw a dark crumb of a figure moving slowly behind some other dark figures, figures so tiny as to be nearly invisible; in a lifetime of looking I would not have noticed them. How Mike Menahan had spot-ted them was beyond me. He looked half blind to me anyway, with those tiny eyes. I said, "Mr. Menahan, how did you know that farmer?"

"Who else would it be on that particular hill?"

"But how did you see him?"

"I *saw* him," he said.

It occurred to me that Mike Menahan was just the person to ask about Bridie O'Daly. "She lives near you," he said. "Her husband is under the clay only a few years now. She's an oddball. Never talks. Her son lives with her. He's an oddball too."

Mike's foot came down with a stomp, dangerously near my own foot. A mare and her foal approached the fence and stared at us, twitching their creased and rubbery lips. Then they bent their heads to the grass and yanked it out of the ground. Their munching sound-ed like water sloshing in a bucket.

We carried on, and soon Mike prepared to turn off on the lane to his cottage. He said, "You have a long way to go to Ennistymon, but when you get beyond the crossroads you'll be all right. If you'd been out here on a weekday you could have caught the bus bringing the scholars home from Ennis."

He meant the high school students. I said good-bye to him, and he went off toward his little cottage with his stick and his fire.

THE NEXT CAR that passed me stopped, and the driver, a middle-aged man, offered me a lift, which I accepted. It was impossible to walk an Irish country road without being offered a lift from every passing dri-ver, and if you refused the lift, the driver peered at you with skeptical surprise, as though you might be mad. Few country people walked for pleasure. Walking was primarily a way of getting from one place to another, and only a fool would decline the gift of a free ride. There was a casual indifference in the way Irish drivers offered pedestrians a lift. On my first day in Corofin an elderly farmer slowed his rusted Ford Escort alongside me, said softly and without looking at me, "Coming with?" and continued rolling down the road. I had to jog to keep up with him just to give him my response. Often a driver would crank down his window and say simply, "Seat to Mass?" or, "A mile do you any good?" and sometimes they simply got out of the car and opened a door without saying anything at all.

Hitchhiking, too, was common in rural Ireland. Old women, young children, and everyone in between hitched freely. Once, when I had rented a car, I picked up a middle-aged woman who was thumbing with three plastic shopping bags dangling from her arms. The woman climbed breathlessly into the car, fitting the bags around her feet and onto her big lap. They were heavy, awkward bags bursting with potatoes and rolls of toilet paper. The woman said nothing and stared gratefully through the windshield as we proceeded down the road to Ennistymon. She had a big red face and smelled of coal smoke. It delighted me that a lone woman could stand at the side of the road and put out her thumb without trepidation. To me, hitching was a bygone freedom, and that I was able to do it here contributed to my feeling that Ireland lay just beyond the corrupting reach of the modern world.

The man who gave me the lift that day drove a Toyota with a cattle trailer in tow. He wore a suit and a short red tie, the tip of which was level with his heart. He had blood blisters under his fingernails. "I just drank a lot of wine with my lunch," the man said as we started off down the road, and I thought to myself, *Oh, great*. Fortunately he drove very slowly and stayed on his side of the road, working the steering wheel with a single index finger curled over the top of the wheel. He asked me what I was doing here, and when I told him, he said, "Want me to tell you how to write a book?" He had a big face and a purplish complexion and bloodshot eyes. "What are you doing about Ireland?" he said.

"What do you want me to do about it?" I said.

"You should study Maud Gonne."

"I'd like to."

The man pulled over and parked the car on the shoulder, apparently because he couldn't talk and drive at the same time. There were newspapers on the floor of the car and on the dusty dash were a bunch of plastic roses, a comb, matches, an umbrella, and bits of paper. "And you should go to Mayo and find out about our President Mary Robinson's origins. Don't bother going to see her. That woman started out in the Labour Party, but she never came from a Labour background. She never came from unions. She only used Labour as a way to get ahead. She had rich parents."

The man sat slumped low in his seat with his elbows in his lap and the palms of his hands together in a praying position on his knees. It was the posture of a man sitting in a beach chair at the ocean. He seemed sleepy and slightly depressed. I felt oddly annoyed by him, and it took me a few minutes to realize that what annoyed me was the strong sense of defeat he radiated, a defeat mixed with a degree of presumption and self-importance. His teeth were rotting, and several were framed with threads of gold, which would have made him look sly and deceitful if he hadn't seemed so helpless. We talked about the business scandals rocking the Irish government at the time. I wanted to provoke him. I said, "Women rarely get involved in political and business scandals."

"They do," he said.

"When was the last time you heard of a woman involved in a scandal here?"

"Never. Women aren't in business and politics here."

That was, for the most part, true.

"I have my own business in Sligo," the man said. "If you had a business and it wasn't doing well, would you be happy to let your employees go off on maternity leave and pay them for the time they weren't there? No, you would not. You'd hire a man instead and avoid all that."

The man told me he had five sisters, that he had never married, that he didn't know any girls, and that he was desperately lonely. He said, "If paternity leave came in, as they are proposing, I would only ever hire a man who wasn't married. Or one who was only living with a woman."

The cow in the trailer behind us shifted its weight, and the whole car rocked gently.

I said, "Do you mean to say that if I had a child and had to leave work . . ."

"And God knows I'd like to be the father of that child," the man said, staring out the window at the fields ahead of us. He was so helpless and drunk that I didn't feel threatened by the comment. In fact, I pitied him.

"Women can't do the same work as men. That's why they don't deserve to get paid as much as men."

"What can't women do?"

"Women couldn't lay a pipe under this road."

"Why couldn't they?"

"They haven't the strength."

"They do it all the time in China," I said.

We argued about that. He brought up Michael Collins, the assassinated Irish hero. He said, "No one has ever told the true story about Michael Collins. Collins sided with the British. He got a twenty-one-gun salute from the British when he died. Few people get that, and he got it from the *British!* He stole the wife of his best friend. He was a bad article. Nobody seems to realize that."

The man's name was Richard. He asked me if I would come to Ennistymon with him and have a drink. I told him I couldn't. "Well, we'll have dinner tomorrow night, then. How about that?"

"I'm busy tomorrow night."

"Well, lunch then. And no strings attached. Though God knows I wouldn't mind having a few strings attached to you."

This was like being stuck at a drive-in movie with an overheated adolescent. The man had the raw, pleading sort of loneliness ubiquitous in Ireland. He said, "Where do you live? Could I knock on your door sometime?"

I said good-bye, and when I got out of the car he leaned across the seat trying to see me, his hands between his knees and his tie curling up on the seat I'd just been sitting in. He looked up at me sideways. "We'll just have lunch with no strings attached and I'll bring you right home and let you out of the car. I promise I won't rape you!"

"I'm relieved," I said.

So many men in the country acted as though they'd never seen a woman before. There seemed to be many more men than women, and they were desperate for someone to listen to them. But as lonely as they were, they were also very gentle. They talked and rarely acted. A man like this would not deter me from taking a ride from a stranger again.

❊

THAT EVENING AS I returned home I met Mrs. O'Daly on the road. She was moving a cow and its calf from one field to another. She wore a navy blue greatcoat that had molded itself to the shape of her body and was so worn that the wool was like felt. The long sleeves of her coat hid all but the fingertips of her hands. She wore knee-high rubber boots, and on her large gray head she wore a scrap of knitted wool that I realized was the raveled sleeve of a sweater. She moved down the road behind the cow, tapping the road with a long stick. The calf could not have been more than an hour or so old, for the bloody umbilical cord was still hanging from his belly, swaying and wrapping around his legs as he tried with great difficulty to follow his mother. He fell and had such trouble getting up that Bridie picked him up and gently set him on his legs again. As I passed her, I turned and looked at her face. It was wide, soft, and appealing. I had never been so close to her before. I was afraid to speak. Self-consciously I said, "Hello, Mrs. O'Daly." She didn't look at me, but she raised her stick in salute, and as I passed beyond her gate I was startled to hear her say in a soft, chalky voice, "Hello, Rose."

Whoredom in Kimmage

I NEVER SAW Bridie O'Daly in the village, and I never saw her conversing with anyone. The longer I stayed in Corofin the more it seemed that women were at a slight remove from the mainstream; I saw them behind walls, in doorways, and peering out of windows, and this contrasted sharply with the experience I had had in Dublin, where all I ever seemed to meet were women, and all they ever seemed to talk about was women's issues and concerns.

I first became aware of Ruth Riddick when I read her name — misspelled, I later learned — on the door of a toilet stall at Dublin's Trinity College. The notice, printed importantly in thick red letters across the top of the door, read: "Ruth Ruddick's Open Line: 6794700." I often stopped into that bathroom on my way home from the library, and each time I did, these words confronted me. The other messages on the door were not so easily discerned, for they were written in tiny, crabbed handwriting, in smudged pencil or ballpoint pen, were contentious, required concentration, time, even physical effort; I had to crouch down in the stall, chin on my knees, to read the lower messages. Though I had no idea who Ruth Riddick was or what a phone call to her number would get me, these other messages seemed to suggest that she was either a lesbian or an abortionist. The messages read:

> Are there condoms or any other form of contraception for women besides the pill? Please let me know. The pill is so much hassle.
> I recommend abstention.
> Information available in Well Woman Centre.
> Abortion is murder.
> I'll decide that for myself.
> Only God can decide.
> Lesbian line, Thursday, 7-9 pm 613777.
> Lesbians make my stomach turn.
> What a small-minded but honest individual.
> Closet dyke if ever I heard one! Are you so insecure about your own sexuality that you feel threatened by lesbians?

On the left-hand wall this question was answered in angry black ink:

> Why is she "threatened," as you put it, and insecure just because the thought of two girls making love repulses her? I think, and I honestly believe this, that if most straights were totally honest about the situation, they'd admit to a certain degree of repulsion regarding homosexuality. A few decades ago it was lesbians/gays who were shunned because of their views. Now it's more those who admit that they are not pro-homosexuality that get the abuse from the "liberals." It's not "insecure" to dislike the idea of lesbianism. It's perfectly natural. I admit to this dislike and I don't give a shit what any "Trendy" "Liberal" thinks or has to retort—I'm not going to change my views just because it's becoming more and more trendy to approve of homosexuality. Phew! Now I've got all that off my chest it's time for all you "open-minded" sorts to stamp all over my views.

To the right of this someone had responded in what must have been eyeliner pencil:

> First, I wish you'd introduce me to the people who think homosexuality is trendy, because I certainly have not met them. Second, nobody asked you to change your views. In fact, all that has sparked off this homophobia and "stomach turning" is the writing of a phone number on the back of a door. We are not forcing our views down your throats, merely getting on with our lives. You have made the attack so it is only reasonable to expect to be answered. You

wait, you say, to have someone stamp all over your views. Lesbians and gays live in a society full of heterosexual propaganda: Happy men and women kissing, making love, etc, in ads, books, cinema, TV, etc. It is our views that are being stamped on. If we so much as dare to suggest that we exist, all these wonderfully honest people start telling us how much we disgust them. You seem to be proud of your honesty and think it important, yet you despise ours. We do not want homosexuality to have to be "trendy" or "liberal." We merely want it to be accepted. I am 18 years old. I don't want to go on fighting for the rest of my life. I ask you not for open-mindedness but for some basic humanity. 1 in 10 is lesbian or gay. We are not creatures. We do not have horns. We are part of this university, this city, this country. Maybe you should start giving a shit.

Point taken. I apologize for degrading your sexuality and sounding unreasonable.

Cen fath as Bearla, ar fad? Nach Eireannaigh sibh ar chor ar bith? ["Why use English anyway? Aren't you people Irish at all?"]

When I read these notes I found all but the last astonishing. Thirteen years before, as a student in Dublin, I never saw debates of this nature on bathroom walls. I rarely heard mention of homosexuality, except in arch or embarrassed tones, and as for abortion and contraception, they were issues, but by all appearances distant and impersonal ones. Now these subjects were everywhere, were being discussed openly and by individuals rather than by groups. Every day the headlines of the Irish newspapers held the words "condom" or "abortion information" or "gay." In addition, I had noticed upon my arrival in Dublin an alarming increase in the number of rape and sexual abuse cases reported in the newspapers. The pious, circumspect, prudish Ireland I remembered seemed in the process of being altered by realities that would not, despite a magnitude of prayer and hope, remain suppressed. I saw everywhere evidence of two Irelands engaged in heated conflict. Daily the letters to the editor page of the *Irish Times* included letters titled "Homosexuality," "Contraception," "Rape Crisis," and "The Third Secret of Fatima"—religion lay in some way at the heart of all of them.

After seeing Ruth Riddick's name on the bathroom door, I began seeing it in newspapers and on posters in bookstores. I heard her name in pubs and on radio talk shows, but most often I heard it in private conversations with women. Ruth Riddick, I discovered, was neither a lesbian nor an abortionist but a steadfast and dedicated leader of a small effort to provide Irish women with information and counsel on the abortion services legally available in Britain. For this she was both famous and infamous.

In 1983 Ruth Riddick founded Open Line Counselling, a nondirective pregnancy counseling service in Dublin, and to a younger generation of Irish women and men she was the object of great admiration. Wherever I went, young Irish women urged me to speak to her, to read her pamphlets. Women who had never met her spoke of Ruth Riddick as one might speak of an intimate friend. She was a banner and a landmark of sorts. One woman I knew wore a T-shirt with a colorful and appreciative reference to Ruth Riddick printed across its front; another once offered me directions to a certain pub by saying, "You know the place I mean. You do. You do. You know it. On Morehampton Road." When I confessed that I still did not know the place, the woman cried with model exasperation, "Of course you know the place! Everyone knows it! Ruth *Riddick* lives around the corner from it!"

Ruth Riddick was also—and for a far greater number of people—the object of animosity and contempt. Although she neither advised nor discouraged abortion and concerned herself only with providing information, her very name was an affront to the majority of Irish citizens who support the right to life of the unborn. On September 7, 1983, after a divisive referendum whose acrimonious debates are still galloping across Ireland, 841,233 Irish voters (66.45 percent of the 1.2 million who voted) agreed to adopt an Eighth Amendment to the Constitution of the Republic of Ireland. This became Article 40.3.3, which banned abortion absolutely in the state. The article reads: "The State acknowledges the right to life of the unborn and, with due regard to the equal right to life of the mother, guarantees in its laws to respect, and as far as practicable, by its laws to defend and vindicate that right."

In a 1988 pamphlet entitled "Making Choices: The Abortion Experience of Irish Women," Ruth Riddick detailed the history and facts of abortion in Ireland. Irish law has long placed an unequivocal prohibition on abortion and on all activities and information related to it.

The 1861 Offences Against the Person Act prohibited homosexual behavior and made abortion, or assistance in abortion, a crime punishable by penal servitude. This law was assumed by the Free State and eventually by the Republic of Ireland, whose 1937 Constitution provided that existing laws would continue to be respected as long as they were consistent with the Constitution. In 1956 an Irish nurse was sentenced to death for attempting to induce a miscarriage. With the British Abortion Act of 1967, which legalized abortion in Britain, Irish women began traveling to England to obtain abortions. In such a climate, professional involvement in the facilitation of abortion could nearly be seen to be un-Irish.

In June 1985, at the request of the Society for the Protection of the Unborn Child (SPUC), and as part of a further effort by those who were instrumental in effecting the 1983 amendment, the attorney general of Ireland brought a case against the two organizations that continued to offer nondirective pregnancy counseling services in Dublin: the Well Woman Centre and Ruth Riddick's Open Line Counselling. Both organizations had stated clearly that if requested, they would provide clients with information about the availability of abortion in Britain. On March 16, 1988, the Irish Supreme Court issued an injunction ordering them to stop the counseling and "the making available of abortion information." The two organizations maintained that the injunction breached the European Convention on Human Rights—which guarantees basic rights such as life, liberty, and respect for private and family life—by interfering with their right to impart information, with others' rights to receive information, and with the right to private life, and they claimed it further violated privacy rights in that only women would be affected by the denial of information.

The European Commission on Human Rights, based in Strasbourg and operating under the twenty-five nation Council of Europe, is accessible to the citizens of any European member state who believe their rights have been denied and who have exhausted all domestic legal recourse. In response to the Supreme Court's injunction against them, the Well Woman Centre and Open Line Counselling lodged applications for complaint with the commission. When I met Ruth Riddick in August 1991, the commission had already made a preliminary ruling that the denial of abortion information was indeed a breach of the Convention on Human Rights in relation to the right to receive and impart information. It was expected that the full court's decision, which would not be delivered for another eighteen months, would agree with this finding.

❦

BY TELEPHONE I arranged to meet Ruth Riddick in her home, and on the appointed day, as I walked up Waterloo Road toward her house, I realized I had formed an elaborately detailed picture of her in my mind. She would be a tall, thin, peripatetic woman in black jeans and a leather jacket, less identifiably Irish than generically European. I imagined her standing angularly in a stark basement room furnished with nothing but a humming photocopier and a three-legged couch propped up on a stack of newspapers. She would chain-smoke and speak with a nasal, faintly leering Dublin accent. She would be blunt and forbidding, cynical, angry, intelligent, and — to the discredit of my own imagination — menacing.

The day was uncharacteristically bright and pleasant for Dublin's August. A soft breeze carried the sweetly burnt smell of cooked hops all the way from the Guinness Brewery in St. James's Gate to the patrician streets of Dublin 4. The afternoon sun was reflected sharply in the fanlight windows above the colorful doors of the Georgian houses. A heavyset nurse standing at a bus stop grinned maniacally in the unaccustomed sunlight and moaned to her companion, "Merciful Jesus, 'tis fuckin' roastin' out, Marie. I'm persecuted with the heat."

Red-haired Marie flapped a folded newspaper hopelessly in the direction of her own saintly, shiny face and murmured her simple concurrence, "Fuck. Roastin'."

It was not roasting. It was merely warm — Dubliners will never have any idea what it is to be truly persecuted by heat.

The two nurses leaned against a billboard advertising Batchelor's Baked Beans. The ad, which had popped up all over the city, depicted Batchelor's famous cartoon characters, Barney and Beaney, soft-shoeing around a can of beans taller than themselves. Dressed in tuxedos and trenchcoats, they looked like two simple-minded detectives on their way to the opera. Batchelor's ad campaigns often appealed to the Irish mother's intuitive ability to know a superior bean when she saw one. In big black letters at the top of this ad was the simple Irish phrase *Bean an Ti*, "the woman of the house." This coy play on the

English word "bean" and the Irish word for woman, *bean*, surprised me every time I saw it. The message was clearly that it was the responsibility of the woman of the house to choose the bean of the house. And in using a little Irish, Batchelor's had, in a brilliantly sidelong way, reinforced the popular appeal to traditional values.

I turned up Marlborough Road and got my first surprise of the afternoon. Ruth Riddick did not live in a tenement basement; she lived in a pretty salmon-colored stucco house at the end of a row of similar houses on a quiet, affluent street. The house was hidden by a large, leafy tree in the yard and by a high wall that ran alongside it and out to the street. The tree's weeping branches threw the yard into deep shadow and kept it lush, green, and damp. The stones of the walkway looked slick and mossy; I half expected to slip on them on my way up to the door. The place had the feel of having been long ago abandoned, and as I approached the door I felt the fine threads of a cobweb break across my forehead, which seemed to confirm my impression. Neither of the two doorbells to the right of the door was marked, but a shingle on the front of the house said "Fiacc Ó Brolchain, Architect." I made note of this ancient and deeply Irish name; to me such names always suggested an admirable patriotism and cultural pride in the parents of the person who bore them.

I pushed the first doorbell, got no reply, and pushed the second. Several minutes later a white-haired woman in a black dress opened the door and smiled silently and expectantly at me. Her pale, perfectly round face radiated softness and warmth. When I explained myself, the woman told me with a disarming shyness that Ruth wasn't home, but that if Ruth had made an appointment with me, she would certainly be back straightaway, and she urged me to go upstairs to Ruth's flat and wait for her there. When the woman stepped back and let me into the dark hallway, I had a strong feeling of being embraced by the house, of walking into another world. The hallway was cool and quiet, high-ceilinged, lined with old photographs and a large shelf of books. One photograph just inside the front door—an oversized sepia print of a funeral early in the century—caught my eye. Approximately forty people were visible in the photograph, and each one was pictured with equal clarity. There was a familiarity to this photograph, an emotion in it that I had seen and felt before. It was reminiscent of Irish news photographs taken during the Easter Rebellion and the eventual civil war, photographs depicting the grave and hopeful faces of people acutely aware that they had allied themselves with the nation's future martyrs.

As the woman led me down the hallway, I got a glimpse of a dark sitting room full of old and elegant furniture. I felt I was being led back in time, partly because of the darkness of the house, partly because of its antique appointments, and partly because of the Old World manner of the woman herself. She was calm, gracious, and soft-voiced. She walked with her hands clasped before her, like a cenobite.

At her direction I went alone up the narrow staircase to Ruth's rooms. It didn't surprise me that Ruth wasn't there. This fitted my picture of her. And it fitted what I had learned after several months of similar disappointments: lateness was a particularly Irish characteristic. The Irish took their social appointments remarkably lightly. When they said they would meet at 7 o'clock, what they really meant was 7:40, or better yet 8 o'clock, or, really, any old time they got around to getting there. There seemed to be no conventional concept of time here, no concept of having made a promise or a commitment, and they showed not the slightest embarrassment or remorse over their tardiness. Too, the Irish were always delighted to put things off to a later date, even the most pleasurable things—vacations, parties, picnics. Procrastination, indecision, and stalling were symptoms of a chronic national disease that seemed related to a deeper fear of allowing themselves any expectations at all, and I thought it was as a result of this fear that the Irish appeared so deceptively supple and easygoing.

Living in Ireland amid such seemingly casual unconcern, I began to wonder if my own hyperpunctuality wasn't a terrible psychic burden. In my mind I *had* to be on time. But in an effort to meet the Irish standard I tried to cultivate lateness in myself. For a 7:00 appointment I would leave my apartment promptly at 7:30 and struggle to keep myself from running. I would walk frantically six times around a block to prove how late I could be, pawing all the while at my watch. My lateness was as forced and calculated as my punctuality.

One afternoon not long before I left Ireland, I overheard a woman saying to her friend as they ambled down Baggot Street, "I told the committee we'd be there at one, Fionnula," in response to which Fionnula lifted her watch to her face and said breezily, "Ah, sure, 'tis only one forty-five. We're all right, so."

I wanted to catch Fionnula by the ear and shout, "You're not all right! The committee is *waiting* for you, and you're incredibly late already!"

In nearly a year of trying I never succeeded in assuming the Irish laxity about time.

I stood awkwardly in Ruth Riddick's foyer, which connected six small rooms and a short staircase leading up to a little glassed-in garret. Directly before me were a pair of curiously tiny rooms, little more than two coffins stood on end; one of the rooms held nothing but a toilet, and the other nothing but a sink. In the office a computer monitor displayed a glowing menu, and on the office wall were four or five photographic portraits of female movie stars with identically beautiful faces and dreamy expressions. A bookcase in the hallway and a long wall of books in the sitting room appeared to be holding twice their capacity, with books crammed in this way and that. The books included *Banned in Ireland: Censorship and the Irish Writer*, various books on film, books by Angela Davis, Elizabeth Bowen, Kate O'Brien, Willa Cather, Kay Boyle, Andrea Dworkin, Martha Gellhorn, Sylvia Plath, Anaïs Nin, and Grace Paley.

Standing in the sitting room, I felt intrusive and oddly as though I were watching myself. On the coffee table was *Vanity Fair*, with Demi Moore startlingly naked and pregnant on its cover, and a copy of *Cosmopolitan* with an article headlined "The 101 Uses of Sex." Both seemed entirely pertinent. On the wall an old-fashioned propaganda poster published by the Anti-Amendment Campaign pictured three starved-looking, bedraggled children tugging at their mother's skirts. The caption read, "It's life that needs amending, not the Constitution." There were watercolors on the wall, a stuffed leather desk chair, and two large junglesque plants that looked exhausted and eccentric. The upholstery was blown out of the arms of one of the armchairs, and on the rug, just below the coffee table, was the outline of a violent spill. The place was both refined and worn—a cross between a men's club at an Ivy League school and a graduate student's apartment. It had an intensely private quality, and I felt guilty standing there unattended.

The floorboards, ancient and dark as church pews, creaked loudly as I wandered around the room. I thought of the woman downstairs; was she wondering why in God's name I was ranging around up here?

Then, almost as though she had read my mind, loud music came dancing up the stairway; it seemed calculated to cover the sound of my footsteps and spare us both self-consciousness. The music, which had a lot of lightfooted oboe in it, was like the soundtrack to a 1930s adventure film, the sort of cheerful, whimsical music that accompanies the protagonists' drive through the French countryside. It only increased the strangeness of the situation.

I sat in the armchair and flipped nervously through a magazine. Twenty-five minutes passed. Ruth Riddick had forgotten me, that much was plain. I went downstairs, ran into the elderly woman coming out of her kitchen, and told her I thought I should be on my way. She apologized for Ruth. As we traveled together down the hallway, I felt compelled to comment on the appeal of the house. The woman said modestly, "My family has owned it for years." When I asked about the photograph by the door, she told me it was taken at the funeral of the nationalist O'Donovan Rossa. I had read about this funeral. The year was 1915. We stood before the photograph and she pointed out Padraig Pearse, delivering a eulogistic poem. I said clumsily, "Are you in this photograph?" and she said with what I thought was a trace of disappointment, "No, love, I wasn't born until three years later. But my grandfather is there." She indicated her grandfather by putting her thumbnail proudly up to his bushy beard.

I suspected that this woman was the mother of Fiacc Ó Brolchain, Architect, and again, as if she had read my mind, she said, "Fiacc is my son," and with such pleasure that I couldn't bring myself to ask how Ruth Riddick and her apparently antithetical beliefs fit into all this sober Irish nationalism.

Later that afternoon Riddick called me to apologize and to set another meeting for the next day. And so the next day I tromped skeptically back to Marlborough Street. The mother of Fiacc opened the door again, said happily, "You're back," turned halfway around, gestured to a woman coming down the hallway behind her, and said, "And here is Ruth."

The image I had created for Ruth Riddick was smartly shattered. The woman who stood before me, a long slender hand outstretched, was dressed in a rust-colored skirt, a white cable-knit sweater, and open-toed sandals. Her wavy hair, the same color as the skirt, was held back from her face with a large black satin bow and fell delicately to her shoulders—a surprisingly old-fashioned hairdo, like that of a girl in a fairytale. She was brown-eyed and pretty, with the sort of pale Irish skin that could tolerate the sun for no more than three minutes; as if to prove this, there was an unlikely splash of sunburn across the top of her forehead and slightly upturned nose. The sunburn, along with a mild plumpness, made her seem vulnerable and younger than her thirty-seven years.

Ruth apologized again for having missed the first appointment and invited me upstairs, to the already familiar sitting room. She brought us each a mug of tea and settled into an armchair. She toyed with a strand of pearls that hung majestically around her neck—the pearls were the size of pinballs. On each hand she wore two large silver rings side by side. The rings looked heavy and utilitarian, like hardware. Her earrings were big cameo brooches, and on her wrist was a futuristic watch nearly the circumference of a hockey puck, with geometric shapes instead of numerals.

I asked Ruth about the case she and her colleagues had brought before the European Court of Human Rights and whether she thought the full court would agree with the recent favorable finding of the Commission on Human Rights. She curled one sandaled foot up under her on her chair and let loose a long, vocal sigh. She spoke without looking at me. "It usually follows that way, yes, but the commission has more freedom in the sense that it's not as politically ruled as the court might be, because obviously it's a very serious matter when you're talking about the constitution of the country."

Among Dublin's educated classes there is a manner of speaking that has a decided Britishness about it, a defensive sophistication, a slow precision, with each word separate, a dragging of the vowels that seems to bespeak disdain, undue effort, ennui. Ruth Riddick had this manner. She leaned into certain words and pushed them heavily across at me. She was articulate and incisive and a shade wary, and when she talked I felt that she was talking not to me but to the nation, to all the people who had come before me.

I asked, "If the European Court of Human Rights decided in your favor, decided that you do indeed have a right to distribute abortion information, wouldn't that decision hold here in Ireland?"

Ruth laughed silently and without pleasure. "Not necessarily," she said. "Ireland is a signatory to the European Convention on Human Rights, but that is not in any way binding. Now, we've seen that very recently, for example in the case of male homosexuality, where Senator David Norris won an historic victory. The point about David's victory is that it was unequivocal in terms of human rights, but nothing has happened here as a result."

Among Dublin's tiny gay community I had heard the joke that there was only one homosexual in Ireland: David Norris. Not true, certainly, but he did seem to be the country's only public homosexual, which was a measure of the degree to which homosexuality is despised in Ireland. In the Norris case the Court of Human Rights had found that Irish laws forbidding male homosexual practices in private infringed on the European Convention on Human Rights. In response to the case, legislation had been promised in Ireland, but now, three years later, still no bill to amend the law had been published. The Irish government was dragging its feet on the issue, and conservative Catholic groups were working openly to oppose any change in the law.

Ruth said, "I'm relatively optimistic about how the court will decide in our case. I do think there are serious questions to be answered about freedom of information and freedom of expression and the rights to impart and to receive information, which are taken seriously in the European context, although they are not taken seriously here. Here in Ireland we have a background of censorship. We *expect* to be censored. I don't know what it will mean in the long term, but a European court case seemed the right road for us to go down."

I asked Ruth how the case had originally been brought against the pregnancy counseling services. She said, "The Society for the Protection of Unborn Children took the case under the constitutional amendment of 1983. They argued that the provision of nondirective pregnancy counseling—where abortion was discussed as a legitimate option that women might consider, and where specific practical help was afforded to women—was in breach of the constitutional guarantee to the unborn, and the Irish courts upheld that."

I had heard a great deal about SPUC in the few months that I'd been in Ireland. They were a powerful conservative group who had support from all but the most progressive and liberal-minded. Their detractors spoke of them with fear and urgency, as one might speak of a plague. That summer, at a public meeting in Trinity College, I had heard an impassioned student representative saying of SPUC, "There's a lack of awareness of what's going on here. They have a sinister and hidden agenda. Their agenda is not just the abolition of abortion, and not just the hindrance of freedom of information. It is not just women. They are against the whole of the working class. Their ultimate goal is complete oppression. We must never forget that."

Ruth said, "Essentially SPUC is the most visible of a whole range of new-right parties that became visible here in the early eighties, and who have decided that they have a specific agenda around—well, they chose the abortion issue rather than the women's movement— but they also have campaigns around divorce and homosexuality, and less engagingly around condoms and how and where condoms might be made available. That resurgence of the right was something that happened in force here in the late seventies and early eighties. Many people felt that Irish society had been too liberalized in the seventies, by the women's movement especially, that the whole thrust and force of the seventies had been towards liberalism, and they were disturbed by it."

This sense of disturbance had fueled the push for the 1983 amendment banning abortion. There was also concern at the time that liberalizing trends in the United States were having a direct and adverse effect on traditional Irish attitudes and laws.

I asked Ruth who was funding the Society for the Protection of the Unborn Child.

"We thought at the time of the abortion amendment they probably were getting funds from America, and I think that that still holds, but in terms of their day-to-day operation they probably aren't getting American help. The amendment was a particularly important campaign for them, and it carried on over a period of approximately eighteen months, so they would have needed serious funding for that."

When I told Ruth that I had tried to arrange an interview with the spokeswoman for SPUC and that my efforts were three times ignored, she nodded calmly and said, "One of the characteristics of the new right is that they are not at all concerned about talking to people, because they don't need people to establish their agenda. And one of the fascinating things about the 'eighty-three referendum campaign was how they managed to get the agreement of all the people in power to push this amendment before it was ever mooted in public. They are people who don't have annual general meetings, they don't have public meetings, it's not easy to join up with them, even if you want to, because their basis is fundamentally antidemocratic."

"Family Solidarity, I assume, would also not be sympathetic to your cause."

"Not at all. They are very similar people and there's a kind of overlap between them. Mary Lucey is the president of SPUC, and her husband is very involved in organizations like that. Solidarity and groups like it are all very similar kinds of people with similar ideas and aspirations and agendas."

During the summer of 1991, when Dublin's Rape Crisis Centre was threatened with closing because of insufficient government funding, the *Irish Times* columnist Fintan O'Toole wrote an editorial criticizing the organizations that claimed to speak for the Catholic majority, the ordinary people of Ireland: SPUC, The Pro Life Amendment Campaign (PLAC), the Anti-Divorce Campaign, Family Solidarity, and Responsible Society, which opposed government funding for the Rape Crisis Centre. O'Toole wrote, "The majority of ordinary Catholics do not really understand the ideology of those who purport to speak for them, an ideology as hermetically sealed, as paranoid, as self-righteous, and as intolerant of the great tradition of Christian humanism as Stalinist Communism ever was."

The Irish conservative organizations seemed to believe that Ireland was being undermined by a foreign conspiracy. As these organizations saw it, the source of the conspiracy was the International Planned Parenthood Federation and other groups that urged better sex education, contraception, rape awareness, and counseling for child sexual abuse. According to the conservatives, such efforts and their attendant publicity encouraged abortion and threatened the Irish family. In 1981, when Responsible Society succeeded in curtailing the level of state funding for the Rape Crisis Centre, its spokesperson said: "It is our belief that in funding the Rape Crisis Centre, the state is funding and lending respectability to the promoters of abortion, even though the amount [of funding] is small and it cannot be proved that the Rape Crisis Centre as such is in any way connected with abortion or with abortion referral."

On this Fintan O'Toole commented:

This is the sort of darkly fantastic conspiratorial thinking that characterizes fringe groups of self-righteous crusaders of all sorts. The difference is that these people are the most effective and powerful pressure group in this state over the last decade, strongly connected to the forces of both church and state, in spite of the fact that their views are not only bizarre but also what can only be called totalitarian.

The complaint among Irish liberals was that Church leaders and politicians were afraid to oppose the conservative ideologues and therefore had forsaken their responsibility to protect the rights of the individual.

I asked Ruth how the average Irish person felt about SPUC and similar organizations.

"Well, you have to look at the particularly Irish response to these issues. Irish people are overwhelmingly supportive of the right to life of the unborn. It's a specific issue here, and all the teenagers in all the second-level schools are shown the film *The Silent Scream*, and without any kind of discussion or any kind of alternative view being proposed, so it's not surprising that they respond to that kind of emotional appeal, particularly at a time in their lives when they are feeling very idealistic. But as a general principle, I think that while Irish people are absolutely satisfied that the right to life of the unborn should be enshrined constitutionally—and this is a very fine aspiration by us—we don't actually want our sister or our daughter or our wife stopped from going to England to have an abortion if she thinks it necessary. There's that dualism there."

I said, "I think there's great social pressure on women in Ireland to have abortions, particularly due to the stigma placed on the unwed mother, and it seems plain that if the attitudes toward single motherhood were changed or relaxed, fewer women would be traveling to England for abortions."

"I would agree that there's a lot of pressure on Irish women to have abortions. I would agree. You have obvious situations of women in professions like nursing and teaching, where they're terribly, terribly vulnerable." In Ireland an unwed teacher can be fired from her job for becoming pregnant.

Ruth added, "I understand that in the nursing profession one still actually signs a sort of morals clause which specifically refers to not getting pregnant out of wedlock. And I think there are a lot of those kinds of pressures on women. In a situation like that you are obviously under immense pressure, and I would go so far as to say that I think this society is very abortion prone in that it is very negatively inclined towards women and their feelings and their situations and their circumstances. But it is very difficult to deal with the fact that on the one hand we have this entirely antiabortion ethos, and on the other hand we have four thousand Irish women annually who terminate pregnancies legally in England."

I guessed that the true figure was probably higher.

"It is probably higher than that. But that also is a figure which disguises the infanticide rate, for example, and all the other things women do, like jumping down stairs and taking hot baths, and so on. So, I would say that the—shall we say—*negative* response to pregnancy is very much higher than that, but even so, the official figure of four thousand is very high in a country of only three and a half million people."

In her first pamphlet Riddick had responded to the wording of Article 40.3.3 this way:

> During the [abortion] debate it was argued that this form of words was essentially meaningless in that it afforded an absolute right to an entity which it did not define and established a further absolute right which, under common and recognized circumstances (e.g. ectopic pregnancy, carcinoma of the uterus), would be in conflict with the first named absolute right. It was tacitly understood that it would be left to the courts to clarify these issues.

The difficulty of this situation was illustrated in February 1992 in the case of a fourteen-year-old girl who had become pregnant, allegedly after being raped by a classmate's father. According to her parents, the girl had repeatedly threatened to kill herself if forced to carry out the pregnancy. Under any other circumstances the girl would have traveled to England, had an abortion, and returned home without unusual publicity or obstruction. In this case, however, because the girl's parents had inquired of police authorities about using samples of fetal tissue as evidence in a rape prosecution, the attorney general was alerted to the situation, and an Irish High Court judge issued an injunction barring the girl from traveling to England to have an abortion. The court's decision—the first time the government had attempted to prevent a citizen from going outside the country to get an abortion—caused an international controversy and divided Ireland's coalition government. In Ireland there was tremendous public sympathy for the girl and her family. The family appealed the case to the Irish Supreme Court, which found that the girl's life was indeed at risk and that therefore she should be allowed to travel for the abortion. Consequently the Irish government has been forced to consider whether changes in the wording of the constitution will be necessary to allow due regard for the mother's right to life in some cases.

In 1990 Attic Press published Ruth Riddick's pamphlet "The Right to Choose: Questions of Feminist Morality" as part of a series on contemporary issues and controversies by Irish women writers. The pamphlet was an attempt to raise the moral issues surrounding the abortion question and to interrupt the silence that the subject had engendered among women. Ruth's argument was not that abortion should be made available to Irish women but that women's abortion decisions are moral decisions. "Abortion," she wrote, "as the ultimate exercise of individual fertility control, is the arena in which women have least social acknowledgment and support; it is, therefore, the context in which women's right to choose, that is, women's right to act as moral agents, must be argued." She stressed that women have too long been defined strictly in relation to men, and that this is particularly so in Ireland. The Irish Constitution refers to women only three times and in a restrictive and paternalistic fashion. The first reference is in Article 40.3.3. The second is in article 41.2.1: "The State recognises that by her life within the home, woman gives to the State a support without which the common good cannot be achieved," and the third in Article 41.2.2: "The State shall, therefore, endeavour to ensure that mothers shall not be obliged by economic necessity to engage in labour to the neglect of their duties in the home."

I said to Ruth, "I am constantly hearing the opinion that Ireland is a matriarchal society. Is it?"

She said, "I think that the powerlessness that women have in the public sphere is seized in the private domain. I think that Irish women have probably been quite successful in doing that. The less power we've had publicly, the more power we have insisted upon privately. Further than that, though, I think that Irish men particularly have used the myth of the matriarchal Irish mother as an excuse for their own sort of bad behavior, really. And at the end of the day it's fairly meaningless, because at the end of the day she's only Mammy.

Mary Lavin has a marvelous book called *Mary O'Grady*, which is about the Irish mother, and it gives us a portrait of both the power and the powerlessness of the Irish woman. But having said that, I think there is an enormous tendency among Irish people to blame the bad behavior of the boys on the Irish mother."

"What is the bad behavior of the boys?"

"Drunkenness. And irresponsible sexuality. That sort of thing. I think there's a real tendency to blame that on the mother, for spoiling them, or whatever. I find that very objectionable."

When I asked Ruth what kind of responses she had received to her pamphlet, she shoved the baggy sleeves of her sweater up on her fore-arms and laid her arms regally along the arms of the chair. The crooks of her elbows were the bluish white of the inside of a clam-shell. A light stain on the sleeve of her sweater answered the lived-in mood of the room. Ruth peered absently at the coffee stain on the rug while considering her answer, then with an ironic smile said, "None."

"No one responded?"

"No."

"How many people have read it?"

"Well, it's a bestseller." At this she leaned forward in her chair and laughed so heartily I couldn't tell whether she was joking.

"I'm not joking, no," she said.

"So people are reading it?"

The laugh died. She looked silently at me for a moment, then said, "I don't know. I suppose I occupy a curious position in Irish society in that I am an obvious scapegoat, and I'm used as one, there's no question about that, but also I'm used as a resource, and probably occasionally by the same people. Because we have this enormous social reality—four thousand abortions annually—there's got to be some way of dealing with that, and to an extent I and my colleagues and the information we provide are the way we deal with it. But we don't like that answer either, so we have to have a hate figure based around that."

"You?"

"Oh, I think so, yes. But not personally. I mean, I don't suffer any personal abuse at all. Very occasionally there are abusive messages left on my telephone answering machine, but not other than that, no."

The distance from which Ruth Riddick discussed her unpopular position in Irish society surprised and impressed me. Her argument depended not on emotion but on fact and reason, and from this it derived its force. There was no overt anger in her assessment of the present state of Irish affairs. She was calm but determined, opaque and resolute.

When the Irish feminist journalist Nell McCafferty's name came up in our conversation, Ruth said, "I've never worked directly with Nell, but she's the author of the happiest quote of my whole litigation saga. She was writing a piece about . . . well, I think we were in the High Court, and one of the interesting things about our case is that we're all of a certain generation, and the SPUC people are all old enough to be our parents, and when you're sitting in court it's terribly marked that there's a generation gap, and Nell was up there, and one of the SPUC women said into Nell's ear in reference to us, 'Oh, those *women!* Those women encourage *whoredom* in Kimmage!'"

At this, Ruth's face, which had been consistently inexpressive, was transformed by a sudden theatrical energy. Her hands flew up into the air, her eyes rolled skyward. She drew in her breath and spoke in the gasping, hissing, scandalized whisper that Irish women employ with stinging mastery. There was true comedic genius in her mimicry.

Ruth laughed at her own interpretation and at the utter sanctimony of the statement; she seemed to be warming to her subject. She said, "In its day, you see, Kimmage was a very notorious working-class area, and the Dublin Corporation had a policy of dumping so-called problem families over there. It was one of the new working-class ghettos. So this remark had a resonance for Dublin people."

We discussed the legalization of contraceptives, which did not happen until 1979, after the establishment of the Irish Family Planning Association and because of pressure from the women's movement and family planning clinics. Ruth said, "And there was pressure from the fact that just so many contraceptives were being imported into this country and being used. The figures themselves told a story. That's why there was legislation at that point."

"Is there anywhere in Ireland where a woman can go to get an abortion?" I asked.

Ruth peered at me incredulously. "*Absolutely not!*"

I had heard this before, and still I found it difficult to believe.

Ruth said, "I've been involved in this area for thirteen years now and I've only ever heard whispers about that. I would not know how to put a woman in touch with an illegal practitioner of whatever nature. I wouldn't know how to do it. Now, I wouldn't approve of it either, and I've always said that to women who contact me. '*Don't* try to do that,' I say to them. 'Go to a proper medical practitioner.' My feeling is that if there's any illegal abortion at all, there's very little of it. But I would be worried, on the other hand—and it's a political point—that the less access Irish women have to legal abortion in Britain, however that might be structured—I mean, it might just be a denial of information, which is what we're laboring under at the moment—the greater the demand we'll have for illegal services here, and that's what I would be worried about, and I think it's an important political point. You see, you have to look at the history. We are accustomed in this country, because of our colonial past, to exporting our social problems to England, and it makes sense in an historical way that we would go to England for a service like abortion, particularly when we consider it to be completely out of bounds here."

Too, it is in the nature of a postcolonial state to be conservative and inward-looking.

I asked Ruth about the famous public meeting held by the Women's Right to Choose Group in Dublin's Liberty Hall in 1981. Public meetings in Ireland are often tumultuous because Irish audiences are emotional, opinionated, and outspoken. According to numerous accounts, the Right to Choose meeting, chaired by journalist Mary MacAleese, degenerated into a raucous free-for-all, with audience members hurling venomous personal attacks at the panelists and at each other. One of the leading women in SPUC attended the meeting disguised in a wig, and at some point in the meeting the wig was yanked violently from her head. At this meeting Ruth Riddick, then twenty-five years old, stood up in the audience and voiced her opinions forcefully enough to be noted in the *Evening Herald* the next day:

> A woman, who admitted having an abortion, spoke out strongly in favor of a woman's right to control her own body last night. Ruth Riddick said that the men of this country are not enlightened enough, or choose not to be, when it comes to the question of taking positive steps to avoid pregnancy. They have a right to choose whether they will take responsibility for their actions or not. So why should the basic right of control of one's body be denied to women, she asked.

Ruth said, "The meeting was organized by the Women's Right to Choose group. I would have thought that even at that time it would have been quite clear what such a group stood for. Among the panelists were the Irish journalist Mary Holland, Jill Tweedie, also a journalist, a spokeswoman from the pregnancy counseling center, and one or two others. You could not have misunderstood the nature of the meeting or the auspices under which it was being held, and there was a SPUC picket against it and all of that. But it was a very stormy meeting. A horrible, horrible experience. In many ways it foreshadowed the experience we would go through over the amendment. For example, Mary Holland was one of the speakers at that meeting. Mary Holland then as now was a respected journalist. She had written in *Hibernian* magazine about having had an abortion herself and in that piece she had appealed to other Irish women to join her and make a statement, as Simone de Beauvoir and others had in France. At that meeting Mary Holland eventually excused herself with the apology that she had to go home because it was a child's birthday, or something to that effect, and some woman in the audience actually stood up in Liberty Hall and said, 'I *want* to say to Mary Holland while she is still here, I *want* to say that there is *one* child *missing* from that party this evening!' And that was actually what prompted me to speak that day. I got so *angry* about this."

In her pamphlet Riddick wrote,

The primary social identification of women is not in ourselves, nor as "persons" or "citizens," but in our relation to the patriarch. This means that the first right we must assert for ourselves is the identity of personhood, not simply in a spurious equality with men but as an elemental involvement in the world of morality, decision-making, responsibility, social accountability.

I asked Ruth if she felt that Irish women agreed with that statement.

"It may be irrelevant," she said. "It may be that the arena in which we live our lives in this country is just sideways to that." She paused and sighed heavily, preparing to move on to what she saw as the great Irish problem. "You see, I think the most important thing to be said about this country is that the Roman Catholic Church claims the allegiance of up to 95 percent of the population of the country. Now I think that is a statistic that is *loaded* with meaning because, of course, within that 95 percent there are all of us: us feminists and socialists, us disaffected, and *whatever* we are. Fundamentally we are Roman Catholics, and that involves a certain very specific arena of thought and belief and thought structure, and indeed even an underlying philosophy that we maintain because the pain of working through it really is impossible on an ordinary day-to-day level."

The statistic that Ireland is 95 percent Roman Catholic was forever being brandished as evidence of one thing or another, but many people told me they were not practicing their religion, that they hadn't been to Mass in years and hadn't been to confession in even longer. I wondered how their experience fitted with the official figure.

"I actually think that that's irrelevant," Ruth said. "I'm not sure where the Roman Catholic Church gets that statistic—probably from the important things such as births, marriages, and deaths, which are registered according to religion, but I think that attendance at Mass or going to confession is entirely irrelevant. The point is how you structure the way you think and what values you transport into your thinking, and what are the arguments that you feel you have to answer, and I think that in this country, overwhelmingly, the Roman Catholic Church is at the root of all of that. All of that."

"So even the most liberal people are thinking in a way that is still, at its foundation, Roman Catholic."

"That would be my view. And I think it's evident in my work. Although I'm absolutely anathema, and indeed possibly the embodiment of *all* that is anathema, there is no doubt that my work betrays a fundamental Roman Catholicism."

I told Ruth about having found her phone number on a bathroom door. I told her how I had seen posters pasted up all over Dublin on telephone poles or on streetlights, with the number for abortion information printed on them, and how the very next day, without fail, the posters would be ripped down or covered over with black paint.

"The bathroom walls . . . that's a wholly appropriate response of the women's movement, I think. But equally it horrifies me in the sense that I do not think that it's appropriate that the most important decisions about women's lives should be conducted in toilets. Of course, it's quite right that the women's movement responds in that way. You're left in a situation where you're dealing in informal networks, where you're dealing with people ringing you up who may have got your phone number from a *toilet*, and they have an attitude towards you that's based on that."

"How is that attitude expressed?"

"Most of the people who ring me apologize for ringing. Their introductory remarks are apologetic. They're not apologizing to me. They're apologizing to themselves. The most important thing that's happened since the order of the Supreme Court of March 1988 has been the total devaluation of counseling and the counselor-client relationship, and the equality of that relationship. What I've really noticed since is that people ring me desperate for the sort of information that they should be able to read in *Cosmopolitan*, rather than ringing me looking for an arena where they can talk about what's going on in their lives, and what their other options are, and how they feel about what they're doing, and how they're going to reconcile how they feel about God, and whatever the issues are, and you cannot do that kind of work on the telephone."

Ruth's reference to *Cosmopolitan* was pointed. In the January 1990 issue of that magazine a publisher's note read:

> Following complaints from the Office of Censorship of Publications in Dublin, this page, which is usually devoted to advertisements providing abortion advice and help, has been left blank in all editions of this magazine published for distribution in the Republic of Ireland. We deeply regret that we are unable to provide the relevant information, but we are advised that if we continue to publish these advertisements it could result in this magazine being made the subject of a prohibition Order under the Censorship Publications Act 1946 as amended by the Health (Family Planning) Act 1979.

Ruth told me that her Open Line Counselling service was still operating in a number of ways, that she ran training workshops nationally under the Open Line banner, and that access to counseling services was still available through her telephone number. The women who availed themselves of Open Line Counselling came from all social classes, were urban and rural, and were of all age groups, though most were in their mid-twenties.

"There is no rule at all, except that for most of them it is a very difficult process or a very difficult decision to have an abortion. Generally, in the public arena, there is no longer access to information. But on the subterranean level there is, of course. You cannot have a rate of four thousand women per year having abortions without that being an indication of a huge availability of information. It's out there . . . on a very informal or private level, but I think there's a lot of information out there on that level."

"Are you counseling now?" I asked.

"I myself no longer counsel. I stopped that quite some time ago, because I found that I personally got so angry about the conditions of individual women's lives. I got angry on a political level, and I thought, 'Right, the way to deal with this is on a political level,' because it's got nothing to do with your client, so you can't lay it on them.

"I got involved in the whole area of pregnancy counseling by accident. I would not as a feminist have chosen it as my arena. I had previously always thought of violence against women and the whole area of rape crisis as being the elemental issue for feminists. My thinking on that has probably not so much changed as evolved over the years. I actually now see the abortion issue specifically as a site where whole dramas are played out about the meaning of being a woman in our society, and the hatreds that are directed towards women are played out, and I suppose when I first became involved I wouldn't have seen it that way. I do now, and that's why I'm interested in developing the sort of moral inquiry around that. That's particularly important."

I told Ruth that a few months earlier on a radio call-in talk show I had heard a conversation about whether women should be allowed to be ordained as priests. A middle-aged woman had called up and said irritably, "Of *course* women should not be ordained as priests! What person in his right mind would say confession to a woman?" I told Ruth how disappointed I had felt when I heard that, and how betrayed, and I expressed the sense I was getting that in Ireland the people who were most outspoken against the rights of women were women.

Ruth nodded knowingly. "I think the most visible people are women. But when you look behind that there are a lot of male puppeteers—no question about that—who are not interested in publicity and don't have their photographs in the paper. Mary Lucey's husband,

Michael, is a very good example of that—the shy, retiring type. But Michael Lucey is actually running the show. Or this character called John O'Reilly who more or less singlehandedly gave us the abortion amendment. These are the shy, retiring types that you don't see much, and they are actually running the show. But I do think that historically Irish society has done a very complete job of alienating women from themselves and from each other. I think that may have changed over the last twenty or twenty-five years, and I wouldn't want to promote a stereotype because I do think that there have been changes, but having said that, we are still a very deeply conservative society, and a conservative society relies on women being the custodians of morality."

"How will things change here? What will happen with the abortion issue?"

"Oh, the court cases will run and run without any conclusion. At the absolute end of the day we'll have to take Article 40.3.3 out of the Constitution, there's no doubt about that, because it doesn't work, it's a bad law, it's been seen to be a bad law, domestically and at the European level. Ultimately we're going to have to get rid of it. This of course is a prospect that no politician will touch. We're going to have to deal with that or not deal with that. As long as Irish women have access to legal abortion in Britain, as long as it isn't curtailed any more than it is now, there won't be any lobby for abortion rights in this country. You see, when you look at the makeup of it, anywhere that abortion has been achieved as a legal right it has been achieved by a mix of a strong women's lobby, certainly, but even more important by a medical lobby of doctors who are very upset at having to tidy up botched illegal abortions, and they have been the most vocal, and they are not arguing a moral right, they're arguing a pragmatic right. And that's the thing that has achieved legal abortion in various places. Now, we don't have that in this country. There isn't a constituency in this country which is tidying up after illegal abortions, because Irish women have access to medically safe abortions in the United Kingdom."

"Why aren't you satisfied with that, then?"

Long moments passed before she spoke again, then finally, and softly, she said, "Goodness, am I *dis*satisfied? I mean, my level of debate really has always been around the counseling area. It's probably wrong that women have to leave their country and have to negotiate with a culture that is not their own, especially in times of stress or crisis, but that's not the major focus of my work and never has been. I sort of take that as being a bit of a fact of life, if you like. I would prefer that there'd be proper services available here, structured through the health boards, but I've never particularly argued for abortion in this country. The area that I really feel very strongly about is that of counseling. And the empowerment of women. And the whole area of morality—morality of decisions and having support for that, and I think that that's what we particularly lack in this country."

I told Ruth I had gotten the impression that Irish women didn't talk very much about men. I'd been working with the Irish branch of the Women's International League for Peace and Freedom, and I'd noticed that the women in the group, who were anywhere from thirty-five to sixty years of age, rarely mentioned men. In addition I had spent a lot of time with the women in the Irish Housewives Association, most of whom were elderly and widowed, and they never talked about men either, never talked about their husbands, never referred to a life spent with a man.

Ruth stared at me, as though something was dawning on her. She said, "Yes, that's true, I think. I think that's really interesting. Yeah. I think perhaps that historically marriage has been a fact of life rather than anything more important, and your answer might lie in that."

"Well, it is possibly that Irish women don't take men seriously?"

"I think there's a lot of that. If we talked to each other in our secret language, would we completely dismiss men?"

"Perhaps women don't want equality with men but rather sovereignty over them."

Ruth smiled. "You're getting into a very interesting area there. I think it's probably true that women live in a separate sphere from men and that we consort with them for whatever purposes, for social purposes, for financial purposes, for sexual or procreative purposes, but I think it's probably true that women actually—even where it's least acknowledged—live in a separate sphere and speak a different language. I know that certainly among various of my clients over the years, mothers and daughters have engaged in the most incredible subterfuges so that Daddy doesn't know that his daughter is pregnant. We're not telling him. The premise there is clearly that an equal relationship does not exist between the two. Because if you were genuine partners, such a subterfuge would never arise. You wouldn't expect it. You wouldn't assume that you'd behave that way, and I think that it's probably true that women speak a language that men don't know and understand. But, of course, if you go very far down that road, then you get into areas that are very difficult to reconcile with the public, social, political sphere, which is where we're also trying to equalize but which is naturally, under patriarchy, dominated by men."

BEFORE I LEFT Ruth Riddick that day I asked her whether she was from Dublin. She told me she grew up in Sandymount, down the road. "I went to Scoil Chatriona on the North Side, where I did my secondary schooling through Irish," she said.

This surprised me, for while Irish was a mandatory course, relatively few students attended Irish-speaking schools, and those who did usually did so out of true devotion to Ireland and its culture. "So you speak fluent Irish?" I said.

Ruth smiled and nodded.

"Who is Fiacc?" I said.

She smiled again. "Fiacc is the man I live with."

J. J. Smythe's

I F THERE WAS LITTLE TOLERANCE for abortion rights in Ireland, there was next to none for the rights of homosexuals. On a trip to the Aran Islands, one of the most secluded places in all Ireland, I fell into conversation with a middle-aged man who, like me, was leaning back against a high stone wall, watching a tiny red fishing boat slide through the flat waters of Kilronan Harbor. We stood with our boots sunk ankle-deep in mud. Though the day was warm, the man wore a wool cap and a heavy overcoat with the collar up, as though against a winter wind. The great wings of the collar hid the lower half of his face—all I could see of him was a black brow, a long, graying sideburn, and an enormous hairy ear.

The man addressed me without introduction or preface and without taking his eyes off the red dot of the fishing boat. I thought he was speaking Irish and stepped closer, the better to hear him, but it was English he was speaking, his second language. Aran Islanders—indeed most native Irish speakers—speak English in a mournful, faintly suspicious way, as though it pains them to be speaking such an unwieldy tongue, but this man's tone was exceptionally gloomy; it made him sound like the spy he resembled. We stared at the sea as he spoke. The water was the same milky color as the sky, and the entire stone-strewn island seemed to have gone pale gray with the weather. The Aran Islands were so bare and wild that even indoors I felt exposed to the elements.

The man was born here on Inis Mor and had spent eight years in New York City working as an elevator operator. He was recently offended by the unflattering things the newspapers had to say about Ted Kennedy in connection with the William Kennedy Smith rape case. He believed the press had been hounding the senator, the press had always hounded the Kennedys, and lately they were dragging the memory of Jack Kennedy through the mud with a lot of clattering chatter about women and the Mafia. What was more, when Ted Kennedy drove off a bridge and plunged into the sea they crucified him and recrucified him.

The fishing boat approached the pier with melancholy reluctance.

"Didn't they?" the man said; he expected an answer.

"Yes," I said, "they did."

"That's right," he said, "they did."

The man's idolatrous feelings about the Kennedys were directly bound up with his feelings about Frank Sinatra. Why was Frank Sinatra never hounded by the press the way Jack Kennedy was hounded by the press? Everyone knew Sinatra was in thick with the Mafia. (He drew his huge hand out of his coat pocket and held it up for me with the middle and index fingers tightly crossed in illustration of how thick.) Turning his head slightly in my direction, he said bitterly, "And everyone knows that animal cannot sing."

I could see the man's dark eyes now over the top of the coat collar—contempt had reduced them to slits. His sinister discontent was puzzling and a little unnerving. In a spitting, petulant, childlike way he proceeded to discuss Frank Sinatra's daughter. "And the little wop always had his vicious daughter up in public, singing that brutal song about her boots. 'Twas an ugly song. Put me off songs altogether. She was a nasty little streel, whatever her effing name was."

A streel, I knew, was a slatternly woman. The man stared at me, waiting. I could think of nothing to say. The fishing boat bumped against the pilings of the pier. "I think her name was Nancy," I said.

"Same as that other vicious voodoo doll."

I moved closer to him, my boots slipping in the mud, sweater snagging on a sharp rock in the wall. "*Voodoo* doll?" I said. He was very hard to understand.

He nodded. "That old cowboy's wife."

I stared at his ear. "You mean Nancy Reagan?"

He made a venomous hissing sound. "Nancy *voodoo*," he said. "And the Sinatra girl was forever in the public eye, but the Sinatra son was never heard about. They kept Sinatra's son's life very quiet. Shall I tell you why? Because Sinatra's son is bent as a hoop."

"Bent as a what?" I said.

"*Hoop*," he said impatiently. "Hoop. Hoop. Bent. *Queer.*"

He put a blistering Gaelic spin on the word "queer," heaping it with so much disdain it came creaking out in two long syllables: "*kwee*-yar." He lifted his cap to two men climbing off the now docked fishing boat. "I hate the queers. The goddam bum-blasters. Sinatra is a queer. Both them Sinatras was queers. But the Kennedys was never a queer."

Without excusing himself he wandered off toward the pier, then stopped and turned to look at me. "What are you?" he said.

I studied his long, narrow face, the deep-set eyes, the lantern chin. I wanted to provoke him, to say, Italian, Jewish, *and* queer. Instead I said, "What do you mean?"

"You're American?"

I nodded.

"What kind?"

He had, after all, lived in New York—he knew it never stopped at just plain American.

"Not Italian," he said suspiciously.

"No."

"Irish then."

"I'm not Irish," I said.

"You are Irish," he said smugly, his hatchet face splitting with a smile of derision. "You are Irish. The Yanks never come to this godforsaken place unless they are Irish some way or another." He leaned back contentedly on his muddy heels, sizing me up. "Irish," he said, and before turning away he pointed a finger at me. "You mark me," he said, "the Kennedys was never goddam queers."

HOMOSEXUALS WERE among the people living in Ireland's tiny margins, and the mainstream was so large, so strict, and so unanimous that its margins struck me as particularly cold and lonely. I wanted to talk with Irish homosexuals, to know how they endured. When I returned from Aran to Dublin, I went to the women's bathroom in Trinity College and took down the number of the lesbian hotline written on the back of the door. I called the line and asked where in Dublin gay women congregated. The pleasant, bored voice on the other end said, "J. J. Smythe's Pub."

"Where's that?" I said.

"Aungier Street."

"Every night?"

"Saturday nights."

"Anywhere else?"

"The Parliament Bar on Friday nights."

"Anywhere else?"

"No, love."

"Any other nights?"

"No, love."

"Are you sure?"

"I am, love."

Two pubs, two nights a week.

I went to Aungier Street to look for J. J. Smythe's. It was a dingy place, with little amber windowpanes that were frosted and pimpled and impossible to see through. It looked like a shanty, like any other pub on that street. From the sidewalk I could hear the driving pulse of rock music pressing at the windowpanes.

The following Saturday night I returned to the pub but was too self-conscious to go in. I found it difficult to walk into any city pub alone, let alone a lesbian pub. I stared at the place from across the street. Two women in army jackets went through its doors, and three women in leather followed. My fears were powerful and troubling and annoyingly vague; I couldn't establish exactly what it was that frightened me. I had no idea what to expect, and I feared that I wouldn't fit in, that I might be rejected. Later I realized that this was precisely the feeling the lesbians in Dublin had to live with every day of their lives. I turned from the pub and walked home, disgusted by my failure of courage and resolving to return the following Saturday night.

When that night arrived I walked apprehensively across the city to

J. J. Smythe's. I walked the longest route I could think of, and the closer I came to the pub, the weaker I felt my resolve. I stood outside the door, wet-palmed and breathless with anxiety. Several women breezed by me, pausing just long enough to glance quizzically at my face before they swung through the door. I decided it was worse to stand staring in the street than it was to go in. I plunged through the door, and when my eyes adjusted to the near-total darkness I found myself facing a long, narrow staircase. I took the stairs two at a time, my heart pounding stupidly in my throat; I knew that if I slowed down, I would never make it in. At the top of the stairs was another door—I flung myself through it, again into darkness, and music so loud it filled my lungs with a thump, like a gust of wind. I could make out tables and booths here, and people smoking. As I approached the bar I felt a hand fall heavily on my shoulder. I jumped and heard a woman saying sternly behind me, "You're very welcome, of course, but there's a door fee of two pounds." I searched in my pockets and paid the woman, apologizing profusely. She stared impassively at me, jingling in her fist the pound coins I had given her. She had the harried, irritated look of a mother blessed with many children.

"American," she said.

I nodded.

"Welcome to Dublin," she said unconvincingly.

At the bar I was served a drink by a woman I thought was a man, and looking around the very small room I wondered if I had come to the wrong place. This was supposed to be a lesbian pub, but I seemed to be seeing both men and women. After watching the room for several minutes, I decided they were all women; I had been misled not simply because so many were dressed like men, but because some of them had extraordinarily masculine features and mannerisms. I turned from the bar and sat down at the table closest to me. Two powerful, pale-faced young women in jeans and T-shirts sat with their chairs tipped back against the wall and their crew-cut heads— one blond, one red—lolling against the greasy wallpaper. They were both pretty. They held their beer bottles clamped between their thighs. Their posture and their impressive size gave them a faintly challenging air.

The redhead, the larger of the two, scrutinized me as I sat down. I said, "Mind if I sit here?" and without a trace of warmth or encouragement the redhead replied, "Nuh." She and her friend stared stonily at me, and under the crushing pressure of their stares I had no choice but to look away from them. I was stuck. Now that I was seated, with a beer in front of me, it would have been exactly as difficult to stand up and leave as it had been to come in.

I sipped nervously at my beer and looked around the room. It was a dark, hot, smoky place, appointed in the manner of a brothel: the carpet was red, the vinyl booth benches were red, the velvet curtains were red, and there were tiny lamps with little red shades all along the upper half of the wall. The place smelled like boiled peas, the result of years of beer spilled on the carpet. Approximately twenty women were sitting in small groups, most in their mid-twenties and early thirties, a few of them older, and there was a clubbish attitude among them, as though they had all known each other for years. I realized I was probably the only newcomer in the room and probably the only person who wasn't Irish. Several women looked at me critically. One woman whispered something to her friend, who responded to the whisper by twisting around in her chair to peer at me—the pair were so unsubtle that I tossed them a decidedly impertinent wave. Fear can make a person reckless.

At the far end of the room a tiny patch of dance floor and a big, pony-tailed DJ were illuminated by colored lights. Everyone here looked settled and as if they were not going to talk with a stranger. Giddy with unease, I began to gibber at my two tablemates. My hands, gesticulating over the table, looked like someone else's hands. I made comments about the price of the beer I was drinking, how much cheaper it was here than in other pubs I had been to in the city, how you never knew what a pint might cost, how it usually cost around a pound sixty-nine, but a half-pint—which for some odd reason was only ever referred to in this country as "a glass"—cost around one pound five pence, which didn't seem right, if you stopped to think about it, and how a person could become thoroughly confused by pubs and prices in today's world.

The redhead smiled skeptically at me, showing a broken front tooth. She tipped her chair forward and put her big arms squarely on the table. I saw the sleeves of her T-shirt tighten around her biceps. There was a tattoo of an ivy-entwined crucifix on her upper arm. I heard myself saying—unbelievably—*So, what do you girls do?* to which the redhead replied, *Work in a prison,* to which I said, *Prison! Nice!*

The conversation slogged on in that asinine fashion for another five minutes, and it became clear that these women neither trusted nor wanted to talk to me. Eventually the redhead said, "You're not American or something, are you?"

I said, "I am."

"What are you doing here?"

"Visiting."

"Been here long?"

"Pretty long."

"*How* long?" The question was unmistakably threatening.

"Long enough," I said.

"Long enough for what?"

"Who wants to know?"

"Aoife. Aoife wants to know."

"Oh, really?" I said. "Who's Aoife?"

The woman leaned forward. "Bleedin' Aoife is *me!*"

The delicate, ancient name didn't fit this contrary article. "Nice name," I said and was alarmed by the sarcasm in my own voice. The way the woman grabbed her beer bottle, I thought she might hurl it at me. Her thick neck was like a plinth. "Ya like it in Ireland, do ya?" she snarled.

For my own safety I relented. I said, "I like it a lot. I really do. It's interesting."

Aoife softened suddenly. "I like it too," she said sadly, and her wide shoulders collapsed into a slouch over the table. "I live in London. But I come home to visit as often as I can. I go mad missing Ireland. London's a kip."

"Kip" was the Irish term for a dumpster.

"What do you do in the prison?" I said.

"Keep records. It's stupid."

Like every last person in Ireland, Aoife said "schewpid." She told me she was in a bad mood that night because her best friend had just had an abortion. She herself had twenty-one or twenty-two nieces and nephews, and though she would never have children of her own, she loved children and felt abortion was a terrible crime. I was surprised to hear this. I had assumed that the lesbian community would be in favor of the right to choose, but I was learning quickly that in Ireland the strong feeling against abortion was not merely a generational phenomenon; it transected age, class, and gender.

Aoife said, "It was like a slap in the face when my friend told me about the abortion. I took it as a personal insult." She added that she didn't want to go back to London and was hoping to be transferred to a prison in Belfast. "I'd be happier there," she said. "It may be the North, but it's still Ireland."

The blond tipped forward in her chair and pressed her smooth, angular face against Aoife's tattoo. Aoife pointed at her and said, "This is Maggie. She used to be my girlfriend, but we're not together anymore."

Maggie sucked resentfully on the mouth of her empty beer bottle and stared through me.

The room was filling up. Alone at a table to my left sat a short-haired woman in an electric-blue track suit who had picked the labels off four empty beer bottles and was starting in on the fifth. She did not appear drunk, nor did she seem to care that she was alone. She was lost in open-mouthed thought. The lenses of her glasses—the thickness of sliced bread—were like a wall between her and the world. As I stared at her, she leaned across to me, pressing the glasses to her face and grinning with the strain of trying to see me in the dark. Without warning she reached out and struck me on the shoulder, trying to capture the attention she didn't know she already had.

"Mind me seat for me while I go to the loo?" she asked.

Minding her seat was a struggle, as chairs were growing scarce. Women glared and muttered "Shite" when I told them the seat was taken. I threw my jacket over the chair. When the woman returned she thanked me with a nod of her head and went back to clawing at her beer bottle. I turned my chair toward her and, for lack of anything else to say, I said, "How much did that beer cost?" She winced at me; she seemed unnerved by the question, unnerved at having been spoken to. She leaned forward, trying to find my face. "I don't actually know how much it cost, to tell you the truth," she said.

The woman was long-legged and slender, had a sad, spade-shaped face, a pointed chin, and a lipless mouth crowded with sharp little teeth—like a shark's mouth. Her features were bland and blurred, and her pale skin was porous. Her short hair looked laid on in clumps, like sod, and her beautifully soft voice was marred by a heavy Dublin accent, an accent that often sounded leering and defeated. "You're not American, are you?" she said.

We chatted. I said it seemed as though everyone here knew each other. She said, "I been coming here for years and I don't know a soul in the place. I usually come in with a friend, but she's not here tonight." She explained that she and her friend would normally talk only to each other, because they felt excluded by the other women. "I hate coming in here alone," she said, "and I've been coming for years. It's hard. I don't know a soul. They're not friendly here. They exclude you. They judge you."

I was relieved to meet someone who felt as bad as I did, and I told her that I had felt a bit nervous myself coming in here alone.

She listened with her mouth open and her head tilted to one side, as though hearing the miracle of speech for the first time. "But I thought you knew these people," she said. "The way you just came swannin' in and sat straight down with them two things across."

"I forced myself to do that," I said. "I hated doing it. I don't know anybody here."

"Well, you'd want to have a power of confidence to do that. Especially in this place." She shuddered. She said she would have no trouble going alone into a pub full of men, because men didn't judge a person. Men didn't care who you were. Men just talked to you. But Irish women were unfriendly, and they were always judging you and comparing you to themselves, and they wouldn't talk to you. She thought Irish people were secretive and unfriendly because they felt inferior. "I don't know why that is, but I hate it about us," she said. "I think it's because we're an island, and nobody ever comes through here in history. And we never get any sun. Not like in France, where everything's nice. I wish I could go to France or someplace like that. But I could never leave Ireland. I love it too much."

The woman spoke in a softly sorrowing way, and without confusion or irony. She seemed personally pained by her nation's character. There was puzzlement and anxiety in her voice, as though these were thoughts that kept her awake at night. She spoke the way one might speak of a difficult daughter who years ago had run away from home and never returned. She had few physical gestures and sat perfectly still as she spoke, both hands clutching the beer bottle. Her lack of animation was oddly attractive. When I asked her if she had any children, she said, "Where would the likes of myself get children?" I was struck by her gentility and her seriousness. She was forty-two years old. Her name was Freddy. When I asked what Freddy was short for, she lowered her head in a sweet sulk and said, "Never you mind what it's short for."

The name was short for Frederica, which she pronounced "Frej-ri-cah." She said, "'Tis a fuckin' schewpid name," and she peered intently at me, waiting to see whether I would agree.

"I agree," I said. "Frederica is a very stupid name."

She wagged her head at me and grinned, showing her shark's teeth. "Hardy-har-har, very fuckin' funny, Rose." Emboldened by my teasing, Freddy leaned over the table and mooed, "*Stoo-pid*. That's what *you* say."

I laughed, and she persisted. "And Yanks say 'Toosday' and 'noose-paper' as well." She cackled at her own disrespectful approach to me, then said seriously, "Rose, do you not think the women in Dublin are very butch?"

"Straight women or gay women?" I said.

"Gay."

I looked around the room again at the anomalously masculine faces. A tall woman stood near the bar drinking a pint of Guinness — drinking it fast, I could tell by the many white rings the creamy head had left on the near-empty glass. The woman looked for all the world like a fisherman up from the Blasket Islands. She had a jutting chin, a collapsed mouth, a heavy brow, and long flat cheeks like slats. The oversized bones of her face looked battered, as though they had been misshapen and distorted by the trauma of her birth. She stood silently, feet apart, big gentle eyes staring diffidently at the other women, free hand stuffed into the pocket of her baggy mechanic's trousers.

Lamely I said to Freddy that I thought there might be a few mannish women here. She said, "Well, I wouldn't want to judge, because I once asked a friend that same question, and she said to me, 'But sure, aren't you very butch yourself, Freddy?' And I suppose it's true that I am, but I'm not like some of these women here tonight who dress like men and have men's attitudes and are snobby as well."

Freddy had the unmysterious androgyny of a high school basketball coach. She said feminine women occasionally came into this pub dressed in skirts and other pretty clothes, but before many Saturdays had passed they would switch to jeans and leather jackets in order to fit in.

"A woman gets forced to be butch around here," she said. "You don't fit in if you're not butch. I don't like it. They ought to accept you for what you are. These women look like men and they act like men. But if I wanted a man, I'd go out and get one. I like what's soft and gentle about women. That's what makes us special." She lifted her chin and studied me for a moment. "For example," she said, "you seem very feminine to me."

I sipped my beer and smiled.

"These women," she continued, "they should be happy they're women. They go home and get their period anyway"—she uttered the word "period" so forcefully that her breath gently lifted the hair on my forehead—"and no matter how they act in here they still have to be a woman."

Freddy, like so many Dubliners I knew, was not working at the moment. She had recently bought a house with money provided by her mother under the condition that the mother could come and live with her. "I feel sorry for my mother. She's going senile. Every last one of us has to get old, and we should remember that," she said.

I asked Freddy if she had ever considered moving to the country; the idea horrified her. "I've never been out of Dublin," she said.

"You've never been to Mayo?"

"I've never been beyond Rath*mines*. I've never even been to visit my brother in Kerry."

"Where in Kerry does your brother live?"

She tipped her face up toward the ceiling and sneered, "Ballygo-backward. Who fuckin' knows? Country people are nice to you. Know why? They never see you. They never see you but once a week. You look out the window: grass and a cow. Look out the other window: grass and a cow. And I hate all the shit all over the place. And it's boots all the time. I hate the country. That's all I know."

Freddy spoke of Ireland's rural life with utter contempt. What she wanted more than anything was to be a chef. "A cook, like," she said, "a person cooking food for people. I have heard about this cooking course that would end you up a certified chef. The problem is, and I don't like to make myself fail a thing before I even get started at it, but you see, in this cooking course you would have to cut up animals, and I am a person who is for animal rights. But don't get me wrong. I don't like animals at all. I hate them; it's connected to the country. But I believe they have their rights, so I'd be in a dilemma cutting them up just to get the certificate."

Freddy said she had a dog, but she didn't really like him; he was dirty and busy and a nuisance, but he had his rights, certainly.

Freddy was one of the more judicious people I had met in Dublin.

When I told her that, she spun one of her empty bottles on the table-top and tried to stifle a smile. She said shyly, "I don't actually take compliments very well."

Over the sound system Cher was singing "It's in His Kiss." Two women danced hard into my chair. Freddy was talking eagerly now. She said, "I left school too young, Rose. I was only fifteen. I left because what good is a diploma in this country? How are you going to get any jobs? There's no jobs. Nothing changes."

I admired the nerve—or perhaps it was simply the terrible force of loneliness—that had motivated this woman to come here by herself on a Saturday night when she knew that no one would talk with her.

"I haven't talked like this in ages," she said. "I don't talk much to my mother. She doesn't know I'm gay. She wouldn't agree with it. She wouldn't understand it. She would think I was sick or perverse, or that it was her fault, or maybe my fault. I think my brothers and sisters know about it. They don't like it. I was always on the outside of my family. You're gay yourself, Rose?"

The question startled me. It was the question I'd been dreading. It was put with great eagerness, and I should have been prepared for it but was not. I had thought a great deal about what I would say if asked to define my sexuality that night, and still I had no answer. I looked at Freddy's ingenuous face. If I said I was not gay, would she grow wary of me? If I said I was, would it not be a lie? And between those poles wasn't there the possibility that everyone was capable of homosexual feelings, that there was an element of sexuality in every relationship? If I explained my reason for coming here, would my interest seem clinical and voyeuristic and false? Why did she need to know, and why should I have to define myself? But even as my mind spun down that path I knew my defensiveness was born of the fear that I would be spurned if I revealed that I was not gay. I feared my presence in this pub might be offensive to women for whom it was a haven, that I might seem to be disrespectful of the seriousness of their situation. Trapped by what I did not know, I lied and said yes and felt a muscle in my face twitch with the lie.

The room was dangerously overcrowded now, with many women standing between tables or in the doorway or dancing wildly on the patch of dance floor. Beside me a snappy, big-toothed blond in cutoff shorts that reached to her knees hung drunkenly around the neck of an older woman in a sheepskin coat. The older woman looked depressed. She was overweight, and her fuzzy hair stood on end. The blond released her and began to spin recklessly in place, like a top. A young woman who had been standing with her hip against my shoulder bent over and shouted, "I can hear you're American. What's the gay scene like in America?"

I had no idea what the gay scene was like in America, but I knew I could safely say, "It's bigger than this." My deceit filled me with dread. The girl's name was Siobhan, and she was slight and pretty. She introduced me to her friends: Nora, whom I had seen earlier pretending to dab beer under her ears as if it were cologne, and a woman named Shleen, who looked like a jockey.

"Shleen?" I said. "How do you spell that?"

Siobhan said, "C-e-l-i-n-e. Shleen. I think it might be French. You can pronounce it two ways: Shleen or Shayleen."

Either way it sounded Irish.

"French names always sound better than Irish ones," Siobhan said.

What was this obsession with France? It reminded me of Samuel Beckett saying, "I preferred France in war to Ireland in peace."

I realized I was a little drunk, and I was smoking a cigarette, something I hadn't done in years. I asked Siobhan if she minded the cigarette smoke, and she laughed loudly in my face and said, "Cop yourself on, Rose. You're in Dublin now." Siobhan, with her overfriendliness, had squeezed Freddy out of the conversation.

Two seats opened up at Freddy's table, and a pair of women no older than high school age flung themselves into them. The taller of the two had a pretty, plumpish face. She hugged a paperback book titled *The Pogues!* to her chest. "I love the Pogues to death," she said. She held the book up and kissed its cover. She talked a great deal and happily: she had been to New York with her father, and it was there that she discovered she was gay. "I was never attracted to men," she said. "I only went out with them because when you're just beginning you don't really know what you are. But I just did it because my friends did it." She looked around the pub and said cheerily, "It's always so dykie in here! But if you got these women alone they would be very different. Irish people always get into a rut. They need a good shake."

She said she liked feminine women, and it puzzled her, as it did Freddy, that women would want to dress like men. "Oh, Christ!" she gasped. "There's that creature Aoife home from London. What a piss artist. I s'pose she can't help herself—the women who go to work in London always develop an awful problem with drink. They get lonesome and want to come home. I loved New York because it was exciting, fun, and you could be gay. But I would never ever leave Ireland."

The overhead lights came on in an ugly flash, a message to the patrons that it was 11:30 and time to leave. The DJ shouted, "Go home to yer husbands and yer wives!" in a tone that suggested she would show us all the back of her hand given half an opportunity.

I went into the bathroom, where two middle-aged women were discussing how early they had gotten up that morning—ten and eleven, respectively. "I got up at seven," I said absently and a little drunkenly, and immediately I regretted it, for the women twisted their faces at me and one of them yelped, "Shite! What in the fuck did you do that for?"

I told them I had wanted to hear Mary Robinson speaking at a morning conference in Parnell Square. The women's faces grew suddenly reverent, and the shorter one cried, "Mary Robinson is grand! She is the best president Ireland ever had! She is one of the people!" Her friend supported that proclamation by hollering mawkishly at her own dark-eyed reflection in the mirror, "And you're dead right, Una!"

Una's hem was hanging. She teetered on her high heels and gripped the edge of the sink with both hands. "That woman has brought Ireland into the twentieth century!" she cried, then, frustrated that it was broken, she dealt the chrome hand dryer a savage blow that nearly knocked it off the wall.

Just outside the bathroom door I ran into Freddy, who had been waiting for me. In the bright lights her skin was gray. She was a head taller than I. She held her hands clasped behind her back and stood with one sneakered foot covering the other. She raised a hand at me in a half wave and said softly, "Well, I guess I'll see ya sometime, Rose."

"See ya, Freddy," I said.

Freddy plucked hesitantly at her lower lip. "Can I ask you something, Rose? If you saw me again sometime, would you talk to me?"

"Of course I would," I said, "and I hope I do see you again."

"I hope so too, Rose," she said. She waved again and went forlornly out of the pub with her head down and one hand visoring the side of her face, as though she expected a heavy object to come hurtling through the air and hit her in the glasses.

Siobhan caught my arm as I was going out the door. "Are you coming to Ulysses with us, Rose?" she said. "It's a nightclub. Stays open all night. Gay. Men and women both."

I went down the stairs and out to Aungier Street with Siobhan and her two friends, Nora and Shleen. The streets were crowded with people streaming all at once out of the city's many pubs. It struck me that Dublin's streets at midnight were exactly as crowded as they were at noon, but now, unhindered by automobile traffic, pedestrians strayed off the sidewalks and weaved dreamily down the middle of the wide streets. The relative absence of cars made the familiar streets seem soft and quiet, and comforting as half-lighted rooms in a beloved house; voices and footsteps echoed off the shadowy buildings, and the pavement, studded with chips of glass, glittered brilliantly in the glow of the wrought-iron streetlights. That night the heavy mist that had traveled up from the Liffey hung yellow in the lights of Aungier Street.

Strange events occurred in Dublin when the pubs let out. I had witnessed, at different times, a group of people hoisting a body like a rolled-up carpet into the back of a tiny car; a slack-jawed, glassy-eyed face pressed against the inside of a storefront window; a man in a tuxedo peacefully asleep in the doorway of the Bank of Ireland, head pillowed by a marble step. In groups of three and four, people strolled, arms slung around each other's shoulders. And every night at half past twelve the streets were festooned with empty glasses placed on curbsides, doorsteps, and windowsills. They were placed with great care, as though the people who put them there did not want them to break. The glasses were like mushrooms that had sprung up through the pavement during the night—they made the streets look strange and magical.

A group of men passed by, and Shleen shouted at them, "Hiya, fellas!" An aging bum with pitch-black palms begged us for two pence so he could buy a bed in the shelter that night. When I turned toward him, Siobhan grabbed my arm and pulled me away. The man shouted after me with inspiring clarity, "Fuck you, fuck you, fuck you, ya lousy bleedin' motherfuckin' old hoor! Fuck you! Filthy old filthy old filthy old hoor!" I was spellbound by the rhythm and imagination of his cursing—it had all the musicality of a nursery rhyme—and fascinated at being addressed in this fashion. The invective was like steam spraying out of him. "Filthy old bleedin' hoors the lot of ye!" he shrieked.

Ulysses, the nightclub, was the low-ceilinged stone cellar of a restaurant on Parliament Street. It was half the size of J. J. Smythe's and twice as loud. People were sitting on every inch of the floor, chins on their knees like refugees, or standing two deep along the walls. Siobhan went to the bar and brought me back a tall can of Heineken, which I couldn't drink.

Nora jeered, "Americans don't know how to drink at all. You're always seeing five of them huddled around one glass of Coke in a pub."

Nora's hair was like Spanish moss. She was jocular and coarse and had a barking laugh. She stood swaybacked, with her belly pushed forward. She was forty-four, and she reminded me of working mothers in the streets of South Boston: harassed and slightly overweight. Stress, disappointment, and indomitable humor were evident around her eyes; her fingernails were bitten so close to the root that they were raw and inflamed. "Where's the accent from, Rose?" she said.

I told her where it was from and guessed correctly that hers was from Donegal. "I left Donegal ten years ago. The only way they could get me to go back to that fuckin' place is if they dragged me in a pine box."

I asked her why.

"They couldn't handle my homosexuality. They just couldn't handle it. I made them sick. I was the village monster. I think they wanted to kill me."

Most of the men in the room were dressed neatly in ties and jackets; they looked smooth-faced and well fed. The air was thick with smoke and sex. I watched a couple kissing passionately against a pole that seemed to be holding up the ceiling. Their hair was matted with sweat, their damp shirts clung to their backs. It was minutes before I realized they were women. I saw hands sliding up under blouses, a man standing at the bar with his hand slipped down the front of another man's trousers. The pub's two DJs (female) were locked in an infinite kiss in front of the turntable, the taller of the two running her hand up the inside of the smaller one's thigh. Siobhan hissed in my ear, "I think the tall one is gorgeous, but she never says hello to me."

I sat on a tabletop and listened to Siobhan's vaporing. The room was so loud that she had to speak with her lips half an inch from my ear. She had opinions about every woman who passed by us, and she took great care to point out which women used to be hers. She said, "Nora has it on for you, Rose. Watch out."

"How do you know that?" I said.

"I know Nora. She's a snake. Here she comes. Hi, Nora."

Nora had swaggered over to ask me to dance. I demurred. She grabbed my hand and yanked me off the table and into the middle of the room. The song was deathly slow. Bodies crowded around us. Nora wrapped her arms around me, and I thought to myself, *You deserve this.* Nora's hands traveled slowly up my back. She put her cheek against my sternum and pressed herself into me. Her lips were wet on my collarbone, and surprisingly cold. I couldn't help imagining her family sitting bitterly on the steepest hillside in Donegal, couldn't banish the image from my mind. I had a powerful desire to make a comment about Nora's shortness but checked myself. Nora's exploring hands traveled ever higher up my side, thumbs approaching my breasts. "You're too thin, Rose," she said.

"And you're too short, Nora," I said. Fortunately Nora thought this was funny. She snorted, "Ha!" into my shoulder and stepped on my foot.

When the song was over I went back to sit with Siobhan and met Deirdre, a short blond woman in a skirt. I talked to a young man in a cowboy hat who said, as though this fact haunted him, "I always felt like an outsider in my family, even though they accept my homosexuality. I was always the quiet one. I was always the weird one. I remember looking out the window and thinking: I got born into the wrong family; I got born into the wrong country." As I listened to him, Siobhan kept tapping me on the back and saying, "Don't talk to him. He's an awful bore." When finally I turned from him, she said, "Rose, are you by any chance bisexual?"

"Why are you asking me that, Siobhan? Because I was talking to a man?"

"No. I thought it before, back in J. J.'s. I didn't think you were completely gay."

"How come?" I said.

"It's something about you." She squinted at me. "I don't know what it is."

These questions irritated me. If this were a straight bar, would people be asking me if I was straight? And why did they need to know? I thought it was none of Siobhan's business. But more to the point, I was uncomfortable at having lied.

"You're bisexual, right?" Siobhan said.

"Right," I said, hoping this was the answer.

"I hate bisexuals." She wasn't joking; her harshness puzzled me.

Siobhan's friend Deirdre said, "What do you mean by bisexual, Rose?"

"Boyfriends and girlfriends," I said pathetically.

"Ever had both at once?"

I had an urge to laugh. I said, "Nope," and stared into a corner of the room, where a small man was sitting in a bigger man's lap, crying.

"I'm bi, too, so I can understand you," Deirdre said. "But I could never have a man and a woman at once. Too much hassle."

The snappy blond in the cutoff shorts whom I'd seen spinning in J. J. Smythe's fell against me on her way to the bar. " 'S'cuse me, love," she muttered. "I'm a little bit twisted is all, and I'm avoidin' Aoife, if you know what I mean."

I knew what she meant. She said, "Aoife used to be my girlfriend."

Siobhan went off to dance, and Deirdre said, "Watch out, Rose. Your woman's gone off with somebody else."

"My woman?" I said.

"Yours. Siobhan."

I shrugged. "She's not mine. I only met her an hour ago."

Deirdre said, "Did you not come in here with her tonight?"

"Yes, I did."

Deirdre lit her skinny, self-rolled cigarette and killed the match with a ferocious whip of the wrist. She blew smoke into my ear. "Then she's yours, and you're with her."

That was how it worked. Alliances were fierce but lasted all of an evening, and everyone was everyone else's old girlfriend. This was a pickup joint as insidious as any other. I felt a mild panic coming over me.

Deirdre introduced me to Mary, a good-natured, vivacious woman who had spent four years working in Connecticut and Florida. Mary had been arrested in Connecticut. She said, "This little dot of a cop at the side of the highway tried to wave me over for speeding, and I just carried on with me foot to the floor, because it frightened me, you know, the way he pointed his bleedin' finger at me."

Cigarette drooping from her lip, Mary demonstrated the way the cop had pointed his finger: legs apart, arm outstretched, one eye squeezed shut, as if training a pistol on a target. "And didn't the bastard come after me with his siren blowing a bloody blue circle to waken the dead. Pulled me over. Shouted, 'Out of the car!' like in films. Told me to put me cigarette out. I dropped it on the ground. He made me pick it up and put it in the ashtray in the car. Honest to Jesus, I was so nervous I nearly shook the hole off meself."

The hole Mary meant was, to put it plainly, her asshole. Dubliners were always talking about what certain emotions or events had done to their "hole." They were either laughing the hole off themselves, or vomiting the hole off themselves, or shouting their hole off, or having the hole scared off them. I could never get accustomed to this trope; each time I heard it, it was, with all its microscopic precision, newly arresting.

The cop took Mary to jail and handcuffed her to two prostitutes.

"One of the prostitutes had nothing on but a pink shirt down to here"—she pointed to her crotch—"and when I told them what I was arrested for they laughed in my face." Mary slapped the table on behalf of herself. "I'd've thumped the both of 'em if I wasn't chained to the bleedin' bitches." She paused to catch her breath and smooth her wild hair. "And, by the way, what religion are you, Rose? Because I'm supposed to be Catholic. But I guess I'm not Catholic, judging from my lifestyle."

As she talked, Mary kept reaching accidentally for my beer, and when I told her she could have it, she laughed so hysterically I could see her tonsils. "Jays, Rose," she hooted, yanking on my arm, "you're the master of codology!"

Mary expatiated then on Jews and blacks. She said in London blacks would undress you on the street with their eyes. She, for one, had no right to cast stones, being gay as she was, but still she had reservations about blacks and Jews. She interrupted herself to stare at a woman going up to the bar. "Wait a minute," she said furtively, throwing an arm across my shoulders, "d'you see Pat there? That's Pat. Always wears a skirt up to her arse. It's really not a skirt. It's really just a waistband with an inch of fringe, and when she goes up to the bar she still stomps like a fuckin' man anyhow. A leopard cannot change its stripes. Pat is a professional narcissist. Thinks every woman wants to slip between the sheets with her." Mary gave me a hortatory grimace. "Tell me, Rose, would you favor climbing into bed with a person like that?"

When I left Ulysses that night, Siobhan followed me up to the stairs to the door. "You and Deirdre hit it off grand, didn't you, Rose?" she said coyly.

I shrugged. "Deirdre seems nice," I said.

"She's nice, but she's a user. She used to be my girlfriend."

❖

THE STREETS on the west side of the city were bathed in the smell of the Guinness Brewery. The smell was like chicory, like a vat of coffee and chocolate burning slowly over a wood fire. It was kind and inviting and gave me the feeling that something useful was being accomplished while Dublin slept. It accompanied me all the way home, like light.

The bells of three churches struck three o'clock, and the sky was already livid with the approach of the sun. As I turned up Baggot Street I saw a young couple coming out of a basement restaurant, the man blind drunk, the woman in a fury, shouting at him to for fuck's sake come on. She hit him on the chest with both fists and knocked him to the ground. She bent over and shrieked into his face. She grabbed him by the necktie and began to pull him up, as though lifting a bucket of water out of a well. He sat up like a marionette. His head rolled backward, his arms were limp. The woman screamed, "On your feet!" I couldn't stand watching them, but I felt compelled to. The woman's movements, gently lit by a streetlight, were so incongruously careful, so graceful, that it was like watching a ballet or a dance occurring underwater.

Ancestors of Our Own

No two pubs in ireland could be more unlike than J. J. Smythe's in Dublin and Dillon's in Corofin.

One Sunday evening I went into Dillon's Pub and found Conor MacNamara at a table with his sister, Eileen, and Eileen's husband, Matty O'Shea, and their cousin John Pat Lynch. They sat in their overcoats, though the pub was warm that night. The coats made them look bereft and needy, like war victims huddled in an air raid shelter. It was a strange fact that in winter people in rural Ireland rarely removed their overcoats in the pub.

Eileen and Matty O'Shea, in their early seventies, were the parents of Donal O'Shea, the man who owned Dillon's Pub. The pub was otherwise empty but for Francis behind the bar and the pestering little man who was forever begging me to play darts with him, the coyote, whose name I had learned was Joseph and who was exactly as drunk as he had been every other time I had seen him.

When I asked Francis for a glass of Guinness, Joseph staggered up to the bar, reached into his pocket, and said, "That drink will be on me."

This irritated me. The Irish habit of buying drinks for other people sometimes seemed aggressively intrusive, an effort to grab one's attention and cause one to be obliged. Francis, sensing my irritation, refused to accept Joseph's money.

Conor MacNamara was dressed in a suit and tie, and behind his glasses his eyes were bright with drink. He called out merrily to me, "My little friend! Come over and give us all a hug!" I sat next to him at the table, and he clapped his arms heavily around me and shouted, "Friend!" into my ear. He smelled like after-shave lotion, motor oil, and stout. Joseph picked his way through an obstacle course of stools and stood just behind me, his knees touching my back. He muttered something about darts. I ignored him.

I commented on Conor's tidy appearance, and he said with genuine surprise and pleasure, "Do I really look nice? I don't mind if I do. I was burying the dead in the company of my family. A first cousin it was that died."

Francis called to me to pick up the glass he had filled, and when I went up to the bar, Joseph followed. "Will you play a game of doubles tonight with me?" he said. His eyes were nearly shut, his head was tipped back on his skinny neck, and he peered laboriously at me through his long, pale lashes.

"What's doubles?" I said, suspecting a coy euphemism.

Joseph's eyelids fluttered open momentarily in disbelief. "It's *doubles!*" he cried. "It's *darts!*"

I turned and stood directly before him. His thinness was startling. He was like a two-dimensional figure, a cardboard cutout, something collapsible. His mouth was a beak and his hair stood on end. He looked less like a coyote tonight than like a wind-whipped seagull. I said firmly, "As I told you before, sir, I don't play darts," and sat down again at the table.

Conor was saying venomously to his sister, "If I ran into that cunt, Eileen, do you know what I'd do, Eileen? I'd kick her from here to Ennis, and I'd put fuckin' brains in her some way or another."

Eileen had short, curly hair dyed auburn and little dangling earrings that wiggled distractingly as she moved her head. The earrings, jade, were the shape of tears. She turned to me, smiling sweetly. "And what might your name be?" she said.

"Rosemary," I said.

"Hello, Rose, darling." She grasped my forearm warmly by way of a handshake, the way many Irish women greet each other. She was a small woman with a round face and pert little features. Her big eyes had the same slightly popped aspect as Francis's, but hers were more mischievous and less sad. Her chin was sweetly pointed, her small nose youthfully upturned. She had probably been beautiful when she was young. She was drinking half pints of ale followed by short glasses of rum and was amiably drunk. She held her ultra-long cigarette slightly away from herself, clamped between middle and index fingers, thumb pressed against the filter as though it were a hypodermic syringe. On her left hand was a large diamond ring. She was a powerful presence in the room, and I could see that the men deferred to her. With mock formality she said, "Rose, darling, I am a sister of the proprietor, Francis MacNamara. And this"—she pointed a finger so energetically at Conor that her finger hit the lens of his heavy glasses and knocked them crooked on his face—"is also my brother. My illustrious brother."

"We've met," I said.

"And I am also a mother of the owner of the pub. Which is Donal O'Shea. Fix your specs, Conor."

Conor straightened his glasses happily, curled his long hair behind his ears, and introduced me to the others at the table. Eileen's husband, Matty, was a skinny, quiet, harassed-looking man with a black toupee perched precariously atop his high, pointed head. The cousin, John Pat Lynch, was tall, balding, and moon-faced. He sat slumped in his chair, grinning, his chin resting on the knot of his tie.

Eileen tried to introduce me to Joseph, my admirer, and I said, "I've met him too."

"Jesus, keep away from that man," said Conor. "He's an awful sexy bastard. He's a sexy bastard. A slyboots. Keep away from him, Rose."

In the sage and prophetic tone of a fortuneteller, Eileen O'Shea said, "You are American, Rose. But you are also Irish. I can see that from where I am sitting." I nodded. "And may we ask, Rose, what is your second name at all?"

"Mahoney," I said, bracing myself for the ridicule I knew would follow.

Eileen and Conor covered their smirking mouths with their hands. Even quiet Matty O'Shea smiled. "Mahoney!" shouted Eileen. "Ah, God, Mahoney! The way ye Americans pronounce your own names, 'tis not to be credited! Mahoney!" She slapped the table and sputtered, "Pah!"

"Sure, the way ye Yanks bring it out it sounds like a big round goddam thing rolling down a hillside!" cried Conor.

"A big rolling thing going tumbling, tumbling down!" cried Eileen.

That was why, in Ireland, I sometimes adopted the Irish pronunciation of my name, which turned it into little more than a nervous gasp. The Irish throw all the emphasis hard onto the first syllable and roll the last two syllables into a single disappearing one, dropping entirely the sound of the *o* and giving the *h* too much breath. They made the name sound like a stage sneeze. *Ma*h'nee. And when they were really keen to correct me, they added peremptorily, "But, of course it's really O'*Ma*hnee."

Conor noticed that I had the *Irish Times* under my arm. "That's very difficult reading altogether," he said. Francis had expressed the same opinion only a few days before. No one in Corofin seemed to read the *Irish Times*. They found it too serious and boring and preferred the more gossipy *Independent* or *Press*.

Eileen yanked the paper from under my arm and held it close to her face, staring at a front-page photo of Ireland's then prime minister, the Taoiseach, Charles Haughey. "Jesus above, spare us the face of this divil. He's the spit of a snake and those awful beady eyes." Then, airily, she said, "And what do you think of the politicians in Ireland, Miss Mahoney?"

I thought the politicians in Ireland were even more self-righteous, long-winded, untrustworthy, unctuous, prevaricating, pugilistic, and ridiculous than any American politician I could remember, but I loved the former prime minister, Garret FitzGerald, for his bumbling honesty and his modesty, and I told Eileen that.

"I love him too!" exclaimed Eileen. "All the women love him. He's curly-headed. And he's absent-minded. Doesn't he show up in the Dail with one sock blue and one sock green?"

Conor said somewhat anxiously, "Tell me one thing, Rose, did my son go out to dinner in the castle with you last Sunday?" When I said, "He did not," Conor looked relieved, then annoyed. "So the little chancer lied to me," he said.

Eileen said, "I was last out in that castle in 1945, when the goats were in it. Before Bob Brown's time. Before your time, Rose. I remember going right up them old winding stairs. Ah, God, I have heard them same stairs is there this long time."

Suddenly Conor said, "Say, Rose, have you much money?"

"Don't get personal, Conor," said Eileen.

"I have to get personal."

Eileen ignored him and said with renewed sobriety, "Rose, we are only just after burying our first cousin."

"Yes," said Conor eagerly, "and he was cre*mated*. He came out of the church in this little coffin." He held his hands up before him to illustrate the length of the coffin, approximately that of a shoebox.

"We don't believe in that at all in Ireland," said Eileen.

"No, we do not," said Conor, shaking his head thoughtfully.

I reminded Conor that cremation was exactly what he had planned for himself when he died, that he intended to have his ashes scattered in Galway Bay. He answered brightly and as if he hadn't contradicted himself at all, "That's right! Cre*mated*. And my ashes scattered in the bay, since I spent my whole life taking people out fishing there. And I'll take you out too, Rosie, my darling." He said this sweetly, then, wiggling in his seat, he threw off the mantle of affection and was all business again. "But anyhow, this little different coffin was only a foot long. They done it different, but all the usual Mass was said. 'Twas in a church, of course, but the dead man's sister carried the ashes."

"Maggie Butler," said John Pat Lynch, helpfully identifying the sister.

"And Maggie said she felt very happy about carrying him out like that," said Eileen. "I don't know why. Probably because she was the eldest daughter in that family. She felt a bit like the mother, I suppose. You might do it different than us across in America, Rose. But we don't do it that way here in Ireland. I am only telling you my view. Your culture is different than ours."

"Are ye Catholic in America?" said Conor.

"Some of us are and some of us aren't," I said with appropriately Irish equivocation.

Eileen said, "We here are much more into burying the body in the ground." Then, as though to herself, she added, "Maggie Butler felt happy carrying her brother in a little box."

Conor asked Francis for new drinks for all of us, and when I told him I didn't want another drink he lifted his fist and said, "I'll give you a bunch of fives, Rose. A bunch of fives if you don't have one."

Joseph the drunk came silently out of the shadows again and put his face an inch from my shoulder, so that when I turned my head we were eye to blurry eye. He mumbled hotly into my collarbone, "I hope to play one game of darts with you, miss."

I told Joseph gently, and as though it were the first time I had ever told him this, that I could not play darts. I told him I was so bad at the game, so uncontrolled, that if he dared to play darts with me, he would finish the evening with a dart embedded deep between his eyes. This was a lie. I am very good at darts. I simply didn't want to have to go into the back room and stay with this maundering drunk for an hour.

With great relish Conor shouted, "A dart between the eyes! Rose, that is exactly what he'd want at this moment!"

Joseph's paw came down heavily on my shoulder. He staggered against me, pleading, "When you come in again some night, we'll play a game of darts? Will we? Will we?"

"Yes, we will," I said, which might have been the truth; some evening when there was no one to talk to, I would play darts with the suffering creature.

Conor snapped at him, "There. You're shot down, ya fucker. Satisfied now?"

Eileen said, "Shush, Conor. Keep yourself under control. Keep your emotions under control."

"I should keep my jealousy under the table, Eileen."

"Emotions under control, Conor."

Francis came out from behind the bar, opened the door of a closet that contained a pile of coal, and with a tiny metal shovel, like a beach toy, he scooped up some damp coal and slag and threw it on the fading fire. The fire hissed and crackled pleasantly. Francis picked up the empty glasses from our table and glanced warily at his wayward siblings. He said gently to me, "Everything all right, Rose?" And with the way he looked at me, sadly and solicitously, he seemed to be asking if these people were too rough for me. He seemed angry at his family, and fearful of them, seemed to want to bang the little shovel down hard on the table and give them all a fright. Presently he returned to his place behind the bar and began washing glasses. Matty O'Shea got up and disappeared.

Eileen said, "Rose, Matty and I are the parents of Donal O'Shea, in Ennis. Have you been in his antique shop?"

I told Eileen I had been in Donal O'Shea's shop, and that I had seen an old photograph there that I liked, but that Donal hadn't wanted to sell it to me. Eileen leaned back on her stool, wide-eyed, her fine-boned hands pressed flat to her chest. "Not sell it to you? Why ever not?"

I told her the photograph was part of a news series that Donal planned to sell as a set. Eileen leaned forward, elbows on the table, and lowered her voice. Her face was alight with scheming pleasure. "Come here to me, Rose. Do you know what you'll do? You'll go in to Donal one day and you'll say, 'Donal, is your mother Eileen Mac-Namara O'Shea?' and he'll say, 'God, she is,' and you'll say, 'I met the woman, and Jesus she is an awful old boozer!'"

Eileen stared so intently at me I thought she might reach out and grab me by the collar.

"Will you do that, Rose? Will you, hah?"

I smiled at her. She was thrilled with her own idea. "You say to Donal, 'Your mother would kill for a drink. Jesus save us, she loves her drink.' And if you get him in the right spot, he could sell you that photo, whatever it's of."

It was a photograph of the Irish patriot Constance Markievicz, chatting with a reporter at a rally in 1915. In a wide-brimmed hat and with a pistol in a holster slung around her hips, Markievicz looked like a Canadian Mountie. In the photograph she looked large and lifelike and startlingly modern.

John Pat Lynch, who had said little so far, leaned forward meaningfully in his seat. He was like an oversized adolescent. His perfectly round face was pampered and smooth, and he was bald but for a glistening band of gray bristles around the crown of his large head. He had a docile manner and looked as though he'd been dressed by a fastidious and competitive mother. His shirt was brilliant white, his tie was knotted too tightly, and the stiffly starched collar of his shirt seemed to be choking him, cutting off the circulation to his head. He was slow and smiling and simple, and he was easily worried. Anxiously he said, "Eileen? Hey, Eileen? Where's your husband gone to?"

Eileen gripped the edge of the table with both hands, the long cigarette dangling from her lips. Suddenly wild-eyed, she screeched horribly, "God help us, he's gone, John Pat! He's gone, oh!"

Much the way a person can incite a high-strung dog to bark louder and more fiercely by imitating a fierce bark, Eileen's performance threw John Pat deeper into his fit of terror. "Ah, God, where's he *gone* to, Eileen?" He looked frantically around the room, clutching at his tie, his hands, his head.

"Jesus, he's gone to Mass, John Pat! My God, we're abandoned!" Eileen said, swinging her beer glass loosely over her head in the wide circular motion one would use to swing a lariat, and without spilling a drop.

John Pat looked stricken, on the verge of tears. He pressed the tip of his tie to his mouth and whined through it. "How are we gonna get *home*, Eileen? Who's gonna drive us *home*, Eileen? Who?"

Eileen spun youthfully on the stool until she faced the bar and Francis behind it. She spoke in a stabbing way. "Francis will drive us! No problem! Francis my little brother will drive us!" She snorted at the utter comedy of this, stomped her high-heeled shoes on the flagstones, pressed her knees together, and folded herself over at the waist, choking on her own cackling. I took from this that Francis didn't drive.

Eileen turned back to the table, calm and serious now, and obviously irritated by John Pat's fussy timidity. "We'll get back all right, John Pat, boy," she said dismissively. She had a heavy Clare accent, words running together breathlessly.

I said, "Your husband's gone to Mass at seven o'clock on a Thursday evening?"

Eileen raised her hand to the side of her mouth and leaned into me. "My husband," she whispered, "goes to Mass several times a day."

"Does he really?"

Eileen gave me a pitying look that said, *Of course not, dolt! You fell for it too?* Then, apologetically, she said, "No, Rose. He does not. I was only taking the mickey out of John Pat. Matty's only gone off down the road for a bag of crisps."

Joseph was murmuring incoherently into my ear again. "Remember when you and me were in the pub down the road, and you asked the pub owner my name in there? You. I'm asking you to go back there and you ask the pub owner, Bofey."

"Ask him what?" I said.

"Well. I'm only saying. I don't mind. I'll bring you home tonight."

One of Joseph's eyes had snapped completely shut. His glass had tipped in his lax grip, and beer splashed onto his boots.

Eileen rolled her eyes and said to Joseph in a patronizing voice, "Not at all. Not at all. The girl is all right. She's taken care of. We'll take her home tonight."

Joseph persisted. "You remember the night I asked you to play darts?"

I nodded, and suddenly Joseph was heartbreakingly lucid. "Well, I meant no harm. Maybe you thought I was just messing around. But, well, I do fancy you. Right? Yes. Yes. And I was trying to buy a pint for you. And I only wanted to talk to you. But I didn't know how to say that. And now I have made a mess of it. But then when you went out of that pub you asked the bartender my full name."

Joseph's chin was grazing my shoulder and his hand was heavy on my back and he was murmuring as though he was already lying in bed with me.

I said, "Yes."

"*So?*"

"So I just wanted to know who you were."

"*So you never play darts?*"

"I never do."

This was too much for Conor; he stood up beside Joseph and shouted, "And you will never play darts with that girl anyway, because that's my girl!" He raised his hand as if to strike Joseph. I stood up. This seemed somehow false and fabricated to me. It wasn't me they were interested in, it was any woman who stepped through the door. There weren't enough women in Corofin, and the men were exceedingly lonely.

Eileen O'Shea stood up and shoved the men apart in a bored, perfunctory way, as though she had done this a million times before. We all sat down again, and John Pat Lynch leaned back in his seat, grinning hugely and patting his tie now that the conflict was over. With the self-satisfied air of a man being interviewed on a talk show, he said, "You see, Rose, when a stranger comes into this country, they go mad about her. Same thing happened to me."

A silence ensued in which all at the table considered this curious statement. Conor said disgustedly, "For Chrissakes what the fuck are you going on about now, John Pat?"

John Pat winced and bowed his head. Meekly he said, "Well, I was only thinking of when I came home after all those years in Canada and everyone went mad about me."

Conor ignored him. Eileen ignored him. Eileen said, "Conor, remember the time I saw Mrs. Haran's ghost with the rosary beads in her hands?"

Conor tried to nod his head as he drank from his glass—the stout splashed onto his chin. He swiped at his mouth with the sleeve of his coat. "And when I ever heard that I fecked off out of there fast, Eileen. And those days you had that long mop of hair, and your hair was standing up on its feckin' ends after you ever saw that ghost of Mrs. Moran."

"Mrs. Haran."

"Mrs. Haran."

Eileen explained that as children they used to help out at the Harans' farm. Conor and Eileen milked thirteen cows between them, racing to see who could do six the fastest; whoever lost had to milk the thirteenth. "I was a star for milking cows," she said. "And you can go straight in to my son, Donal O'Shea, and tell him, 'Donal, your mother is a right old boozer.'" Eileen changed the subject as swiftly as Conor did.

Conor jumped to her assistance. "Rose, here's what you tell him: 'I met that blathering old boozer in Dillon's, and every one of her relatives was drunk.' Tell him we told you you might get an old bargain off him." Conor looked at Eileen for approval, then, as if realizing the futility of the plan, he said with a deep frown, "Ah, but Donal's so tensed up, isn't he, Eileen? He has to know you."

This brother and sister were like two cronies deep in collusion against the world. They loved jokes and social experiments, they loved guessing games, and it was difficult to know when they were being serious, or whether they believed what they said. They reminded me of members of my own extended family. They were sharp and excitable, funny and vaguely disappointed.

Eileen, watery-eyed with rum, said, "Well, he has to build up a little relationship. That's the way the Irish are. We really are. We have to build up a little relationship before you get any bargains off us. Tell him you know me, Rose." And again she slipped into the charade she was finding irresistible. She pulled an inquisitive, slightly puzzled face, the way I was supposed to do when I had my encounter with Donal O'Shea. "'Is that woman your mother?' says you. 'Well, God, I thought that was your sister,' says you to him."

Eileen was using a very Irish tactic; she was rehearsing my lines for me, showing me how I should approach her son, and she was proud of the lines she had created. It was like a little play, a fantasy that had taken over momentarily. This was a device that could be applied to the past as well as to the future. Stories were retold with all the appropriate dialogue assigned to each character, and with the same emotion, tone, facial expressions, and gestures of the original.

Eileen poked me in the elbow with her cigarette lighter. Conor slapped me on the back so hard it took my breath away. They were a dangerous pair to sit next to, and they were having the time of their lives entertaining each other. Eileen said, "That Donal, he could kill you, and then he's very soft at the same time. He's like himself across the table." She pointed at Conor.

Conor said, out of the blue, "Now I am a great-grandfather. I christened a little baby last week and became a great-grandfather." At sixty-three this seemed nearly impossible. Conor turned to Eileen, suddenly keen on a new subject. "Eileen," he said urgently, "did you notice anything today when they were carrying that small little coffin out of the church?"

"I never saw that before. Such a small little coffin."

"Yeah," said Conor, "and when she was carrying this little foot-and-a-half-long coffin out of the church — or maybe it was nine inches long — my first cousin, his sister, was carrying her own brother out, and did you notice who in the name of Jesus came strolling down the bloody street? Only my little granddaughter and her daughter, my great-granddaughter, and I said, 'Monica!' because there she was with the new little infant inside in the pram coming down the street as bold as a little monkey, and she's only seventeen years of age and a kid and doesn't know any better, and says I to her, 'Don't you go down past the church, for the little coffin is coming out and 'twould be a cross for you to do that, and 'twould be bad *luck*. To cross a baby with a coffin would be bad *luck*.' And Jesus she did not obey my orders and she did not go back, and there was Maggie Butler walking out with the small little coffin on her hip, and away went Monica with her little baby and made a perfect cross in front of the coffin. Jesus." Conor looked ready to spit.

Eileen said to me, "It's different cultures, you see, and we wouldn't do that sort of carry-on here in Ireland, Rose."

Matty O'Shea came through the pub door, and Eileen hooted, "Well, here is my husband home from Mass!"

"Eileen," Matty said wearily, flopping down into his armchair, the stiff strands of the toupee falling over his eyes, "you know I only go to Mass on Easter and Christmas." He tossed her a bag of potato chips.

"That's right," Eileen said, tearing the bag open, "they began the collections in Mass and he couldn't afford to go anymore!" She shouted, "Ha!" and launched wholeheartedly into Irish Gaelic. "Sigh sios agus do scith a ligean! Nil aon tintean mar do thintean fhein! La bhrea buiochas le Dia!" Sit down and rest yourself! There's no fireplace like your own fireplace! It's a fine day, thank God! These were the platitudinous sayings that people flung out with bold authority when their Irish was rusty or incomplete. The habit was known as the *cupla focail*, the few words. Eileen looked over at me with new interest. "Cailin dheas, muise," she said. You're a nice girl. She rested for a minute, elbow on the table and chin in her palm, and looked curiously at me. "I am speaking Irish, Rose. You wouldn't know what I'm saying at all."

"Tuigim. Ta beagan Gaeilge agam," I said.

Eileen clapped her hand over her mouth. "For the love of Mike!" she cried through her fingers.

"For the love of Mike," Conor said, equally astonished.

Had a dog come into the pub singing a little song they would not have been more surprised.

"Did you learn that across in America?"

I told them I learned it here in Ireland, when I was younger. I told them the truth: my Irish was terrible. Conor looked at Eileen. "Think of it, Eileen! A Yank spouting Irish!"

That was the usual reaction to any outsider who bothered to study this archaic, fading language—it was seen as a silly joke or a trick.

Eileen started to say something, and when Conor interrupted her she told him to shut his mouth and go back on the wagon. She said, "My great-aunt married a man named Hurley who was the postmaster general in Boston. When you go home, Rose, will you research that for me?"

Enviously Conor said, "How did Hurley get that big job?"

"Wait till I tell you about them, Rose," Eileen said, thinking hard, trying to remember what she knew about these characters in her personal history. She narrowed her eyes, tipped her head to one side, stirred her curls with a finger. She tapped her cigarette lighter on the table. "My genetic factor is working," she said. "Ah, well, I don't remember that part, but I remember my great-aunt wouldn't let Hurley have anything to do with the MacNamaras, because the MacNamaras were all alcoholics."

Eileen said she had eight children and that if she could have more, she certainly would. "We had them all and we loved them all. We loved our kids, all of us. We just loved them. And we're still minding them. I love them. If you had a child in the morning, Rose, I'd mind it for you!"

Everyone laughed uproariously over this.

"Haven't we MacNamaras got mad old ways?" said Conor.

"Ah, God, we loved all the children and would never harm them. We would never harm them. We loved them, all of them."

Eileen's voice had taken on a faint tone of protest, as though someone had accused her of neglect or immorality. The conversation turned then to abortion and illegitimacy. Conor said softly, shaking his head, "Remember Mick O'Laughlin? Jesus. We do love kids. Remember Maeve? And remember the baby died?"

I said, "What baby died?"

Eileen leaned over and whispered in my ear, "Illegitimate," which didn't explain what baby. "But Jesus we do love kids. We cuddle them up and we love them. Every one of us needs love. Every baby needs love. And all the fighting there is in the world. It's like Charlie Haughey. Nothing good comes out of the men politicians."

I agreed and expressed my far-fetched opinion that Mary O'Rourke, then minister for education, should be the next Taoiseach, and Conor concurred with great relish. "Oh, I'd like to see that! She's good and honest and very capable, and I'd like to see that. Weird-looking face on her, but she's shrewd and clever. Fianna Fail she is. Poor old Jack Lynch was the best of them all."

At that point I sensed John Pat Lynch across the table trying to get my attention. He was leaning so far forward his cheek touched the lip of his beer glass. "Rose," he was saying softly and pleadingly. "Rose. Rose. *Rose*. Hi, Rose. How about our president, Mary Robinson, Rose?"

Before I could respond, Conor exploded with stunning contempt for Mary Robinson. "Ah, no! Not that old bitch! You should not have a fuckin' president when you don't own your own country! We have a half a cunt of a country! We have a borderline case across our country! And you should have no president when you do not own your own country! England still owns six counties of it!"

Conor sounded sickened by this state of affairs, but it was difficult to tell how deep his feeling was. At times his emotions seemed skewed and misdirected, merely imitations of emotions.

John Pat said timidly—and rather recklessly—"But *I* voted for Mary Robinson, Conor."

Conor placed the heels of his fists dramatically against the edge of the table, as if to keep himself from punching John Pat. He lowered his voice to a threatening growl. "Well, ya dirty rotten tramp, ya. You should not have. You do not vote for the fucking president when you do not own your own country. And we do not own this one! So therefore we should have no president."

"Dun do bheal," said Eileen gaily, sweeping her hand across the table. She was telling him to shut his mouth.

"It is as simple as that!" roared Conor. "There is a borderline case across our country. We do not own it. Therefore you should not have a president in a half a country. I am IRA. I came out of the Irish army, and I joined the IRA in 1953. I am a member, so I know what I am talking about."

This I didn't believe. "What do you think of the IRA's tactics?" I asked.

"Their tactics are good! Their brains are fantastic. We'll fight and we'll fight and we'll fight until our dying day, but we should not have a president." Conor put his elbows down hard on the table and stuck the tips of his two little fingers into the gaps in his teeth. He breathed heavily around the fingers and stared into an ashtray. He seemed to be thinking, *What's next that's good to say?*

All Conor's self-righteous, determined talk about fighting seemed like a parody of the supposedly belligerent Irish temperament. I didn't believe Conor MacNamara was capable of harming anyone. I said, "But Conor, if you shouldn't have a president, then you shouldn't have a prime minister either."

"We shouldn't, Rose! That's right!" He was grabbing onto anything now. "Do you know how much that bitch Mary Robinson is costing us each year? I don't give a fuck how smart she is. She shouldn't be there. That's a dirty rotten bitch there anyway. She's costing us one dick of a heap of fuckin' money. We don't own our own country. We don't own our own country. *We don't own our own country!*"

Conor was incapable of differentiating between Mary Robinson the woman and the office of the presidency, and he spoke as if all of Ireland's problems were Mary Robinson's fault. He was probably the only person in Ireland who didn't adore the new president. "England is still inside in a part of our country. There should be no such thing as a fuckin' president in Ireland."

Having worked himself into a frenzy, Conor was on his feet again, barking and spitting and waving his arms. "We're only a cunt of a misfortunate bastard of a fuckin' thing. And why should we have all those great big things such as a president? First of all we have to get a proper country. Sack every one of them fuckin' leaders. How? I'll tell you how. A big machine gun. And give me a machine gun and I'll put 'em up agin' the wall and I wouldn't even give them coffins. I'd give them a big strong river like the Shannon. I'd put 'em up along the side of it, and in they'd go and out to the fuckin' sea. Then I'd hire twelve good business people to run the country. Sure, aren't we governed by Brussels anyway?"

Francis, deeply upset by all this shouting and cursing, turned the six o'clock news on loud on the television. I could see him shaking his head sadly in the other room, his back turned to all of us. He couldn't stand Conor's bad behavior and vulgar language, but he feared his brother and was helpless to make him stop. The pink face of Ian Paisley, the leader of the Loyalist cause, appeared on the television. I drew Conor's attention to it and asked what he thought of Paisley.

Conor was quiet for a moment, sizing up Paisley's heavy, angry features. He said, "Not *that* cunt again! I don't like him at all." And then he spun around in his seat and announced, with characteristic self-contradiction, "But, no! Wait a minute. I think Paisley is great in a way, because he keeps the fuckin' thing going. I'd give him a clap on the back if he stopped in here. He keeps the shit stirred up is why."

Eileen said absently, staring at the next segment of the news, "Three and a half thousand people dead in the Philippines tonight."

Conor said, "You know what they done for me in Africa? They put me up agin' the wall and they were going to shoot me for preaching the gospel the same as I'm preaching it now. They are three hundred years behind the times. There are beautiful girls in Africa. One hundred twenty degrees of heat, and the beautiful girls go around with nothing on top and with a baby sucking at the breast and it is beautiful. It makes a man realize what's important."

Conor lost interest in his own train of thought and stared gloomily at the television. Matty O'Shea suggested it was time for us all to go home and offered me a ride back to the castle.

Conor said sadly, "But Matty, you never gave us a single song tonight."

John Pat said, "Matty is a champion singer, Rose."

Matty stood with his hands in his pockets and said, "Time to proceed along home now, everybody."

Eileen stood up unsteadily and said, "Time to proceed."

❊

THE NIGHT was wet and windy. We tumbled into the O'Sheas' car, which was parked crazily halfway across the sidewalk. Matty drove, I sat in the back with John Pat, and Eileen talked from her seat in front. John Pat seemed delighted with this little adventure. I heard him murmuring to himself, "Rose is sitting next to me." We started off down the Gort Road, and as we passed the church, Eileen cried out with false urgency, "Cross yourself, lads! Cross yourself!" and the lads did so, quickly and mechanically. Eileen shouted across the seat to Matty, "Give us a song, Matty!" Matty resisted weakly, then launched into "I Hear You Calling Me." He had a voice of astonishing purity and sweetness, and he sang with that finicky, overdramatic, and slightly fruity elocution of the tenors of the twenties and thirties. The windshield wipers beat out the time perfectly. At the end of the song I told Matty I would have difficulty differentiating his voice from that of John McCormack, Ireland's most famous tenor. John Pat clapped his hands together and giggled gleefully, "Good one, Rose. John McCormack!"

The road was dark. The car's headlights shone through the rain and lit up the high, wet hedges, making their burnt autumn colors more vivid than they were in daylight. It was like driving in a fabulous, shimmering tunnel. Ahead of us a brilliant red fox sailed over the hedge with a dreamlike fluidity, dashed across the road, and disappeared over a wall. His tail was nearly the length of his body.

"There's himself now," remarked Eileen calmly, almost to herself, as though she had been expecting this fox. We passed Bridie O'Daly's farm and Sean Byrne's little white cottage. When we turned into the field beside the castle, the headlights flashed dramatically against the west wall, revealing the castle's dour height in a sudden looming flash. Eileen clapped her hands to her face and cried, "*Jesus!* 'Tis like Dracula!"

Matty and John Pat said at once, " 'Tis!"

When I asked if they wanted to come in, the little car filled up with a long, worried silence. Rain swept across the roof of the car in crackling waves, and the wind strained plaintively at the window cracks. My friends peered apprehensively through the windshield at the great ivy-covered wall before them. Eileen and John Pat's hands had flown reflexively to their throats, as if to protect their jugular veins. Finally, Eileen said, "Well, why not? We've nothing to lose but our lives." Matty parked the car at a dangerous tilt on the side of the hill, and we all rolled out. With the car's headlights turned off, we were left in utter darkness. The howling wind whipped ferociously at our heads, and the rain stung our faces. I led my company toward the pathway. The three of them had linked elbows and were muttering and stumbling through the long grass. Faintly, beneath the voice of the wind, I heard John Pat saying shakily, "I won't be afraid, Eileen. Will you be afraid? Because I certainly will not be."

John Pat was seventy-five years old, yet he seemed like a boy of thirteen.

After much tripping and cursing and exclaiming, we made it into the castle. Eileen and Matty and John Pat stood in the great arched doorway of the first-floor living room and stared in stunned wonder, their mouths hanging open. The room always stopped people still. Human beings were rendered tiny and insignificant in the face of such a magnificent structure, older than just about any man-made thing in Corofin. It was the sort of place one saw only in movies, and the movies had illustrated what manner of catastrophic, blood-bathed events such rooms were likely to accommodate. People felt frightened upon entering the castle, but they also gained a sudden humility and sober respect for the place and for themselves. I had discovered that the castle stirred up a great range of emotions in people. I myself had spent my first days there doing nothing but wandering from room to room, staring and wondering and forgetting myself entirely.

Matty, who had reacted to little all evening, whispered, "Mother of God, take a holy look at this!" and John Pat added, "Christ upon the cross! Shit almighty! Forgive me, Jesus, for cursing."

Eileen said, "For the honor of Holy God and His Holy Mother, 'tis a sight! Little did I think when I woke up this morning that I would find myself in Ballyportry this night! God, I always wanted to see it with my own two eyes." She clapped her hands and grabbed my arm with both hands and cried, "Thanks, Rose!"

The living room managed to be at once lugubrious and irresistible. Its corners were dark and damp, and at the peak of its vaulted stone ceiling it was as high as a two-story house. A wooden balcony the width of the room hung just above the doorway. There were three tall, narrow windows set deep into the wall at the kitchen end of the room and three more in the east wall. The fireplace—ten feet across, five feet high, and three feet deep—held a huge iron cooking crane with a sooty kettle dangling from its arm. In the corners of the fireplace were two pot-bellied cauldrons with mouths the circumference of automobile tires. Directly before the fireplace was a large, low stone table—a perfectly square limestone slab cut whole from the Cliffs of Moher— that held hundreds of fossils in its rough surface. The floor was of the same stone and was covered in places by tattered Persian rugs. There was a lot of old pine furniture and several enormous brass vessels. The heavy wooden dining table was twelve feet long, with wrought-iron candelabra at either end. I lit the candles, threw more peat on the smoldering embers, and suggested we tour the castle while we waited for the fire to quicken.

As we climbed the stairs Eileen said, "These were the very stairs I was on so long ago with my school chum, Janey Crowley."

The stone stairs were steep, and their spiral was so tight the ascent could be dizzying. Each step was wedge-shaped and worn smooth in its middle by centuries of use. Window slits appeared at measured intervals along the staircase, and each windowsill was gently illumined by a candle.

We looked into the various cell-like bedrooms just off the staircase, then went into my bedroom, a large, low-ceilinged room with an enormous fireplace, a king-size waterbed, the famous stone bathtub, and several strange and oversized pieces of antique furniture, including a waist-high silver samovar intended for bathing. I flipped on the lights, which were hidden behind the wooden beams, and lit several candles. I encouraged Eileen to try out the waterbed. She hesitated, then flung herself onto it with youthful abandon. She laughed uproariously and lay back flat, rocking on the waves she had made, her legs crossed daintily at the ankles and her pointed shoes resting on my pillow. "Lads!" she cried. "Will ye have one look at the timber ceiling!"

Matty had walked into the fireplace and was looking out into the stormy night through a tall, skinny window placed, oddly, in the middle of the back of the fireplace. John Pat stared into the bathtub with an expression of disbelief on his clownish face. He touched the stone. "And Rose," he said dreamily, "is this where you bathe at all?" I said it was. He nodded and smiled and said to no one, "And this is where Rose bathes."

John Pat seemed compelled to verbalize the things happening around him, perhaps as a way of ordering them in his mind. All three of my guests were watery-eyed and drunk and emotional over their adventure.

We moved on. Each room was more amazing to them than the last, and the rooms kept coming and the stairs kept going upward, and I began to wonder whether I was overwhelming these people. They were like three obedient donkeys clattering blindly up the narrow stairs. They pressed their hands against the clammy, gently curved wall of the stairway, steadying themselves. Every so often I heard one of them sighing out an appeal to God for protection or salvation this night. Their faces held concentration, pleasure, anxiety, and reverence.

We stepped into a bathroom, and they marveled at the barrel-vaulted wattle ceiling and at the copper bowl of the sink.

In the highest and largest room were two crude wooden candelabra taller than myself; they resembled life-sized crosses. I lit the candles—eighteen of them—and they filled the cathedral ceiling with pale yellow light and deep shadows. John Pat shuddered visibly as he stared up at the ceiling. Softly and quite reasonably he whispered, "*Spook!*"

By this time every shred of Eileen's sarcasm and irony had disappeared. She was serious, fascinated, and puzzled. Her face looked ten years younger. Feverishly she said, "Rose, what did they ever burn in these huge fireplaces at all? And would you not be frozen stiff in here? And Jesus, Rose, would you not be scared to death of it? Ah, God, will you look? That fireplace is so big you could put your feckin' bed inside in it. And what in the name of God sort of people ever lived in here and made it their home? Ancestors of our own, I suppose. Ancestors. Genetic factor. Our history, lads. *Ours.* Jesus, will you help me, I will never get over this night. I will *never* get over it." Her chin quivered, and I thought she would cry.

I showed them the little kitchen on the top floor. On the way back down the stairs John Pat said, " 'Tis harder going down than going up," which was true, though I hadn't realized it before. The fear of falling was always greater on the way down.

I took my friends back down to the first floor, and they sat happily by the fire. John Pat slumped heavily into one of the very low chairs. Its design — little more than a leather sling wrapped around a spindly wooden structure — together with the force of gravity caused the occupant's limbs and bones to be slightly compressed and tugged downward; sitting in one of these very low chairs was somewhat like lying in a hammock. John Pat's shoulders curved inward, his elbows met in his lap, his long forearms lay flat on his thighs, and his knees nearly met his chin; he looked both vulnerable and happy. Though the fire had picked up, the room was still cold. I gave them all Connemara shawls to put around their shoulders. Their aging faces were orange in the glow of the firelight.

John Pat gathered his shawl up to his throat and, staring into the fire, struck up an argument with himself. "Isn't she a lovely girl? I'd marry her. If only I wasn't already married. Ah, well, so I'd live with her, so. But you couldn't really do that when you're married. But my wife, she's a bit wicked, but she's lovely, but she really is a wicked woman."

Eileen said apologetically, "I'm afraid he's talking about you, Rose."

John Pat let his head drop back until his face was pointed up at the shadowy ceiling. He stared at the strange, rippling tracks of the old wicker wattling in the ceiling's stones. He said wistfully, "I wish Maggie Butler and Noreen could be here to see this. To see us here." His voice echoed softly above us. He tipped his head forward again. "We won't be seeing any bats tonight, will we, Rose?"

"Not at all, John Pat," I lied.

John Pat said, "Maggie Butler is a social climber, you know."

Eileen said, "That's right, Maggie is a social climber."

"Who's Maggie Butler?" I said.

Eileen said, "The sister of the cousin we buried. Don't you remember I told you about her?"

While Matty sang songs, Eileen and John Pat drank the whiskey I offered them and looked curiously around the room. Eventually Eileen turned to me and said carefully, "Excuse me, Rose, but I am intoxicated. I am intoxicated, and you were nice enough to bring us here. And how will we ever repay you?" Her eyes seemed to be slipping back in her head, and she had begun to repeat certain phrases in the monotonous and melancholy tone that often accompanies drunkenness.

"You don't have to repay me," I said. "It's nice for me to have you here."

"We have to thank you. We have to thank you. We have to thank you. We were never here before! I have been in Dromoland Castle, and I have been in another castle that's name I forget."

"The one in Limerick," John Pat said, trying to help her.

"Bunratty?" I said.

"Bun-*ratty!*" Eileen said vehemently, stabbing her finger in my direction. "Correct you are!"

John Pat said casually, "Been there, Rose?"

I hadn't.

"I think it is an honor to be here," said Eileen. "Though I am slightly intoxicated."

"I am well intoxicated!" shouted John Pat.

"The MacNamaras were all alcoholics," said Eileen. "But I am trying to thank you in my own way. In my own way. In my own way. And it was lovely meeting you tonight, and when you came inside that door to Dillon's Pub tonight, little did we know who you'd be."

Who, I wondered, did she think I was?

She stretched her arm out and put her hand on mine in an effort to catch my full attention, and there was familiar intrigue in her thickening voice. "Says you to Donal O'Shea, 'Is that old boozer your mother?' I hope Donal will give you that picture. Whatever damn old picture it is."

"He won't," I said. "And it doesn't matter."

"No, he won't. He's a businessman. But, 'Jesus,' says you, 'is that woman your mother, Donal? I had her out in the castle.' Donal would love this castle."

"Should I invite him out?" I said.

Eileen flapped her hand at me and said, "Pffff!" which meant, Hell, no. She clomped her two tiny feet hard onto the table in front of her and stretched out in a posture of cozy repose. She appeared to be reclining in the uncomfortable chair, as if lying in a bed. She pulled the shawl up to her throat and yawned magnificently.

John Pat crooned, "Invite him out, Rose! Invite him out, Rose! Never mind Eileen and invite him out!"

Eileen's chin fell forward onto her chest. She muttered into the front of her blouse, "Too much drink."

John Pat shouted, "Rose!"

"Excuse me, John Pat!" said Eileen, lifting her head just enough that she could turn it and look at me. "When we met you tonight, Rose, it just worked. You were accepted."

John Pat tried again. "Rose, do you ever come to Ennis? Because if you go one mile out the road from Ennis, that's my house. Right out the road across from the Auburn Lodge. Come there. And if my wife is there, say, 'I am acquainted with John Pat.'"

"Won't she wonder how we're acquainted?"

"Well, she might look at you very wicked, like, but if I was there you'd be safe."

"Wicked," Eileen muttered.

"You'd have the best dinner you ever had in your life at my house."

"I am intoxicated," Eileen said.

John Pat pointed at her and said proudly, "That is my first cousin there, Rose."

Eileen clapped her hands. "There is a song about a first cousin. D'ye know that song? 'I Met My First Cousin.'"

"Give us that song, Matty!" John Pat cried.

Eileen squawked dismissively, "Naahp! He wouldn't know it."

Matty sat still and silent in his chair, hands folded in his lap. He stared contentedly into the fire, oblivious to all this drunken chatter. He was like a stranger. From the corner of my eye I caught Eileen looking oddly over my head at something. She lifted her ringed hand from under the shawl, aimed her thumb at a point above my head, and said in a tiny voice, "Is that your mother?"

Terrified, I swung around in my chair to see who she was pointing at, and too late realized she was indulging again in the Donal O'Shea vignette. She was so deep into the fantasy that she was using the past tense for her performance, as though the anticipated meeting had already happened. The sentences were truncated now, tapping out of her like Morse code. "Said you, 'Donal. Your mother. I met. A boozer,' said you."

Hoping to draw Matty out, I said, "Matty, why didn't you ever sing professionally?"

Matty said, "Heh-heh," and stared at his hands.

"Come on, Matty," said Eileen, "give us one song now. Give us 'The Fairy Glen.'"

"No, Eileen. No, no."

"Give it!" she growled.

Matty began to sing, and Eileen and John Pat joined in, howling like hounds. Matty's voice was beautiful, the song was sad and mournful, and though I could hardly make out the words, it made me want to cry. Singing, quiet Matty O'Shea became larger and more compelling than any of his relatives.

John Pat talked through the singing. "You're good, Matty! You're a nice girl, Rose. You're swell, Eileen, boy."

When the song was over I stood up and said, "Would anybody like a cup of tea?"

"I'd like you to sit down," Eileen said, sipping from her glass of whiskey. "I want you to sit down. Sit down. Sit. I can't sing. I cannot sing. Sing 'Skibbereen,' Matty. 'Oh, Father dear, I often fear I will never . . .' Rose, do you know how we'll thank you? We'll take you out to O'Connor's sometime in Doolin. Some Sunday. We'll bring you out, if you want."

O'Connor's Pub in Doolin was famous for its traditional music. I said, "Thanks," to which Eileen responded with true Irish amiability, "Jesus, will you shut your mouth?"

John Pat, excited by the thought of a trip to Doolin, said, "Rose? What's going to happen?"

Eileen said, "I love Doolin. I am sailing at this moment."

"Have some tea, then, Eileen," I said.

"I'll save the tea for later, Rose, thanks!"

John Pat was nervous, afraid the Doolin plan would get lost before it was confirmed. "So Sunday, Eileen, are we going to pick up Rose and take her out to Doolin? Is that what's going to happen?"

"Ah, it's no good makin' promises now, John Pat, for I am intoxicated. In . . . tox . . . i . . . *ca* . . . ted!"

John Pat sighed and repeated his sincere wish that Maggie Butler could see them all here, and Eileen said irritably, "You have an impression, John Pat. About Maggie Butler you have an impression!"

I said, "What sort of impression?"

Eileen said, "It was Maggie Butler's brother that was buried today. Maggie carried the little coffin. We never saw that before. My mother had, oh, this thing about Maggie Butler."

"What thing?"

"An impression. An impression. Of Maggie Butler. My mother was all the time talking about Maggie Butler."

"How come?" I said.

"Because Maggie Butler thought she was better than anyone else."

I said, "Did you say Maggie Butler was a social climber?"

"*She was a social climber!* She was a lovely . . . a lovely climber!"

John Pat looked suddenly worried. Softly he said, "Why do you ask that about Maggie Butler, Rose?"

"Ask what?"

"If Maggie was a social climber."

"Didn't you and Eileen say she was?"

John Pat looked blankly at me, trying to remember what he'd said.

Eileen said, "I could have been a social climber, John Pat. And you could have been a social climber. And I could have been in the paper." Her words sounded urgent, sad, and pleading.

John Pat stared intently at me, puzzled, his brow deeply furrowed. "Why did you say that, Rose, about Maggie Butler being a social climber?" He seemed to be accusing me of something.

"You said it, John Pat."

"You said it, John Pat," Eileen said, head tilted so far to the right that her cheek was resting on her shoulder. "You said Maggie Butler was it, John Pat."

"I never met Maggie Butler," I said. "I was only repeating what you said, John Pat."

"She is a social climber," said Eileen.

I said, "I'm afraid that's what you said, John Pat. 'Maggie Butler is a social climber.'"

Eileen bleated from the corner of her mouth, "Yeeeaaah! Social!"

John Pat looked sad and serious, forced to face the facts about Maggie Butler. He patted his knees and picked at his fingernails, and said, "Ho-hum." He folded his big hands in his lap and studied them. The firelight shone hotly on his bald pate. "You're right, Rose," he said finally, his voice heavy with resignation. "Maggie Butler is a social climber."

"Do you mean she thinks she's better than everyone else?" I asked.

Sadly and sweetly John Pat said, "She's not as good as you, Rose."

"And she's not as good as you, John Pat," I said, and for the first time that evening, Matty O'Shea came to life. He leaned forward in his chair and let out a braying laugh. He caught his pinched red face in his hands and laughed and laughed, his elbows resting on his bony knees.

Swept up on the tide of Matty's mirth, John Pat laughed giddily along with him. "Ha-ha! Did you hear what she said, Matty? She said not as good as me." John Pat's laugh was a muffled, choking gasp; it sounded as though he had a whole boiled egg lodged deep in his throat. And then, just as quickly as the laughing had begun, John Pat was serious and confused again. "Eileen," he said, "Rose said that Maggie Butler was a social climber."

Eileen had already skated way beyond this tedious subject and was annoyed at having been yanked back to it. She frowned at John Pat and banged her heels on the table in time to the words she spat at him. "*Because Rose knows it, John Pat! Maggie Butler is a social, social climber!*"

"Am I a social climber, Eileen?" John Pat said.

"No, you are not, John Pat, for you haven't the brains! And I haven't them either, for that matter."

"Is it good or bad to be a social climber?" I asked.

"No!" howled Eileen. "It is good!"

"But I wouldn't like to insult Maggie Butler," John Pat said. "I wouldn't like to get on the bad side of her."

"Does she have a temper?" I asked.

Eileen said, "She has a tempera*ment*."

"I just wouldn't like to get on her bad side," John Pat murmured. "Honest to God, I don't know why."

Eileen said, "We like her, but we haven't got the brains to *be* like her."

"Is she educated?"

"Self-educated. She's clever. Without education where would you be? Education. Education. I never had any education. Conor and Francis hadn't either. Only our brother Tom was educated, and oh, he was smart, but he's dead. He fell off a roof one time and just died."

Eileen's big eyes filled up instantly with tears. In the firelight the tears were amber; they slid down her round cheeks and tapped onto her blouse. A few trickled down her throat. She dabbed hard at her face with the corner of her shawl, its wormlike fringe falling into her eyes. Her voice had gone soft and uncertain. "Tom was the star of us all, and he fell off a roof, God help us. And died. Even Conor Mac-Namara could not hold a candle to the smartness of Tom. Tom could do anything. He knew books. Could do anything. Was streets ahead of anyone else. The smartest brother in County Clare."

John Pat stared at Eileen, and then he began to cry too. He was the victim of emotional suggestion; if the people around him were happy, he was happy. If they were sad, so was he. He wiped away his tears and said, "What's a social climber, Rose?"

"Someone who feels inferior, I guess."

"Let's sing a song," said John Pat nervously, plucking at his hands. "But no. Wait. Rose, keep talking about what you were talking about."

"That's all I know about it," I told him. "I guess a social climber is someone who thinks there's a world better than his own."

I got up and went to add more peat to the fire, and as soon as my back was turned to the room, I heard a tremendous thump behind me and sensed the huge stone table shuddering violently. I spun around, and there was John Pat lying face down upon the table with his hands stuffed deep in his coat pockets. He lay perfectly still, his cheek flat on the stone, his legs sticking out over the edge of it. I saw two of my pens poking out from under his temple and a pile of notebooks under his hip. So close to the fire, the top of his bald head shone and glowed the color of a pumpkin. He looked peaceful. I stared, the fire poker gripped in my hand, at a loss for what to do next. I felt worried and responsible.

Matty O'Shea got slowly out of his chair and tapped John Pat on the head. "John Pat," he said. "Are you all right?"

John Pat extricated a hand from his pocket and raised it in a half-wave to indicate that he was all right. We lifted him up by the elbows, and when he was finally on his feet he said, "Now why should a person like me fall down like that?" He looked ashen and shaken but otherwise all right. He laughed uncertainly, like a child recovering from a self-imposed fright.

Matty, Eileen, and John Pat took turns staggering into the bathroom, and each one let out a loud exclamation upon coming face to face with the two life-sized marble angels that stood beside the toilet. When John Pat came out of the bathroom and sat down again, I noticed that his forehead was bleeding. There were two punctures above his left eye, weirdly like a vampire's teeth marks. A tiny thread of blood trickled down his forehead. He looked slightly nauseated, grinning in pain. The fringe of hair that circled the crown of his head was ruffled and sticking up in tufts.

"What happened to you, John Pat?" I said.

"Oh, ha-ha! Nothing! I only banged my head on the bathroom wall."

He slapped his hand up to his brow and smeared the blood around, smiling sickly. He must have hit his head on the doorway, which was low enough that even I had to duck my head to get into the bathroom. I got a wet towel and wiped the blood off, hoping to see how bad the cut was. John Pat leaned back in his seat and grinned widely, thrilled with the attention he was getting. "Rose?" he said dreamily, "would you do this for that fella in the pub that fancied you?"

"What fella?" I said, tipping his head toward the light.

"The one that wanted the game of darts with you?"

I made a face and said I most certainly would not, that there were very few people I would do this for. Encouraged and quite beside himself, John Pat said, "And would you ever consider giving me a kiss, Rose?"

I dabbed at his forehead, smiled, said nothing.

Eventually Matty persuaded Eileen and John Pat that it was time to go home. I got a flashlight and led them out into the darkness and wind and lashing rain. I tried to shine the beam of the flashlight onto the path for their benefit, and before long Eileen and John Pat, who had been walking with their arms linked, disappeared entirely from the beam of light. I waved the flashlight around until I found them lying flat on their backs on the side of the hill, arms still linked and the rain pelting their faces. Over the howling wind I heard John Pat wail forlornly, "*Now* what's going to happen, Eileen?"

Eileen's voice came back at him, flinty and sparkling with disgust. "Ah, Jesus, John Pat, you are an awful eejit, and you always were one! A crowned and throned royal eejit."

They were so drunk they couldn't get up. They didn't know which way to lean. I found myself laughing so hard I had to turn away from them. I didn't want to insult them. I crouched down in the grass, thankful to the wind for whipping the sound of my laughter away. I laughed so hard I felt hollow.

Behind me Matty said wearily, like a patient parent, "I *knew* something like this was going to happen."

Matty and I lugged Eileen and John Pat up by their lapels and fitted them into the car. Eileen fell forward in her seat, hands over her ears, head between her knees, trying to block the world out. " 'Tis like Dracula," she gurgled.

Matty climbed into the car, said, "Cheerio, Rose," and with his wheels spinning in the mud he coaxed the car back onto the Gort Road. I turned to go back into the castle, as concerned for their safety as if they were my own family.

PART

II

The True Face

THE CITY OF DUBLIN is crowded with churches. At the turn of the hour church bells ring out from every direction, their various tones crossing and colliding, confusing the listener. Some begin a minute too early, some a minute too late, rendering the ringing interminable and the hour unclear.

During the six months I spent in Dublin I lived in a one-room apartment in a converted Georgian house on Waterloo Road. The apartment was like a waiting room in a dentist's office, a dissolute dentist who had few patients and no assistant to help him. The ceiling was cracked, and the walls, graced with billowing brown and yellow water stains, looked like a nautical chart. My furniture was an armoire, a lamp, and a couch that folded out into a bed. The mattress was the thickness of a paperback novel and had molded itself to the narrow shape of the person who lived there before me. The wall-to-wall carpet—roughly the color of brains—was frayed and worn. The best thing about the place was its proximity to three neighborhood churches, the sound of whose bells drifted through my window each morning, wakening me and reminding me again of the importance of religion in Ireland.

Religion was as pervasive as the currency. It was everywhere. It was embedded deep in the Irish mind, and that seemed most evident in the way Irish people blessed themselves as they passed by a church; an instinctual flutter of the right hand as they studied the headlines of the newspaper they had just bought, or scolded a disobedient child, or made a conversational point to a companion. Sometimes just the fingers moved, twitching above the sternum or passing absently over the face in a barely perceptible wiping motion. Riding in a Dublin bus, I was often gripped by an eerie disorientation at the moment the bus passed by a church (a church I was never quick enough to notice), and I glimpsed, in the periphery of my vision, thirty hands flying into the air in similar fashion. On the streets teenagers' hands leapt reflexively at the sight of a church and then, driven by embarrassment, the hands would inevitably detour to the hair and pat it down, or to an eye to remove a nonexistent cinder. Young people didn't want to be seen to be religious or to be identified with the lack of sophistication that religion had come to signify, but they were unable to rid themselves of the habit. Even red-faced schoolboys could not help raising a hand and passing it absently across their noses as they ran by a church hurling curses at each other. The gesture was as ingrained and superstitious as the national pause for the Angelus.

One of Dublin's distinctions is that it is the birthplace of the Legion of Mary, an international Catholic organization of great power and influence that grew out of a small, informal meeting on Francis Street in 1921. I had heard of the Legion long before I ever set foot in Ireland, had seen it in operation in the United States and in China, but I knew little about its purpose, and it wasn't until I began seeing regular notices in the *Irish Times* about Legion meetings that I took an interest. The notices always said: " 'The Legion of Mary presents the true face of the Catholic Church,' Pope John XXIII."

The idea of the "true face" interested me, for at times it seemed difficult to know what the true face of the Church was amid its many politically motivated distortions. The notices listed the various places Legion meetings were held each week, including Myra House at 100 Francis Street. This was the address at which Frank Duff had started the Legion of Mary seventy years before, so I chose to attend that meeting, although on any given night I could have attended five others in the city.

As I walked across the city to Francis Street the next Monday evening, I passed a young girl playing a tin whistle on O'Connell Bridge. The girl was skinny and long-limbed, with red lips, a pretty face, and scraggly black hair that hung to her waist. She seemed oblivious to the five o'clock crush of pedestrians that jostled her from all sides. She held the whistle to her lips and blew violently into it. The whistle squealed out three wild notes, and the girl responded with a little jig of delight. She twirled in place with one leg held up in the air. In one swift motion she spun around and gave a nearby drunk a spontaneous thump in the rear end with her sneakered foot. She howled with laughter at that, pleased by her own unpredictability. She spun again, hair swirling gracefully around her shoulders like the ribbons of a maypole, eyes ablaze with excitement. She hopped, turned, and panted into the whistle, and then, caught up in the momentum of her own soaring spirit, she wound up and flung the whistle into the Liffey. The whistle rocketed high into the pale evening air and came down, piercing its way into the river, tip first and without a splash. The girl clapped her dirty hands over her mouth. Little bubbles — remnants of her own breath — rose to the surface as the whistle sank to the bottom. Slowly the girl's hands descended to her sides, and her good cheer dwindled visibly as she realized that her whistle was gone for good.

Francis Street, in the old section of Dublin, was a narrow lane of ancient, empty, or burned-out shopfronts, of antique furniture stores and junk shops packed to the ceiling with every imaginable article made from brass. The buildings here were low and old with big windows. I wandered up the gently sloping street and as I passed one shop I noticed, out of the corner of my eye, scores of photographs of naked people taped in the window. I stopped to look more closely. The photographs, clipped from a Swedish magazine, were not pornographic, but looked more like they had come from the newsletter of some nudist colony. There were shots of women plunging into the ocean, a man and woman walking happily hand in hand along the shore, two young girls with breasts the size of limes playing in the surf — all of them displaying the gawky, hairy, lumpy nudity of real people. It was precisely these physical imperfections never evident in models that made the photographs seem seedy.

I walked on past several expensive restaurants. A menu propped up in one window announced smoked salmon and medallions of veal at nineteen pounds, money no resident of this neighborhood could possibly spare for a meal. These restaurants, I soon realized, were for patrons of the theater at the top of the street. It was a strange street where the old and the new, the affluent and the destitute, the holy and the lewd mixed without friction or conflict.

The Legion's Myra House was a small stucco structure not far from the theater. I sat on one of three empty beer kegs standing in the doorway of the house and waited to see who would arrive for the meeting. The street was empty. I watched the sky. No matter where the sun hung, Dublin's light always seemed to be approaching from a sharp angle, lighting the clouds from the side and lending them great depth of color—orange, purple, and crimson against a field of blue. That evening golden clouds flew in from the west, massing against each other like frightened sheep. At the top of the street I could see the sober spire of Christ Church, and beyond the bottom of the street, toward the south, the green humps of the Dublin Mountains were crowned in bloated clouds. Across the street in a vacant lot an abandoned couch lay sodden and gutted amid the rubbish, tall weeds sprouting from its cushions like hair.

A car pulled up in front of Myra House, and three men climbed out of it, one of them a priest. As he stepped onto the curb, the man who had been sitting in the front passenger seat said happily and loudly to the priest, who had been sitting behind him, "Now I will finally have a chance to look at your face, and you can see mine!"

The priest and the driver said nothing; they seemed not to have heard this happy man, or perhaps they were merely tolerating him. The man had an enormous head. A pair of tortoiseshell eyeglasses dominated his big face. On his feet he wore huge leather basketball shoes. I thought I had heard a trace of Poland in his accent. All three men were elderly, and age had rendered the priest unsteady on his feet. With a large skeleton key the driver let them into the house.

I sat on my keg and waited to see who else would arrive. A moment or two later a fat man in a green polo shirt showed up with a similar skeleton key and a bag of groceries. After him came a man on a bicycle, also with a key. I asked this man if the Legion meeting was open to anyone, and he stared at me. "Well, if you're really interested," he said finally, "of course, you're welcome." But from the way he stared, I could see he was skeptical. Nevertheless, in true missionary fashion he could not refuse me. He smiled nervously. His teeth were a dull matte white, as though the enamel had been filed off them.

I followed him into the house and up some dark stairs to a small room on the third floor, where five men were sitting around a table covered in a cloth that had *Legio Mariae* embroidered in it in red gothic script. There was a statue of the Blessed Virgin in the center of the table flanked by two vases of flowers and two candles. Except for the fading sunlight faintly reflected in the eastern sky, the candles were the only source of light here; the corners of the room were veiled in great nets of shadow.

The men looked astonished to see me come into the room on the heels of the bicyclist. They sat gaping for a moment, then politely stood up to introduce themselves. They were Tim Donovan (the driver), Ira Weizmann (the happy man), Aidan Murphy (the man on the bike), Padraig Pearse ("no relation to the martyr"), and Canon Leary (the priest). The fat man in the green shirt introduced himself simply as Bobby. He did not stand up but remained importantly in his seat at the head of the table with his groceries safely by his feet. I guessed correctly that Bobby was the chairman. He was smooth as a porpoise. His black hair, oiled and slicked back, was just beginning to gray over the ears. His gold wedding band was tight on his pudgy finger, and his fat face glistened like porcelain in the candlelight.

I sat in a chair, and Bobby began to speak. He welcomed Ira Weizmann and me as the two newcomers to the meeting. He had a strong Dublin accent, but there was something else in his speech, remnants of another language that had settled in the gutters of his mouth. It sounded faintly like French. "And now we shall say the rosary," he said, and they all scraped back their chairs and knelt on the floor. Ira Weizmann, looking bored already, watched the men drop to their knees. He stayed seated, conducting a private debate in his mind, then moved to kneel with a great grunting effort, leaning heavily on the table, causing the statue and the candles to teeter. I knelt with them, and we said the rosary—the five men, the priest, and me in this dark little room. I felt awkward and hot. The candlelight gave the meeting an intimate, cultlike intensity that made me uneasy. I had expected a large meeting where I would be able to hide at the back of the room. I didn't want to have to talk or explain myself or say the rosary. I heard myself muttering, "Blessed is the fruit of thy womb..."

and was thankful that saying the rosary, like riding a bicycle or skipping rope, is one of those things that once learned is never forgotten. I prayed mechanically, furtively trying to watch the men. Tim Donovan had given Ira Weizmann a child's string of bright red plastic rosary beads, which dangled prettily over his hairy hand as he said the Our Father. The priest leaned against the table with his narrow forehead pressed into the palm of one hand and the other hand counting his beads. Fine red veins fanned across his nose and cheeks; his lipless mouth was like a mail slot.

Ira Weizmann's eyes roved—like me, he was more interested in studying his companions than in praying. He seemed to be comparing Padraig Pearse, Tim Donovan, and Aidan Murphy, and that made sense, for the three men looked remarkably interchangeable; they had the same slight physique, the same freckled coloring, sharp features, reticence, and stodgy clothing. They were like triplets. It occurred to me that the deeply religious often share a similar stubborn lack of interest in fashion.

Bobby, the pudgy chairman, was different. He had short fingers and very thick red lips, and when my mind began to wander I found myself picturing him raising a forkful of food to his mouth.

As the rosary came to an end a middle-aged woman came hurrying into the room. The men said, "Welcome, Sister Keating," and the meeting began in earnest. These people addressed each other as Brother and Sister, though all but Canon Leary were lay members of the Church. Their relationships to one another had obviously solidified long ago. They had a stilted, formal way of relating, and they played their parts in the meeting strictly according to Legion rules. They met to discuss the Legion's efforts—through Social Services and Catholic Action—in their community that week, and they took turns giving presentations and reports. They used words like *praesidium*, *tessera*, *concilium*, *archconfraternity*, and *mediatrix*. They seemed to be following a script, and for a group whose stated mission was to make God loved in His world, a group who saw themselves as a soul-saving army devoted to "crushing the head of the serpent and advancing the reign of Christ," they seemed surprisingly uncomfortable with newcomers. I felt keenly that Ira Weizmann and I were intruding.

Brother Murphy read the minutes of the last meeting. In them were mentioned several visits Legion members had made to the elderly, the sick, and the incarcerated. There was financial business, and the minutes of the Pillar of Fire meeting, a small branch of the Legion dedicated to fostering better understanding between Catholics and Jews.

At the Pillar of Fire meeting a Mrs. Greenberg of the Jewish community had given a presentation on the Holocaust. Brother Donovan read the extensive minutes of that meeting in a monotonous halting voice that began to lull his fellow Legionaries to sleep. Brother Pearse's head tilted onto his right shoulder, and his blue-veined eyelids drooped heavily. Brother Donovan read, "Mr. Nyack, Mr. Weizmann, and Mrs. Tolkin were in attendance. Mrs. Greenberg ran out of the house without the speech she had prepared and realized that instead she had grabbed the rough notes, so her speech was not what it could have been. She talked about the Holocaust . . ."

Ira Weizmann said suddenly, "May I say one thing about Mrs. Greenberg?" All the heads at the table snapped up, startled by the sound of his loud voice. "Mrs. Greenberg is a great lady and she did an excellent job, but just one thing she got wrong—and I know this from a personal fact—she said the Italians were no good, but I actually know that the Italians took many Jews in and saved them, so Mrs. Greenberg was wrong about the Italians."

Everyone stared politely at Ira Weizmann. It was clearly not protocol for members of the Legion to venture into reminiscences or personal opinion; Ira was confusing the order and demeanor of the meeting. But Ira himself seemed not to notice the disruption. He made a fist of his big hand and placed it on the table to help further his point. The little red rosary beads still tangled in his fingers looked edible, like strung cranberries wound around a Christmas tree. Through the window I saw that the light in the sky had faded to a bruised purple, and the room was entirely at the mercy of the two candles. Ira's big face shone. He took a hanky out of his pocket and mopped his brow.

"Only five thousand Jews died in Italy," he said. The volume of his voice covered the sadness in it. "Now, I know Mrs. Greenberg was in Bergen-Belsen, but I had my own personal tragedy. I lost two sisters and two brothers in the gas chamber. And the reason why I became a Catholic, which I am very proud of, was the element of forgiveness in the Catholic Church. I told the father that if he could prove to me that I could become a forgiving person with the help of his forgiving God, I would become a Catholic."

Ira's revelation was followed by what seemed like a remarkably stingy silence. No one responded. Instead they looked away and resumed the proceedings, as though Ira Weizmann had said nothing at all. Brother Padraig Pearse displayed a plastic bag full of lapel pins he had brought along for distribution throughout the community. Ira took one of the pins and held it up to the candlelight. "What the heck is it?" he said.

"It's the Pioneers," Brother Pearse said; his voice was a tiny lilting peep after Ira's. "You wear it on your coat to show that you practice total abstention from alcohol."

Ira let his hands fall heavily to his lap. He turned and looked affably at Brother Donovan. His big eyeglasses were like a mask on his face; their lenses glinted in the candlelight. "May I say this, mister? I don't drink and I don't smoke, but I would never wear a pin in my coat about it. Sometimes in the night I get up and make myself a cup of tea—I am an old man now—and I put a drop of whiskey in it. But I don't drink. I had enough problems with people drinking in my family."

I could see the group wondering what to say to this man. His frankness was startling and his self-confidence surprising, even enviable, but the Legionaries clearly had little skill at fostering the exchange of ideas. As the evening progressed I realized that it was not unfriendliness that made them reticent, it was shyness and a complete lack of self-confidence. Though he had professed his fealty to the Catholic Church, and though he had lived in Dublin for years, Ira Weizmann was still alien and therefore an inhibiting presence. I marveled that the Legion of Mary had managed to take root on every continent of the world, that with such a markedly uncharismatic foundation as this it had found its way out of Dublin at all.

The members moved on to reports on various people who aspired to be Legion members. Brother Murphy said he had talked to an aspirant recently who seemed to be speaking against the bishops and cardinals. This man also seemed to be worshiping a false god in Assisi and had even said that the pope sometimes made mistakes. "They say he's doing good work," Murphy said, "but he just doesn't seem like a candidate for membership."

Bobby invited Ira Weizmann and me to work for the Legion the following week, and I could see this was something we would be expected to do if we hoped to become members. Bobby asked me to work at the Children's Praesidium, a Catholic Education class for young girls. He asked Ira if he would be willing to talk with the men in the Jewish retirement home and bring them information about the Legion. Ira held onto his eyeglasses with both hands and tilted them slightly, the better to see Bobby. "Bobby," he said, "let me just say I'll be perfectly happy to talk to anybody. But since I converted, the Jews don't like me. My sister hasn't spoken to me in forty years. So if you think the Jews in the Jewish home are going to listen to a convert telling them about Catholics, I don't know. I think it won't work." He mugged a face of indifference and shrugged and threw up his hands as if to say, *But it's your club; you decide.*

Canon Leary cleared his throat and spoke for the first time. "Simon Wiesenthal said the Jews missed a great opportunity when they forgot to mention the five million non-Jewish people who were also killed in the Holocaust, that people are tired of hearing the Jews complain, and that if the Jews had co-opted all the other dead souls, they wouldn't be so unpopular with their message today. I think Wiesenthal might be right. Someone once asked where God was when the Jews were being murdered. But the real question is, Where was man?"

All the Legionaries turned and looked at Canon Leary as though God Himself had come into the room. Leary opened the Legion handbook and read this pitying view of the Jews: "St. Michael remains the loyal defender of the Church, but his guardianship of the Jews did not lapse because they turned away. Rather it was intensified because of their need. The Legion serves under Michael. Under his inspiration it must strive lovingly towards the restoration of that people whose doctrinal position has been so undermined by the passage of time. According to the Book of Daniel and all the other prophecies the time for the coming of the Messiah is long since expired. The Temple is destroyed and their Sacrifice has ceased, never to be restored. What, then, is the meaning of their depleted worship, and what divine message has the Old Testament for them today?"

When Canon Leary had finished reading, Ira Weizmann blurted, "No kidding! I say that all the time! I agree with that, Father, but I'm telling you I would have one heck of a time making them folks in the home listen to me. They'd roll over in their grave just seeing Ira Weizmann walk through the door!"

⁂

I HAD TOLD Bobby that I would work for two hours at the Children's Praesidium, chiefly because I was curious as to what the Legion was teaching children. The following week I returned to Myra House to fulfill my duty. This time a tiny boy holding a long pool cue opened the door for me. He had a square red crew-cut and a square freckled face. "Lookin' for S'ta Keatin', is it?" he cried.

"Yes, I am," I said.

"Grand! Come wit' me den!"

The boy led me up the stairs past a room where Bobby the chairman was leading a lot of young boys in a game of snooker. Through the door I could see Bobby laboriously tipping his big body over the pool table to make a shot.

Sister Keating was in the Legion room chatting with a young priest. She nodded as I came into the room and continued talking. I listened but failed to follow what she was saying, for she spoke too fast. She was a small woman with a round face, two shining little eyes, and a slight underbite that gave her a disgruntled, faintly canine expression.

Sister Keating left the priest little opportunity to speak, and when finally he left the room she turned to me and put her little face up to mine and began talking at me in the same rapid-fire way. Her breath smelled odd though not unpleasant; it was damp and milky, like curds. She explained that she and I would be giving the children a few religious lessons, that they were rough girls, most of whom came from broken homes, and that they were often "very wicked." She said, "It's never guaranteed that they'll come. One week they're here and the next they're not because their mother wants them to mind the baby for her so she can go out to the pub. And sure, aren't they babies themselves?"

The girls began showing up in twos and threes. They banged through the door and flung their book bags into a corner of the room. They were little and breathless. They wore tin rings on every finger, and their hands and wide, gypsyish faces were shot with copper freckles. Most were dressed in brightly colored nylon running suits. They chewed big wads of bubblegum and stared at me. They had huge green eyes and flaming red ponytails that sprang out of the sides of their heads like water from an open hydrant. They were irresistible, and I was pleased and surprised when the red-lipped, whistle-playing girl I had seen the week before on O'Connell Bridge blew into the room with her wild black hair streaming out behind her.

The girls inched up to me. One of them whispered, "She's posh lookin'," and the others murmured their assent. They spoke with the dirtiest street accent I had heard in Dublin. They found a way to stretch monosyllabic words into two syllables, sometimes three. They said "ho-wum" for home, "wa-rum" for warm, and for mushroom they said "mush-a-roo-um."

The girl from the bridge elbowed her way to the front of the crowd. Her name was Jane. She pointed at me and said, "S'ta Keatin'? What's she to you?"

"She is nothing to me, Jane," Sister Keating said in an admonishing, correcting tone that stayed with her for the rest of the afternoon. "She is a Legionary and she is going to be working with us. She is called Sister Rose O'Mahony."

Jane looked disgusted. "A person like yourself isn't after joining out the Legion, are you, O'Mahony?" she demanded.

"Not yet," I said.

At the sound of my voice another girl said, *"Lads, did ye hear her?! She's American!"*

Sister Keating brought the meeting to order, and the girls sat in folding chairs arranged in a semicircle. Their knees were bony, and their feet barely reached the floor. Sister Keating prepared the girls for prayer by asking, "Why do we say the Hail Mary, girls?"

With insurrection in her voice a pie-faced girl shrieked, "Dunno, S'ta Keatin'!" and the others tittered wickedly. Sister Keating was unfazed. "Why do we say the Hail Mary, Jane?"

Jane couldn't have been more than nine; on the bridge she had looked older. She had a sardonic sense of humor and the deep, smoky voice of a barmaid. Watching me, but speaking to Sister Keating, she said unctuously, "We say the Hail Mary, S'ta Keatin', to honor Mary, Mother of God!"

The girls began reciting a slovenly rendition of the Hail Mary. They made it sound taunting and lewd, like a jeering chant from an angry crowd at a football game. *Blast art'ou 'mongst wam 'n' blast's da fruit* . . . Their faces were twisted into postures of sarcasm and mirth, and I could see I wasn't the person for this job; I wouldn't be able to keep from taking their side. I would find it difficult to ally myself with Sister Keating and her stern admonishments. Just as I was thinking how much I wanted a piece of their bubblegum, Sister Keating shouted at them to spit the chewing gum into the bin. Jane, the ringleader, cried with brilliant mimicry, "Girls! Put da choongum out in da bin!" and the girls ran over to the tin wastebasket and shot the gum out of their mouths with such expert force it pinged like bullets against the metal.

Sister Keating said, "Before we begin, I want to get to the bottom of who took the key out of the door lock last week. There was a key in the door and one of you took it. I want the culprit to confess to me immediately. Vicki Corrigan, was it you?"

Vicki, a skinny girl in a torn sweatshirt, held her hands up defensively and said, "Wasn't near that key, S'ta Keatin'!" Then her face crumpled and she began to cry.

A scrappy eight-year-old sitting beside me sneered, "Vicki! 'f ya croy it means yar guilty, so for Chrissake don't croy!"

Sister Keating frowned at the girl. "We must never take the name of the Lord in vain, Roisin."

"Oh, right, S'ta Keatin'," Roisin said. "It slipped me mind. I won't never do it again." Roisin batted her bangs out of her eyes and grinned fatuously at Sister Keating. She could not have cared less about the name of the Lord.

Vicki, the guilty party, pulled the sleeves of her running suit over her little hands and pressed them to her damp eyes.

Saucer-eyed with false innocence, Jane said, "Either will I ever again take the name of the Lord in vain, S'ta Keatin'."

Maire suppressed a grin. "Right, S'ta Keatin'," she said, "either will I."

It was a highly skilled act. They heaped scorn upon Sister Keating by pretending to be the obedient girls she expected them to be. They hammed it up and winked at each other over the simple way they could mock and fool her.

Sister Keating read aloud for us the story of the fishes and the loaves, then asked a girl on my right to repeat the story. The girl sat silent for a long time, plucking at her lips, then turned pleadingly to me. "Rose," she whispered, "could ya ever gimmee the *start* at least?"

With all my heart I wanted to give her the start, but I shook my head, no.

Jane jumped out of her chair. "I can tell your damn story," she said.

"Jane, in the Legion we do not say words like damn."

" 'Course we don't, S'ta Keatin'. It slipped me mind, like. Well, anyway, once upon a time there was these five thousand people and they was all layin' on the ground."

That the people were lying on the ground was a curious detail not included in the original story. Sister Keating, pleased that Jane was responding, asked, "And why were the people there, Jane?"

"Lissenin' ta Jaysus. And they was starved with the hunger. And there was this little young fella there, and he had five fishes and two loafs, and says Jaysus to the little young fella, 'Will we eat the fishes 'n' loafs, then, Bucky?' and the little young fella says, 'Right enough, Jays, we will.' And they ate till they was burstin'. Then they had a look at the leftovers and there was twelve loafs now and twelve new fishes, and Jays says to the little young fella, 'Mind if I have the leftovers, then?' and the little young fella says, ' 'Tis all the same to me, Jays,' and Jaysus fed all the five thousand in the crowd wid' 'em."

Sister Keating said, "And what do we call that, Jane?"

"Dunno, S'ta Keatin'. "

"You do know, Jane. Try to remember."

Jane wiggled a loose tooth in her mouth. "Picnic, S'ta Keatin'?"

"Not a picnic, Jane."

Jane wiped her fingers on her shirtfront. "Oh, yeah. Not a picnic. What then, S'ta Keatin'?"

"A miracle."

"Oh, yeah. A miracle."

"And what is a miracle, Jane?"

"Something that happens and you don't know why, S'ta Keatin'."

"And who knows what holy day Friday is?"

"Frank Duff's birthday!" Siobhan shouted wildly.

"Frank Duff's birthday is not a holy day," Sister Keating said. She went on to read us the story of Martha and Mary, and as she read I felt an arm slide gently around my shoulders and across the back of my neck. It was Una Hennessy, the little girl sitting beside me. She put her knee on my thigh and her mouth up to my ear. "Rose," she whispered, "I'm five years old." *Oy'm foive yeeyars owe-uld.* She brought her face quickly around and positioned it in front of mine to catch my reaction. She was beautiful. She had bangs as black as anthracite, a perfectly round face, and enormous black eyes. On one of her cheeks a nasty circular burn was beginning to heal. My arm slipped automatically around her tiny waist. "I believe you," I said.

Una's mouth came down over my ear again; it had the muffled echo of a nautilus shell, the same hiss that mimicked the sea. "H'wold're ya?" she said.

"Thirty," I whispered.

"Hah?"

"Thirty."

The girl's hand was hot on the back of my neck, and her mouth was moist against my ear. "What'd ya say?"

"I said thirty."

I could hear Sister Keating speedily reading, "Lord, don't you care that my sister has left me to do the work by myself? Tell her to help me!"

"Rose! I'm askin' ya how old are ya?"

"I'm thirty, Una," I said.

Una brought her face around to look at mine again. She was utterly puzzled. Abandoning all pretense at a whisper, she screeched, "What are ya sayin' to me, Rose?"

Karen, two seats away, saw the problem. "She said she's *torty*, Una. Are ya feckin' deaf?"

"Torty!" Una exclaimed. "Shite! Older dan me mudder."

Sister Keating put down her book and took Karen and Una out of the room for a disciplinary chat. She asked me to mind the remaining seven girls. On her way out the door, Sister Keating said, "And when I come back I want to hear everyone recite Joseph Mary Plunkett's poem."

As the door shut behind Sister Keating, Jane gave her the finger.

I did my best to appear to disapprove of Jane's gesture. Jane pulled a lock of her long hair across her mouth and sucked on it. "Keatin's a nasty old hoor!"

"She is not," I said. "She cares about you."

Jane made a face, a dog's face, that replicated Sister Keating's with eerie precision. "Why do we say da Hayill Meery, girls!" she jeered.

I couldn't argue with that; I didn't have an answer myself.

The girls were delighted that Sister Keating was gone. They pulled their chairs up so close to mine that our knees were touching and they stared expectantly at me. I was in charge. But I had no idea what to do. I taught them a secret handshake. A hush fell over them as they watched my demonstration. Their mouths sagged open, and I saw in those moments how they must have looked in sleep: pretty and innocent and defenseless. They weren't sure whether they should be evil or good, obstructive or obedient. They didn't know their birthdays, and some of the younger ones didn't know their own last names. I tested the handshake on all of them, and then we took turns reading a catalogue of the various miracles. We practiced our Irish, played guess-the-saints, talked about confirmation, confession, and what a holy day of obligation is. We talked about the Eucharist. They loved the taste of it. "It's brilliant," said one girl. "I love it too," said Maire, and immediately the other girls reminded her that she was too young to have made her first communion, therefore she could not possibly know what the Eucharist tasted like.

I asked them to tell me about Joseph Mary Plunkett, the poet and patriot whose poem Sister Keating wanted them to recite. Kerry Spenser leaned forward in her chair. "Y'see, Rose, he wrote a poem. It goes like this, 'I seen his blood upon da leaf.'"

Roisin gave Kerry a peremptory blow in the chest. "Not *leaf*, stupid! 'Tis *rose*. I seen his blood upon da *rose!*"

Maire, preoccupied with the effort of peeling the paper jacket from a crayon, murmured feverishly at her hands, "Oy seen his blood upon da rose and in da stars da glory of his oys his body gleams amid etairnal snows his tears fallin' down from da skoys oy seen his face in every flower da toonder and da singin' a da boards an' oy dunno da rest a da fookin' pome and how come they called him Mary?"

The Angelus rang out from a church nearby, and the girls faced the statue of the Blessed Virgin and rushed through a prayer. Instead of praying, Jane spun cartwheels across the room, the heels of her sneakers flying past the face of the Virgin. Roisin went to the window and looked out at the couch in the lot across the street. I heard her saying to herself, "'Tis creepy." Margaret, a girl obsessed with her new bra, got up and proved to us all that she could extinguish the candles with her bare fingers. Vicki went one better than Margaret and lit some matches and put them out by holding them half an inch from her gaping mouth and huffing at them. I heard one of the matches sizzle against her wet lip, and then I told everyone to stop fooling around. They heard the order in my voice and looked at me, waiting to see whether this was a joke. Maire put her hand on my thigh and said sweetly, "Rose, are ya playin' at S'ta Keatin'? Is that it?"

Sister Keating returned just in time to hear Jane shout, "Vicki's shirt is sexy."

Sister Keating chastised her. "Don't be saying dirty words, Jane, or other words you don't know the meaning of. It's not nice. It's wrong. If you don't understand a word, go home and ask your mother what it means and is it all right to say."

Jane said bitterly, "Me moodah's dead, S'ta Keatin'."

All the girls looked at Jane with renewed respect.

Karen said, "If I went home and asked my mother what 'sexy' means, she'd slap my face, S'ta Keatin'."

Sister Keating looked at me almost apologetically, obviously unable to control these girls. "They are seeing things and hearing things they shouldn't be seeing," she said. "They know more than they should about the world."

The Smallest People
Feel at Home

I WANTED TO LEARN more about the Legion of Mary, its views and aims and programs, for I was certain that whatever the Legion presented would closely reflect the attitudes and beliefs of a large segment of the Irish population, particularly of the two generations preceding my own. I told Sister Keating of my interest, and she recommended a meeting of the Patricians, an offshoot of the Legion of Mary whose monthly meetings consisted of loose deliberations on Catholic doctrine.

I found a Patrician meeting on North Great George's Street on the north side of Dublin. The evening of the meeting was brisk and windy. Huge banks of clouds raced low across the powdery blue sky, and an occasional downpour blackened the pavement and blurred the shop windows. I hurried down Marlborough Street and up Parnell Street, where a skinny, shivering man with bloodshot eyes and a walrus mustache approached me and demanded, "Where have you been?"

I said, "Nowhere," and instantly he realized I wasn't who he'd thought I was. He followed me up Parnell Street anyway, head bowed, narrow shoulders raised up to his ears, hands stuffed deep into his jacket pockets. His clothes were wet, his teeth chattered, and his mustache smelled of beer. He said, "Are you from Dorchester, Massachusetts?"

"Very close," I said and kept walking.

"I have friends and relatives in Dorchester," he said, following behind me.

"I know," I said.

"*How* do you know?"

"Every Irish person has friends and relatives in Dorchester."

At this the man laughed loudly and gave me a friendly slug on the arm. The ease with which Irish people laid their hands on strangers always impressed me. We walked up Parnell Street and made small talk for a few minutes, during which it rained bitterly, got brilliantly sunny, and rained again. The man's sodden mustache drooped into his mouth, and his pointed leather boots were rubbery in the rain. "Where are you going?" he said.

"A Patrician meeting," I said.

"Ah, Christ, not those fuckin' blowhards," he said, and as we turned up North Great George's Street, he added, "Would you not rather have a drink with me instead?"

I told him I didn't drink.

The man stopped in his tracks and raked his oily mustache with his fingernails. He struggled to see me better between the greasy strands of hair that hung across his eyes like sea grass. "Jesus," he said, "you'll get pissed off at yourself, not drinkin' and talking to Catholics all day."

❉

THE PATRICIANS MET in a Georgian house that was a branch office of the Legion of Mary. I stepped into the hallway and came face to face with a nun hurrying purposefully through an office door with a brief-case under her arm. "Upstairs," she said, and though she spoke softly, it sounded like a command.

Like many of Dublin's old houses taken over by private organiza-tions, the Legion house was not cozy. It was utilitarian and bare, dimly lit, more like a shelter than a home, and stripped of all but a few reminders of its previous splendor. I went up a wide, creaking staircase to the second floor, and from a shelf in the hallway I took a Legion handbook. In the meeting room seventeen people milled nervously about, smoking, staring out the windows, seating themselves, and looking tentatively at each other. All were over fifty, and many had an air of bewilderment and timidity. Their clothing was outdated, ill fitting, and shiny with wear.

The meeting room had many tall windows and a brilliant swimming-pool-blue ceiling embellished with Palladian plasterwork in an elaborate design of white ivy garlands, cameo ovals, and scallop shells that stretched from one end of the room to the other. The ceiling, freshly painted, was luminous as the sky; I almost thought I could smell the paint. The blue traveled halfway down the walls, stopped at the white molding, and from there down the mood of the room changed dramatically; the lower walls, a drab gray-green, were scuffed and nicked and had holes punched in them. The squares of gray linoleum tile that covered the floor were warped and buckling— chips of dried linoleum crackled underfoot like seashells. A fleet of tiny wooden folding chairs arranged in rows looked borrowed from a midcentury Irish grade school. They were light and rickety, like toy chairs, and were hardly wide enough for the slightest fourth-grader. The fireplace had been sealed off by a sheet of scratched tin, and above it on the wall hung a large and particularly gruesome crucifix. I thought how well the warring halves of this room could pass for representations of heaven and hell.

On a small table was the same altar I had seen at the Legion meeting: the cloth with *Legio Mariae* embroidered in it, the two candles, and the two vases of carnations flanking a statue of the Blessed Virgin. The blue of the Virgin's cape was exactly the blue of the ceiling, and I imagined the painters pausing on a whim to dab at the statue with their brushes.

I sat in the second row of chairs and studied the Legion handbook. The Patricians had been established in 1955. Their purpose was to build up the religious knowledge of the people, to teach them how to explain themselves, and to encourage them to engage in apostleship. Their meetings were an attempt to cope with "the root problem of the Church: adult religious ignorance and the paralysed tongues of the laity." I understood that this meeting was to be an opportunity for all to speak freely: neither a conversation nor an exchange but a platform for spontaneous thoughts about the topic in question.

A man sitting in front of me heaved around in his seat and welcomed me heartily. He explained that he would be presenting the paper this evening and that his wife wasn't here because his public speaking made her nervous. "I used to be on the stage," he said. "A comedian. My wife used to die with fear for me every time I went on." He rubbed his fingertips together nervously as he spoke — they were so rough and calloused they made the sound of fine sandpaper on wood. He said, "I always look to see if a young woman is wearing a wedding ring. You're not married, I can see. A girl like yourself, why would she, for example, not be married?"

From the doting way the man smiled at me, I half expected him to reach over and give my cheek a pinch. His teeth were broken, and he had the rufous skin common among Irish men; he looked as though he had spent too long in a scalding hot shower with too much caustic soap, but I could see in his face remnants of a former handsomeness. He spoke as though he had known me for years — the way many Irish people speak to strangers with an ease born of a presupposed universal understanding, as though we were all passing through life together, as though my plight couldn't possibly be any better or worse than his and therefore I couldn't possibly reject him. The man looked swollen and overfed, and his camel's hair coat, too tight for him, restricted the movement of his thick arms. In his lapel he wore a Pioneers pin, the symbol of temperance.

He laid a stiff arm across the back of his little chair and told me a story. One night during his days of heavy drinking he got so drunk that he fell down on the floor of his favorite pub, and as he lay there he realized that his cheek was resting on something soft. He put his hand out and surmised after some minutes that this soft thing was the carpet on the floor. Drunk as he was he thought to himself, Do the publican's children have a carpeted floor, and my children have no carpet on their floor? Is that what it has come to? And the next day he gave up drinking, and three months later his children had a carpet on their floor. He finished the story and looked at me eagerly, waiting for the admiring response he had grown accustomed to.

A priest named Father Monahan entered the room wearing the enormous winter jacket of an Alaskan sled driver, a kind of anorak with bits of fur around the hood. The room fell silent. Father Monahan said, "I apologize for the fact that Father Savio could not be with you tonight. I will fill in for him as spiritual director for tonight's meeting," and he sat at a large table before the fireplace, facing the room like a schoolteacher, and did not remove the jacket.

I was pleased to hear that the topic of discussion this evening was "Is the Church Unfair to Women?" To me the answer seemed clear.

Father Monahan directed the people in the recitation of the Patrician Prayer, which included the declaration that they realized what stamp of men they were, how reluctant was their nature, and how unfit they were to offer their shoulders to the Lord, as well as a plea to Him not to let labor and suffering so great as theirs be wasted.

Father Monahan invited the man in the camel's hair coat, the actor, to read his paper. According to my booklet the paper did not necessarily have to be delivered by an expert. "Expertness may mean too much learning and too great length, which at the beginning of the meeting could ruin it."

The actor stood, adjusted the glasses on his nose, and began to read in an overdramatic tone. "Is the Church unfair to women? First of all, I had a grandmother. Second of all, I had a mother. Third of all, seven sisters, five daughters, three daughter-in-laws, and one mother-in-law, but never in their lives did they ever mention that the Church was unfair to them. When our Lord was on the earth, he had contact with a street girl. Now, I am just talking plain in the language of today: Mary Magdalene. She was a rough sinner. And how she changed when she came in contact with Jesus! She used her hair to wipe his feet. And she never said that the Church was unfair to her."

The man had memorized most of his paper, and this allowed him to press the pages flat against the front of his coat from time to time and look searchingly at his fellow Patricians as he spoke. He paced back and forth between Father Monahan and his audience.

"In this country women have put in so much work since St. Patrick brought the faith to Ireland, and never did anyone think that the Church was unfair to them. The mothers with the husbands—I've seen it in my small town, where the husbands are drinking—the women prayed that the husbands would stop drinking, and they never gave up the prayers, so much faith did they have. Do you think if women thought the Church was unfair to them, they'd be sitting around praying?

"Now I've come with a lot of praise for women and the Virgin Mary. And what I want to come to now is the way women have been unfair to the Church. The first thing that comes to mind is abortion. Isn't that being very unfair to the Church? Sixty million babies born every year. Women who abort the babies are unfair to the Church.

The Church gets power when babies are born. Another thing: there's an awful lot of people today siding with divorce. And you know well that the Church says don't separate the man and the woman. And the last thing I want to say: when I was drinking in the pubs for ten years, there wasn't one woman in the pub. Maybe in the snug there was an old granny having a small one. But now it has come that we have young girls drinking in the pubs and falling down in the street, shouting and roaring about, and losing their dignity, and they are very unfair to the Church. Because the Church loves everybody, and she gets hurt when she sees that happening to young girls. Thank you."

The man sat down in front of me again and turned in his seat and grinned at me, hoping for my approval. I smiled at him, though my impulse was to give his ear a good twist. I tried to remain calm, for I had just read in the handbook:

> A harsh attitude towards erroneous or foolish statements (of which there will be plenty) would be fatal. It would frustrate the Patrician purpose which is to coax each one to disclose himself. Therefore freedom of speech is paramount and is to be fostered even if awkward things are uttered.... If the family spirit is established in which the smallest people feel at home, then the Patrician foundation has been laid.

The first respondent to the paper, a tall and powerful-looking black-haired woman in her early sixties, spoke in a slow monotone with her face fixed in an unwavering expression of defeat. She stood with her bare arms folded across her chest in an X, like the arms of a corpse arranged in a coffin. Though her voice was leaden, an undercurrent of umbrage managed to rise through it. She said, "Christ is not concerned whether it is a male pope or a female pope that would serve Him. His only concern is the response you give. In the Church those who are in the positions of authority, which are priests, have decided that they have a monopoly over women. No way if Jesus was standing here tonight would He address the men only here tonight. He would see that everyone was welcome. But what do we get in the Church? 'Ye are all *sons* of God. Ye are all *brothers* in Christ.' Where does that leave women? If the men had received the same kind of discourtesy that we women have had to live with for years in the Church, they wouldn't go. If they went along every Sunday and were addressed as 'My dear sisters,' I am sure that they would be around in the cowshed. It's been teaching men to think that they are superior to women. If you were in a family"—the woman paused, struggling to control an emotion—"if you were in a family and you never got addressed, you would get an inferiority complex. Thanks."

A man stood quickly and in so doing knocked over his chair, which hit the floor with the clattering lightness of kindling wood. He wrestled with the chair. Reverently he said, "Mary is the best thing in the whole Church. Thank you very much."

A woman added, "The last prayer a Jew says before he goes to bed at night is, 'Thank God for not having created me a woman.'"

A woman in a black shawl said, "God created the world, then men, then women last to be a helper of men. He gave men the power to create, lead, decide, and guide women. The Church is following the truthful steps of our Lord. Woman can do much more for the Church in her own role as child bearer."

Behind me a woman's voice said, "I'd like to say I think the poor women are gone to hell. They are gone mad. It seems there's a terrible hatred the women have for the men."

The voice was familiar, a speedy, yapping chatter that sounded like Sister Keating.

"But God and society have always handed women over tremendous power. There is an old saying: man has his will, but woman has her way. Even in early days. And that's how it was meant to be. But I really do think women are gone to hell on this thing about liberation and fighting and talking about men. And they arrive at Sunday Mass in shorts cut right up to the crotch, and a holy priest upon the altar before them, and they are so bold as to be displaying their legs that way in the Mass. God made woman out of the rib of man, so it is for man to lead and woman to follow and make his job easier."

Another woman stood up. She had great difficulty expressing herself and apologized for her inarticulateness by saying, "Well, that is just my thought. It's just in *my* head and not probably in anyone else's. Maybe I'm just me. Sorry very much."

Father Monahan called on an elderly woman sitting beside me, and the woman rose to her feet. Her tiny face came to sharp points at nose and chin. Though it was not a terribly cold evening, she had not removed her hat and mittens. The hat, designed in the style of an aviator's cap with a strap that ran under the chin, was composed of gray and white tufts of synthetic fur in approximation of the pelt of an exotic animal. The fur resembled nothing so much as the shaggy flap of carpet sometimes fitted around the bases of toilets and sinks. She wore glasses and what looked like her husband's trenchcoat. Red bows had been knitted into the wrists of the mittens. She sighed in a deeply pained way and began her chiding monologue in a high, piercing voice. Her words were clearly directed at the black-haired woman who had spoken earlier.

"I would like to say I do not find anything insulting or discriminating about anything in the readings of the Mass. I feel that our Church has greater respect for women than any other religion. And I resent the idea of the priest dropping the word 'men.' This idea of the equal rights of men and women is an attack on the Church, and it is all coming from those who want to throw down the Church. My consolation is that Christ left the words, so that people who want to change them cannot win. That is the bottom line for me. I listen to Gay Byrne and Marian Finucane and the rest of them on the radio and television. They are all anti-Catholics to the extreme. Violently so."

It was true that popular Irish talk-show hosts often attacked the Church and its practices, but they faced great opposition, and the idea that Ireland could ever be rid of the Catholic Church was fantastical.

A heavy truck roaring by on Great George's Street shook the room and momentarily overwhelmed the woman's words. She clasped her mittened hands together at her waist, stiffened her spine, and talked louder and with increased vengefulness. "This so-called equality for women; the whole idea of that point of view is to tear us down. The Catholic Church is antiwomen, they say; no priests are ever women and all the rest of it. But the very people who want women priests also want divorce, contraception, and abortion."

Here she raised a hand and attempted to point an accusing finger from within the mitten. She looked at Father Monahan for approval. Father Monahan looked bored and uncomfortable. He gave no sign that he approved of anything that was being said.

"Let's face it," the woman continued, "women come out the worst on these evils. Abortion is a despicable abuse of women. And we all know that women end up on the wrong end of divorce. Yet all these people talk about wanting equality and wanting women to be addressed in the Church. What they really want is to be rid of priests and churches! But they can't win! We have God's promise for that.

That is the thing I hang on to. Because nobody can defeat God. You now see around the city girls maybe thirteen and fourteen pushing a child in a pram, or maybe two children, and no marriage. It is all the language of so-called equality that's doing that. What greater insult is there than the kind of society that's evolving on the so-called equality? The holy Catholic Church is the only place where there still is any respect left for women, and the more attacks that are made, the prouder I am to be one."

The woman sat back in her seat, red-faced and short of breath. She stared at the tin fireplace. All her determination seemed to have gathered in the fierce point of her chin, which jutted angrily forward, straining against the strap of her hat.

The meeting continued in the same tone of pain and defensiveness. Among these people there seemed to be a fear that the Church they had received solace and comfort from for decades was now on the brink of disappearing, and their anxiety over this was palpable. The Catholic Church was one of the few things they had always been certain of. Regardless of changes in personal fortune, the Church was a constant; it connected them to the past, to their ancestors, to their own history. Most of the women were grateful to the Church that had oppressed them, and gratefully they would set their faces against the insults it received. They were battered and beleaguered, humorless and serious, proud in the way war veterans are proud, and with these speeches they were defending their identity.

The Patrician meeting was intended as an inquiry, but this was not an inquiring discourse. These people believed what they believed, and no amount of discussion would alter that. Most of them were here because they were lonely and this was a way of being with people. Some were here because at one time in their lives they had drunk too much, or had behaved badly, or had mistreated someone they loved, or had ignored God and His words and had since had a change of heart. A few were here because they had been directed by a confessor to do so as part of their penance, and these few sat at the back of the room, intransigent, unmoved, and scornful.

＊

AT THE NEXT Patrician meeting I attended, the discussion was of divorce. The evenings were growing darker, and the meeting room was exceedingly warm. Many of the same people who had been at the last meeting were there, and several looked as though they had never left the room.

A very small man dressed in a beautifully cut but filthy suit said to a man sitting near him, "Lovely weather, isn't it?" His necktie looked as though it had been laid flat on a greasy griddle.

The other man responded sadly, "It is. So lovely we are not able for it. We are not used to it."

The man in the suit said, "True. We are not able. It took us by surprise. If we had seen it coming, we probably would not be here tonight. We'd be out in the Dublin Mountains, I suppose."

"The Dublin Mountains, of course."

The two men spoke soothingly and without looking at each other, as though reciting lines from a radio play.

One woman behind me said to another, "Very warm, isn't it?"

"Very warm it is indeed. An unnatural warmth, really."

And then a whey-faced little man in a white shirt, black trousers, and a tiny pair of eyeglasses came timidly into the room and said indifferently, "I am Brother Lennon. I am sorry to report that our spiritual director, Father Savio, isn't with us tonight. He went down to the country and could not reach us, and I am sorry to add that Father Gavin has had the flu and he could not complete his paper on divorce. Due to the fact that we have no spiritual director, this cannot be a formal Patrician meeting. However, we can carry on with our own discussion following the usual rules of the meeting."

Brother Lennon read a paper on divorce, which included the following information: "Any suggestion that the laws of marriage having been made by the will of man and therefore can now be changed by man is contrary to the teaching of Christ. Divorce is often sought on the grounds that a person has a right to happiness. C. S. Lewis said, 'To claim the right to happiness is like claiming the right to good luck.' Happiness is partial and fleeting. It is within ourselves and in compliance with what God requires of us. The right of children to a stable family is greater than the right of men and women to have divorce. If we accept divorce into our legal system, that will affect the seriousness with which the marriage bond is viewed and approached."

A woman asked, "Why do nullifications take so long to complete? Can anyone advance a reason that it cannot be speeded up in cases where a husband and wife's views cannot be reconciled? Is it that the

Vatican is flooded with applications, or is it that the Church's scrupulous attention is what's hindering it?"

The man in the suit who wished he was in the Dublin Mountains stood up and said, "I do not know, Madam, but nullity is a serious thing to the family. You couldn't just come along and say to a couple, You can have your annulment tomorrow."

The actor rose to his feet, shut his eyes, and raised his silencing hand. "That lady doesn't seem to realize that when two Roman Catholics marry in the Church they become one person in the eyes of God. That's why the Church takes it so seriously for anyone to come and ask to be separated. That is all I have to say."

A scraggly, toothless, red-haired man in a greasy T-shirt exclaimed, "I would never get married! I am too good to be married! I would not want to beat her up. I'd give them a slap. But I wouldn't want to beat them up, so I'll never get married. I'd rather be by myself." In threading his belt, this man had missed three loops at the back of his trousers, which sagged, revealing the waistband of his underwear. His hands and neck were deeply sunburned. When he said he would never marry, the woman behind him began to heave in her seat, struggling to stifle her laughter.

The tall, black-haired woman from the last meeting said, "Why does the second marriage often work?"

The actor said impatiently, "But we're talking about Catholic marriage here! A second marriage isn't a Catholic marriage!"

The woman said defiantly, "Is that why it works?"

With the nail of his little finger the actor scratched at his ruddy cheek to calm himself. "If a man deserts his wife and his children and is callous enough not to take care of them, and if another woman goes to this man, how could she be so callous? How could they have the capacity for real Christian love?"

The red-haired man who wouldn't marry said, "I agree. They don't go to Mass and don't believe in God. All they believe in is getting married so they can get a certificate and a house off the Dublin Corporation."

A voice at the back of the room said, "What is the use of praying?"

The black-haired woman said slowly, "There is a lot of judging going on here. Unless the man and woman are in union in mind, then they are not one person. The lack of education in our schools and families has led to the state our country is in. If there is no divorce in Ireland, then a person can't get married again. The state doesn't give people a choice in the matter."

Brother Lennon said, "State law may come more in line with the Church law of nullity. One of the cases would be homosexuality, where the innocent party would be free to marry again."

A very old man stood up and said with gentle exasperation, "This word *divorce*. We didn't have this word years ago. Years ago people would be married fifty years. These days there's too much money now and too much education for us to have any real peace. This country has got on well long enough without these other EC countries and their big ideas."

The red-haired bachelor said, "I agree. We have gone materialistic. My parents were poor but they were happy. We didn't have anything. These days people don't want to work. There should be a law against people having sex with a girl and then having a child before they are married and then they marry her. I think there should be a law."

The man in the suit said, "Is it only Catholic marriage problems? Christ said quite clearly that when Moses granted the Jews the divorce it was because the Jews had become so hardhearted that they would no longer obey the laws of God."

The actor complained bitterly. "Why are we worrying about the Jews? This is Frank Duff's meeting. We should be worrying about our own people."

Brother Lennon, sensing that the meeting was falling apart, said nervously, "As I said at the beginning, this cannot be an official Patrician meeting, for we have no spiritual director. We have reached the halfway point, and time for a cup of tea now, okay? And then we will come back and we will talk some more then, okay? And thanks very much, friends, for now, okay?"

I LEFT THE MEETING and headed home. A warm wind whipped candy wrappers and old newspapers up the street. On Marlborough Street a woman I had met weeks before at a party called out my name. I had forgotten hers—Theresa. She was unlocking her bicycle in front of a shop. She told me she was on her way home from Sandycove, where she had been listening to a writer reading short stories, and in the same breath she said, "My sexuality is ruled by the stars. I'm a Scorpio is the reason. The genitals are ruled by the stars, if you are a Scorpio." Theresa held my forearm as she talked in her half-despairing, half-hopeful way. She told me she was in love with a man named Brendan and had expected to see him tonight in Sandycove, but she hadn't seen him. Brendan was fed up with women and lived with his mother now. "He's brainy," she said wistfully. "He's smarter and more talented than I am." She had been waiting weeks for Brendan to call her, had literally sat by the phone for weeks. She said, "He doesn't call. I don't know why. He's fed up with us, Rose."

As I continued on my way alone, I had a strong sense of the loneliness in this city. So many Dubliners seemed starved for company, so many were waiting for someone to notice them.

THE TOPIC OF DISCUSSION at the last Patrician meeting I attended was "Do Angels Influence Us?" I sat beside a very short man named John, who, it turned out, was to deliver the evening's paper. He wore the same odd outfit he had worn at the other meetings. His tiny feet were stuffed into soft blue suede shoes with sharply pointed little toes — the sort of shoes Rumpelstiltskin might have worn. Because the zipper and button of his enormous black trousers were broken, he had cinched the trousers around his waist with two belts, and as an extra precaution he wore a pair of suspenders devised from pieces of hairy twine. He wore a tattered woolen jacket with something the size of a rabbit in each pocket; under the weight of these mysterious objects the jacket sagged and tugged at his narrow shoulders. Tongues of stark white hair lay forward on his balding crown. He had a gentle manner and spoke with a Dublin accent so thick it was like a speech impediment; even the other Dubliners strained to understand him. He stood and read haltingly, carefully separating each word from the next. "Do angels influence us? We all have a guardian angel to whom we should pray more often. Angels were created by God to protect us. They are known as messengers of God. There are angels of God and angels who are our worst enemies. The angels of sin entice us to walk into wickedness. But we must invoke a good angel, especially our guardian one, who will show us how to conquer these wicked temptations. So I think angels will have a big influence in where we spend eternity. It is up to us to decide which way we will go. The way to hell or heaven is in our own hearts. Thanks very much."

The first respondent, the tall, black-haired woman, said, "Angels don't seem to get an awful show these days. All we know is that they are much higher than any of the saints. And we are told several times in scripture that the second coming of Christ will be heralded by an angel. I often wonder that we don't have a more decided devotion to the angels. Angels are very outdated creatures altogether."

A woman in her early forties who was sitting in front of me kept turning halfway around in her seat to peer at me out of the corner of her eye. She had the watchful, uncertain expression of a five-year-old. She peered and looked quickly away again each time I caught her eye. It was clear from her expression that she wanted to smile at me, but, unsure of how I would respond, she hesitated. I had a strong sense that if I didn't smile back at her the rejection would be devastating. I did nothing, waiting for her to make the first move.

There were several young people in the room that night, and they looked bored, vaguely scornful, and embarrassed. I thought that in twenty years, most of the older people — the most trenchantly traditional — would be dead, and who then would be attending these meetings?

The man sitting beside me was from Kerry. His eyes were so unnaturally small they looked as though the corners had been stitched shut. He said, "Each person has an angel to defend them. That's one aspect."

Another man said, "Briefly, I would like to say that angels see the face of mankind. I read that somewhere in the scripture, but really I think it has something to do with children. It means don't scandalize the little ones, because their angels see the face of our father in heaven."

A man who wore rings on six fingers said, "The angels know that the son of man is coming back, but they don't know when. And as far as power or vanity or pride in heaven, there's no such thing as those. There's no such thing as saying Saint Michael was the greatest angel, or some such other was the greatest. There is no pride in heaven. Pride lives in us all. Nearly everyone in this room is proud in some way."

"I am not proud," the Kerryman said airily.

John, the evening's primary speaker, stood up. With his amazingly long yellow fingernails he scratched anxiously at his ear. "Wait a minute, everyone. I forgot to say something. I forgot to say in my speech that there are many things that have been named after the angels. For example: angel cake, Los Angeles, Michelangelo, angel hair, Angela, angelfish, angelic, angel sleeve, angel's trumpet, angel's breath, the Angelus. And thank you very much."

The actor, looking directly at me, said, "I think the young people should speak. The young people should not be shy."

No young people spoke. They looked at each other, abashed and abased.

The man with the rings stood up. From where I was sitting, the rings—simple silver bands bristling with rows of tiny points— looked like miniature crowns of thorns. Idle in his lap, the man's hands looked threatening, equipped to punch and scar. I realized eventually that they were rosary rings. "You have to believe in angels on the word of God himself," the man said. "How many of us believe in holy water? How many of us believe in crucifixes in our homes? Or holy pictures? How many of us believe in the Hail Mary, the Our Father, and the Glory Be? I would find it hard to be a Catholic or Christian without believing in angels, or without believing in the supernatural."

I was always struck by the level of superstition in Catholicism, especially here in Ireland, and I was reminded of the way Aunt Lizzie insisted on drenching me in a shower of holy water at bedtime, as though I might never wake again if she didn't perform this ritual. Lizzie was superstitious and often spoke of fairies. The phenomenon of fairies explained a host of otherwise inexplicable occurrences, and belief in them was still strong in rural Ireland. Fairies were said to be angels who had fallen from heaven during the struggle between Lucifer and God—angels not evil enough to be banished to hell but not quite holy enough to be protected in heaven. They were known variously as the Little People, the Good People, and the People Out-side Us. Though invisible and able to change their size and shape at will, they were supposed to live something like human beings. They lived in the ruins of houses, in hills, raths, and moats. They loved music and dancing and parties. They borrowed food and cows from humans and always returned what they had borrowed. Generally fairies were harmless to humans, and often they were helpful, but sometimes, particularly when they felt slighted, they could be mischievous and hurtful.

The woman who kept turning to look at me stood up and said, "The Jews went forty years into the desert, and I wonder who they had to protect them. The Jews, like. Was it angels? Because they would certainly need something to keep them from having accidents when they were in the desert. Thank you." When she sat down she peered timidly over her shoulder at me to catch my reaction. I smiled; so did she.

Another man said, "I think the angel is the purest spirit and never had any body or shape and can see everything, and can reason everything in a flash right to a conclusion. Therefore, if we have guardian angels—which I believe we do have—then they are able to influence our minds, if we want them to. If we pray to them to guide our minds in all difficult situations and to guard us on our way and lighten our minds every day. This is just my own feeling. The people who wrote the books and scriptures gave angels human shapes just to try and explain them, but who will ever know how Our Lady received the message at the Annunciation?"

The man paused for a moment, and I thought he might come up with an answer to his own question. When he spoke again, his voice had softened. "There is a lot we don't know," he said. "There is a really lot we don't know."

The People Outside Us

THE SUPERSTITION I encountered in Dublin was far more pronounced in the country, and while living in Corofin I found it difficult not to be influenced by it.

One November morning on my way out of the castle I found a man's tweed cap lying near the coal bag in the courtyard. The sight of the cap startled me. My outer gates were always locked — how had a cap gotten here? The night before, I had heard an unfamiliar sound along the west wall of the castle, just behind the fireplace and very near where the cap now lay. I knew it was possible for a determined person to get over the castle's outer wall without undue difficulty. I could imagine a man scaling the wall, swinging a leg over the top, leaping the seven feet to the ground, boots landing with a thud in the gravel (possibly the sound I had heard), him hitching forward under his own weight, and the cap tumbling from his head. I pictured him on his knees searching in the dark for the cap, huge hands patting the ground and meeting nothing but weeds and gravel. Or perhaps it was only the wind that had blown the cap there. Or perhaps someone had thrown the cap over the wall on a mischievous whim. Or perhaps, finally, it was one of the ghosts Francis was always fretting about. I tried and failed to force the cap over the crown of my head; it was small enough to fit a young boy, though Irish boys rarely wore tweed caps like this one. It was, I decided, the cap of a very small man. Satisfied that I was capable of overpowering the cap's mysterious little owner, I hung it on the antlers above the fireplace and forgot about it.

Later in the day I accepted a ride into the village from a farmer who stopped his car for me as I walked along the road. The farmer had an enormous head and thick black hair, and he was sweating heavily, though the day was cold. His shirt was open at the neck, and the hair on his chest glittered with sweat. A black-and-white spaniel paced back and forth in the rear of the car, pawing occasionally at the wire screen that separated him from us. When I asked about the dog, the farmer said he had three more dogs just like this one. I asked if they were hunting dogs.

"They are," he said.

I asked if he was a hunter.

"I am."

What did he hunt?

"Pheasants and woodcock," he said, wiping his forehead with a piece of newspaper that had been stuffed into the crevice between windshield and dash.

Did he eat what he shot?

"I would, but I've no one to pluck the fowl for me."

I took this to mean he had no wife and said, "Why don't you pluck the birds yourself?"

He answered with a loud and appreciative laugh, and he lifted his enormous hands off the steering wheel and clapped them together once, hard, applauding my naiveté. The dog stiffened and tipped his head at his master, trying to discern whether the clap applied to him.

The farmer was inscrutable and said little. He had a strong, handsome face, and he watched the narrow road with his mouth hooked up into a half smile. He seemed to be holding an amusing secret. His hands were scored with deep scratches and cuts, as though he had been braiding brambles, and his fingernails, like mine, were black with coal dust. There were piles of local newspapers on the back seat of the car, a pair of rubber boots, a bottle of milk, and a large steak wrapped in a clear plastic bag. The pacing dog leered at the steak and pawed some more at his cage.

We shot between the hedgerows, nearly killing two rabbits, a goat, and a little dog. Every so often the long hairs of the hedge whipped the windshield, making me flinch; my side of the windshield was violet with blackberry juice. The afternoon sun was bright and hard and threw deep shadows across the road, and from time to time a brilliant patch of glowing green grass flashed into sight through a break in the hedge. I saw sheep with identifying splashes of bright blue paint on their rumps, bearded goats, stone walls white with lichen, Bridie O'Daly's slovenly farm, velvety hills, a copper-haired child steering an enormous tractor through a field, a white farmhouse with a twist of smoke spiraling from the chimney, a shimmering stand of birch trees, a swaybacked horse. Everything looked enormous and clean in the sun, and the sky was like a shallow sea.

On our way into the village we passed a woman walking her dog. I had seen this woman several times before, and once, when a sister of mine was visiting, we had met her in the road, and she had asked us without so much as a hello, "Oh, girls? Who do I look like?" Quickly (and crazily, I thought) my sister answered, "Queen Elizabeth."

"Right!" the woman had cried, beside herself with glee. She was a short woman with a stolid, practical face, a line for a mouth, and wide cheekbones. She wore a carrot-colored turban on her head. I asked the sweating farmer if he knew her.

"I do, of course. That's Mamie Duffy. We call her Mad Mamie. She is always going on about having been raped." He smirked in a wicked way that made me distrust him. "But she was not raped. I suppose she is still hoping. She is what we call an eccentric."

The way he said "we" was an indication of how deeply the villagers considered themselves one, whether they approved of each other or not.

❊

IN THE VILLAGE I said good-bye to the farmer and made my way to Dillon's Pub to return the history book Francis MacNamara had lent me. Corofin's short street sloped downhill slightly as it traveled west. Bowed gutters ran directly in front of the doorways of houses and shops. The small, thick-walled houses were made of stucco or stone and had pale, astonished faces. They seemed to be leaning into one another for protection and solace. In their tiny, lace-curtained windows there was always a statue of the Blessed Virgin, or a lonely geranium, or a large dead fly stiff on the sill, or a bottle of holy water, or an old person with big eyeglasses staring out at the street in a puzzled way. When the doors were open, the smell of bacon and cabbage drifted out onto the street. And just inside those doors hung, inevitably, a lurid picture of the sacred heart.

The names painted brightly across Corofin's shopfronts were Burke, Daffy, Connolly, Bofey, Cahir, Kenny, MacNamara, Dillon, Kennedy, and MacNamara.

As I neared Dillon's Pub I saw Mad Mamie in front of the church with her little white dog on a leash. The dog was a Jack Russell with two-inch legs and a rabbit's winglike ears. Mamie broke into a semitrot in an effort to inspire the dog to run. I could tell by the way she bent her head toward him that she was talking to him, coaxing and encouraging him. When she saw me she cried out, "And here is my little son!" as though picking up the thread of an interrupted conversation.

"I see that," I said.

"I see that," she said amiably. "He's named Spot. He likes you."

Spot had done nothing to indicate that he liked or disliked me.

"Spot is thirteen," Mamie said.

I said, "He doesn't look that old."

"He doesn't look that old. Correct. Because I give him vitamins. I slip them into his meat. I live by the graveyard. Do you know my house?"

"Which house?"

"Which house? Cream colored."

All the houses by the graveyard were cream colored.

"Are you the American lady?" Mamie asked.

"Yes, I am," I said.

"Yes, I am," she said.

Mamie was repeating my words not in a taunting way but in summary, as if to prove she had heard me.

"And it's a creamy house with aluminium windows, and most times you can see my little son, Spot, around there. Now do you know the house?"

I did not know the house but said I did, and to cover the lie I bent

and patted Spot, who shivered with pleasure beneath my hand. His
big ears twitched.

"Yes. And I have a phone," said Mamie.

Many people in Corofin did not have phones.

"And there are some shrubs in front of my house. And you're the
American lady living in the castle."

Mamie spoke softly and sighingly, like a person experiencing
tremendous relief and, like so many villagers, she careered back and
forth between subjects without warning or segue. I introduced myself
to her, and she said, "My name is Duffy. My name is Mamie. My
name is Mamie Duffy." This she said uncertainly, as though trying to
mimic a sentence she had heard on tape. She shaded her eyes with
one hand and pointed to a row of boxy little houses on the hill by the
graveyard. "Up there now. The pink house. That little bungalow is
mine."

"I thought you said it was cream colored."

" 'Tis, but is has a pinky shade to it. You're O'Mahony. Your father
must be Irish something way back."

"Grandfather."

"Grandfather. Where from?"

"Killorglin."

"Killorglin. County Kerry! Very pretty place. Anyone else of yours
Irish?"

I told her I had a grandmother from Ballylanders. She said,
"County Limerick! Oh, very nice. Limerick is very nice."

Spot stood on Mamie's foot and licked noisily at her stockinged
shin, his rough tongue grating against the nylon.

"Anyone else?" Mamie asked.

"A great-grandfather from Fethard."

"Fethard in Wexford or Fethard in Tipperary?"

"Tipperary."

"Tipperary! Also nice. Very nice. Though there's better than it.
Still, Tipperary is nice."

Mamie was like a person at a winetasting, appraising, considering,
comparing. She smiled at me — or possibly she was only squinting in
the sun. Her teeth were traced with brownish cracks, like crockery
that has been shattered and puzzled back together with glue. "Anyone
else Irish?"

"Another pair of great-grandparents from the North," I said.

Mamie nodded knowingly and tapped her lips with the strap of Spot's leash. "And which of these sailed off to America?"

"All of them," I said. It was disappointingly true that with all these Irish grandparents and great-grandparents I had only two relatives left in Ireland, both elderly and both so distant as to have little effect on my heart.

Spot sniffed at a puddle, then sneezed daintily.

"And do you like it here?" asked Mamie.

"Very much."

Mamie patted her orange turban, checking to see that it was straight on her large head. "Very much. The Burren is nice. And recently they broke into my house while I was at Mass and stole my rosary beads and my bus pass. You have nice teeth. And a personality. Anyone ever say that? And you still think I look like the queen?"

It was never I who thought she looked like the queen. "You haven't changed a bit," I said.

"You haven't changed. My house is the pink. The cream. Do you love Spot?"

Before I could answer, Mamie walked off in midsentence. The last thing I heard her say was, "I'm hoping to thumb to Ennis."

❖

DILLON'S PUB had just opened for the day and was empty but for a young man whom Francis had been talking with by the fire and Eamon the butcher, who sat in his usual place at the end of the bar. Francis stood up when I came in and immediately apologized for the weakness of the fire, which he had just lit. He pulled up a chair for me and began denigrating the pub for my benefit. He said there was an awful echo in the room, that the stone floor was cold, and that Donal O'Shea's antique love seats didn't belong in a rough place like this. Francis jerked his thumb at the pair of carved wooden heads fastened to the beams above the bar and said, "Not to mention them effin' creepy two heads." One was an Indian woman in a red turban and the other a pirate with a pipe in his mouth. The dark wooden faces had been buffed smooth and shiny, and their features, so carefully rendered, looked real.

Francis could think of a hundred reasons to hate this pub, but whenever he listed them his voice assumed a gently evasive quality, as though something deep in him secretly embraced the place.

Stomping footsteps marched across the floor above us, and a door slammed shut with such force that the ill-fitting windows rattled in their frames.

"That would be Michael getting up," said Francis.

Michael lived above the pub with Francis, partly because there was no room in his father's house down the road, where three of his siblings still lived, and partly because he preferred it that way.

Most of Corofin's shops and pubs operated out of the ground-floor rooms of private houses, and signs of the proprietors' lives were always in evidence. In the various shops barefoot, moon-faced children in pajamas peered through rear doorways. Corofin's tiny post office was always overwhelmed with the aroma of roasting lamb or baking pie. Often I caught glimpses of disrupted dinners through open doors: half a loaf of bread, teacups, a roast chicken, steaming piles of boiled potatoes, bottles of milk, and the pale freckled faces of sons and daughters staring up from the table to see who had come in, staring with their mouths open, pink tongues showing, spoons and forks gripped in their fists. And the proprietor would appear in the doorway, patting his mouth with a napkin, and say, "Now, then!" Once I heard the postmistress in a back room scolding her son for having brought a rotten cabbage home from the grocery. "Tom Hogan would never have sold *me* such a cabbage!" she howled. "Take it back and get him to give you another!" And she hurried out to assist me with a distracted smile.

THE YOUNG MAN Francis had been talking with was English. He appeared to have made a poncho for himself by cutting a hole in a woolen blanket and sticking his head through it. The poncho was brown and furry and reached to the floor. His name was Giles. He had a thug's face and a wide mouth and would have looked menacing and cruel if not for the amazing thickness of his eyeglasses, which made him look merely helpless and blind. He held a pint of Guinness in one hand and a paperback by Bruce Chatwin on his lap. Francis introduced me to him and began rolling a cigarette.

Giles peered critically at me, then, fingering his eyeglasses, he turned to Francis and continued the conversation my arrival had obviously interrupted. "As I was saying, you never knew whether to believe what Bruce Chatwin said. In actual fact, you never knew if it was true."

Francis, who confessed he had never heard of Bruce Chatwin until today, said, "Yeah, and Bruce Chapman probably thought it was true himself, just like that brother of mine. If Conor MacNamara has had a few pints—say three pints, for instance—he'll tell you there was ten geese standing before him. A few pints more and the geese get to be a hundred. Another few pints and it's a thousand feckin' geese that he saw, and he believes it himself. Isn't that so, Eamon?"

Eamon sat hunched over so far on his stool that his chin nearly came to rest on the oak bar. "Yap, Francis! Yap!" he snapped. He sucked on his long teeth and grinned idiotically. He blinked and hic-cupped. He was like a person on automatic pilot. How could a man like this be a butcher? How could he wield a cleaver without harming himself? And, come to think of it, why was he never in his butcher shop?

Francis licked the edge of his cigarette paper, sealed it carefully around the little twig of tobacco, and settled the twig on his lower lip. I asked him if it was true that Conor had built a submarine, and he rolled his big eyes at me and muttered around the cigarette, "Sheesh. The effin' summarine. Okay. So he did build one. If you want to say that, you can be my guest and say it."

Giles said dryly, "In actual fact, John Holland, the man who in-vented the submarine, was born not far from here."

Giles had recently bought a house in Miltown Malbay and, like most immigrants to any country, he seemed to know more about his new home than the natives did. He had a priggish, condescending way of speaking and an uncanny ability to drain all the interest and life out of the many facts he's stored in his head. Much of what he said he qualified with the pompous British phrase "in actual fact." And he was right: John Holland, the inventor of the submarine, was born in Liscannor on the coast of Clare.

"And it was off John Hollander that Conor got the idea," said Francis.

Francis spoke wearily and irritably of Conor, as though it exhaust-ed him to be forever correcting the portrait of his brother. But there was also something like envy in his tone. No feat of Conor's could be completely denied, and some of the things he had done were truly remarkable. A few days earlier I had stopped at Conor's garage to say hello and found him in his greasy overalls surrounded by television sets of all ages and makes. Some he had repaired and others he had rebuilt; all of them worked. There were boats in the garage, cars, a motorcycle, two trucks, and in the middle of the garage, hanging on heavy ropes from the very high ceiling, was a child's swing, which Conor had rigged up for one of his granddaughters. "My youngest girl has a daughter of her own," he said, "though she's not married. They live with me."

The news of the illegitimate granddaughter surprised me, but more surprising was Conor's willingness to share it with me. Conor said he was "stone mad" about the little girl and that she had red hair down to her waist. He told me he and his granddaughter were look-ing forward to Halloween. Last Halloween he had bought sweets and had hung apples in the doorway of his house, but not a single child had come to his door.

"That was a disappointment," he said sadly, winding the rope of the swing around his forearm. "This year maybe 'twill be different."

I sat in the swing and Conor gave me a push. The arc of the swing was tremendous. I seemed to be flying up into the rafters, swooping down across the garage, then soaring up to the rafters at the opposite end, so close I could see the cobwebs gracing the roof beams. If I were a child, I would have been terrified of a swing like this. I could see Conor's laughing face below, the gaps in his teeth, the widow's peak pointing down at his long nose, and it occurred to me that his interests covered the spectrum from childish to lewd.

THROUGH THE PUB WINDOW I could see the hardware store across the street awash in sunlight with a strip of clear blue sky above it, a blue so dark it looked painted. Watchful jackdaws wheeled above the roof, their huge beaks opening and closing as they released their ugly, grating cries. On bright days like this Dillon's Pub felt darker and smaller than it really was.

Conor MacNamara had told me the name MacNamara was one of the oldest in the area. I asked Francis if that was true. He grimaced to show me how untrue it was. "It *is* not. I doubt that very much. Mac-Namara is old, but I wouldn't say it is one of the oldest. Now as far as old goes, the Burren has been here three hundred million years. It was here before the Andes, the Alps, or the Himalayas ever was." Francis looked from me to Giles and back again. "Hard to believe that, isn't it?"

Francis found it hard to believe that a thing so familiar and so much a part of the local life could also be so magnificent, that the neighborhood was invested with such ponderous endurance and pre-eminence.

The word "Burren" is an Anglicization of the Irish word *bhoireann*, which means "a rocky place." That was putting it mildly; the Burren was an awe-inspiring expanse of smooth sheets of limestone that extended for miles, like near-perfect pavement. From afar the Burren looked like a blank and forbidding place, like a desert of stone, like the moon, but up close it was crawling with life. There were foxy pine martens there, frogs, newts, lizards, badgers, stoats, sparrow hawks, kestrels, and a hundred other kinds of birds. Once, as I walked up Mullaghmore Mountain I came over a slight rise and startled a herd of some seventy feral goats. They scattered from me in the undulating, fanning way birds do and swept up the side of the mountain, kicking loose stones behind them. Their hooves on the rock sounded like hail on a windowpane. They had slanted yellow eyes, weedy brows, long beards, and yellow hair. Just before a turn in the weather the goats would wander down from Mullaghmore and roam the lower land. Sometimes at daybreak I saw them drinking from the stream outside my door.

From the windows of Ballyportry Castle I had a view of Mullaghmore Mountain rising in the distance — a stunning sight, more like the artful product of a potter's wheel than a mountain. Mullaghmore was low and round and gently sloping, a delicately layered bubble of ash-gray stone; the layers were so regular they looked as though they had been poured on in stages. The bare stone was a pure reflector of light; at sunset Mullaghmore was magenta, in the early morning it was violet, at other times it was indigo, or white, or gold, or ocher. The Burren sky was huge, and it was not unusual to see three or four rainbows arching over it at one time. The clouds that massed over the Burren came in off the Atlantic and held in them the color of the ocean.

Unexpected wildflowers, both arctic and mediterranean, grew between the big cracks in the stone of the Burren. The first time I saw a flower there my heart stopped. It seemed impossible for any plant to survive in such a barren place. Later I learned that botanists came from all over the world to clamber over the stones of the Burren and study its strange flowers. This was the only place in the world where spring gentian, mountain avens, shrubby cinquefoil, and dense-flowered orchid—plants that usually grew in very different environments—grew together.

I was surprised at how many stone walls had been built in the foothills of Mullaghmore, for these walls surrounded not grass but more stone—sheets and piles of it. One day I came upon a farmer named Sheedy who was repairing one of these walls. In a crushed fedora and a dirty, buttonless trenchcoat, Sheedy looked more like a failed detective than a farmer. He held a pipe clamped between his teeth and wore a piece of string around his waist to keep the coat from flapping open in the wind. I asked him what the walls were for.

"To hold the cattle within," he said through gritted teeth.

"You graze cattle here?"

"We do."

"What do they eat?"

"Grass."

"Is there grass here?" I asked, giving him the benefit of the doubt.

"There is, of course." And to prove it Sheedy rolled a large stone over with his foot, revealing a few crushed strands of etiolated grass the color of overcooked spaghetti.

Later, reading about the Burren, I was struck by a passage from F. J. Foot, an Irish geologist, who wrote in 1862:

> At a distance these bare rocky hills seem thoroughly devoid of vegetation, and the desert-like aspect thus imparted to the landscape has been compared to that of parts of *Arabia Petraea*. But on closer inspection, it will be found that all the chinks and crevices . . . are the nurseries of plants innumerable, the disintegration of the rock producing a soil, than which none is more productive. So rich and fattening is the soil in the valleys, and often in the barest looking crags, that high rents are paid for tracts for grazing, that a stranger *en passant* would hardly value at two pence per acre.

There were karst caves, holy wells, ring forts, prehistoric tombs, and hundreds of religious monuments and burial grounds in the Burren. Some of the megalithic tombs were nearly six thousand years old. Ruins of medieval churches and castles shrouded in ivy and lichen dotted the landscape like statuary. The Burren was an open-air museum of wonders, and because there were few places like it in the world it cast a mystical spell on its visitors, some of whom moved to the area and grew obsessive and possessive about it.

Once I hitched a ride from an elderly British couple who had moved to Ireland to be near the Burren. They were on their way to a seminar on Burren fauna. The wife had worked herself up into a state of high agitation about what she saw as the imminent demise of the area. When I mentioned the local government's proposal for an interpretive center to be built at the foot of Mullaghmore, the wife bent over in her seat and clutched at her head with both hands, as though I had made a skull-piercing noise.

The interpretive center, which would have videos, books, and experts to explain the natural history of the Burren, was intended to bring tourists to Mullaghmore. Fanatic outsiders hated the idea of the center, seeing it as merely a way to sell tickets and trinkets and ruin the pristine landscape, while unemployed local people were in favor of it and the jobs it would create. Many locals saw the Burren as little more than a pile of worthless stones, and if people wanted to come roaring in on tour buses to stare at it, let them come, especially if they would spend money in the nearby villages. Francis and Conor MacNamara were the only local people I had met who seemed genuinely interested in the Burren, and that appeared to be the one thing the brothers had in common.

I sat stuffed into the back seat of the English couple's tiny car and listened to them complaining that the locals didn't comprehend that under the pressure of so much traffic and building they would eventually lose the very thing the tourists had come to see. The woman said, "The Irish, God bless them, always make the mistake of putting commercial sites smack on top of historical or geological ones." She craned her neck around to look at me. "Have you seen Yeats's tower?"

Yeats's tower, Thoor Ballylee, was a few miles north of Gort. I hadn't seen it yet.

"Don't bother!" the woman shrieked. "They've attached a museum and a tearoom to it. Yeats would whirl in his grave."

※

FROM INSIDE THE PUB we heard what sounded like the report of a rifle just outside the window, followed by loud shouts.

Eamon said wearily, "Is that Diarmuid O'Hagan and his wife fighting again?"

"God, Eamon, it's only a car," said Francis, stirring the fire with a tin curtain rod that had been lying across the mantel. He looked

bored. He relit his cigarette expertly from the glowing end of the curtain rod and asked me if I had been to Aillwee Cave, the most famous
of the Burren's enormous network of caves. I told him I had been to it
but hadn't gone inside.

"Now, why would that be, Rose?" he said suspiciously. "Would it
be because you would not like going into a spooky place like that? Is
that it?"

Something in Francis was determined to discover some natural
phenomenon that frightened me. He couldn't understand why, if he
was frightened of so many things, would I not also be frightened. He
said, " 'Twas only in this century that that cave was discovered."

"In 1944 by Jack McGann, in actual fact," said Giles, passively but
pointedly improving on Francis's knowledge. Giles said the biggest
free-hanging stalactite in the world could be found in a cave in
Doolin, a little village on the coast of Clare. There was a longer stalactite in New Mexico, but that one had met the cave floor. A farmer
in Doolin wanted to put an elevator into the cave and charge admission to bring people down through the narrow passage to see the
famous stalactite. "But if he does a thing like that," said Giles, "the
whole atmosphere of the cave will change, and the moss and the
lichen will die, and eventually it will collapse." He paused to shake his
head, then added, "What a greedy way of interpreting the world."

"I'm *telling* you," said Francis, as though he had made this diagno-
sis first, "the Irish are out to do you. Now, the cave you were talking
about in New Mexico? That is a big one. They could put four or five
cathedrals inside in it. I read that. It's a sheer drop down several hundred feet."

"Which those of us who've been there can vouch for," sighed
Giles.

Giles described how he had crawled for an hour and a half down
the narrow stone passageway into the Doolin cave before getting to
the large chamber. At some points the passageway was so tight he had
to lie on his stomach and pull himself forward on his elbows.

Francis searched my face for signs of the anxiety he himself was
feeling. "You wouldn't go into a place like that first of all and go that
distance, would you, Rose? I'd say you'd want to be practicing in
small bits and gaining your confidence all the time, right, Rose? It's
amazing more people don't lose their lives in that cave. A sudden
downpour of rain and you'd drown. 'Twas the Ice Age that done that

cave. We had four consecutive Ice Ages, and ten thousand years ago was the last one."

"Which means we should be entering another Ice Age before long," said Giles, whose preoccupation with geological phenomena was nearly as great as Francis's and inarguably more developed.

"I am afraid I would have to be inclined to disagree with you just a small bit on that," said Francis.

Giles slid his glasses meticulously up the bridge of his narrow nose. "Well, just consider it: ninety thousand years of Ice Age and ten thousand years in between; we *are* due for another, aren't we."

Francis stared hopelessly at Giles; he appeared to be calculating the years in his head, looking for a way to be right about this.

Giles proceeded to tell us about an Indian tribe in Tierra del Fuego who lived in snow and ice and wore no clothes, and a family in Scotland who lived in an unheated castle dressed only in kilts and didn't mind the cold and never got sick because they ate well. "You get used to the cold, you see."

"But folks have been known to die from the cold," said Francis.

Giles sighed. "But they don't *have* to die. That's my point precisely. If they only knew how to take care of themselves, and if only they weren't so fearful."

Francis smiled tightly. "I disagree. Cold is cold. Your body gets too cold, you die."

"That's rather a limiting viewpoint," said Giles.

Francis stabbed forlornly at the fire with the curtain rod. A Guinness tanker lumbered past the pub window, followed by a priest on a bicycle.

"I wouldn't recommend holding that rod in the fire too long," said Giles. "You'll burn your hand."

"Limiting viewpoint," Francis said, glancing collusively at me.

※

IN THE BURREN, as in other parts of Ireland, there were numerous holy wells and a host of cures and superstitions that came with them. The water from holy wells was said to cure various ailments — warts, painful feet, delicate children, toothache, backache, headache, infertility, rheumatism, and even battles with death. But the great majority of the wells had the power to cure eye illnesses. I mentioned to Giles and Francis that I had visited a holy well just up the road in Kilnaboy, and Eamon the butcher shouted in a bored way, "What's that one for? Eyes again?"

"Warts," Francis said.

Giles faked a yawn. "Eyes."

"I thought it was warts," said Francis.

"Not ringworm?" said Eamon.

Giles sipped from his glass. "Eyes."

"Sure it wasn't warts?" said Francis.

"In actual fact, it was eyes."

From the way Francis held the curtain rod I thought he might skewer Giles with it. This was the sort of Irish conversation that usually ended with one man hurling curses at the other. But this one wouldn't come to that. Francis was too gentle and Giles was too professorial, so they sparred quietly—in their own way they were a perfect match. They were like two people on opposite sides of a swinging door, both pushing to get through at once.

Eamon finished eating a little bag of potato chips, turned the bag inside out, and busily licked at the salty paper. His mouth twisted madly off toward his ear as he licked. "They say holy water from those wells isn't supposed to boil," he said. "I tested it myself."

"And what happened?" said Francis.

"It boiled."

"'Course it did," said Giles.

"But it's been known not to boil," said Francis.

Giles said, "Nonsense," and stood up and found his way to the ancient wooden cigarette machine that hung on the wall. He was so blind he had to put his face up to the machine and walk his fingers across it, trying to find the coin slot. In his long poncho he looked like a prophet. The pound coins he dropped into the machine fell to their destination with a heavy clinking thud. He pulled open one of the little wooden drawers and, finding it empty, he wrapped his arms around the machine, as though preparing to lift it off the wall, and gave it a mighty rattle. He punched the machine, peered at it, and punched it again. Francis watched him with a look of deep satisfaction and finally said, "'Tis broke."

Giles returned to his seat. "I say, Francis, it would be quite easy to fix that machine, you know. It's a mere matter of a spring."

Francis took two pound coins out of his pocket and made a show of reimbursing Giles. "That machine's next to three hundred years old. No point fixin' it."

"But that is impractical," said Giles.

"Ireland is impractical," said Francis.

With a prim smile Giles said, "Quite," and set about cleaning his fingernails with a corner of the Chatwin book. He had to hold his hands two inches from his face to see what he was doing. He said, "Years ago there was a family in Kilnaboy who was supposed to have practiced cures successfully. They were blacksmiths."

I saw my opportunity to jump into this conversation. "That family's name was Curtis," I said. That I knew this seemed to surprise Giles. He looked at me. "You're American," he said. "What are you doing here?"

Few Irish people ever asked me what I was doing in Ireland. My presence neither surprised nor puzzled them. But Giles seemed to think it remarkable. "Touring about on holiday? Is that it?" he said.

"She's not touring," Francis said defensively. "She lives here."

Giles looked amused. "Lives here, does she? Alone?"

Francis snapped, "She's not alone," and was clearly surprised by his own answer.

"What do you do, Giles?" I said.

Giles worked away at a thumbnail. "Do?"

"For work."

"Not working at the moment, I'm afraid."

"Well, how do you live?" said Francis.

"Say again?"

"How do you live?"

"Live?"

Giles hated being questioned.

"Yes, you know, *live*. Money. Food and fags and drink."

"Oh, yes, yes, yes, I see your point," Giles said, and with false assurance he said, "Actually, at the moment I'm catching the dole — as you Irish say."

Francis flinched. Nothing irritated him more than an able-bodied young man on the dole. "Why work if they'll pay you not to?" he said.

Steering the conversation back on track, I said, "I read that Curtis the blacksmith could cure liver problems and cows that had swallowed raw potatoes. He made his patients lie across the anvil and said an Irish prayer." I considered reciting the prayer, but Giles beat me to it.

"An t-ucht a bheith socair, is do schairt a bheith reidh. In ainm an Athar agus an Mhic, Agus an Spioraid Naomh. I've read that book, too, and I'm quite fluent in Irish, you see."

Francis winced at Giles and said to me, "There was a cure for warts that said if you got somebody to count your warts, the warts would leave you and land on them."

"Or you could cut the head of an eel," said Giles, "and rub its blood into the warts and bury the eel and while the eel was rotting, the warts were curing."

Determined to have the last word, Francis said, "Or you could count the warts, and then put the same number of pebbles in a cloth and leave it at a crossroads. The person who found the cloth and counted the pebbles would get the warts."

"Or cure a burn by finding a person who had licked a lizard nine times and asking him to lick the burn," Giles said.

Francis looked at Giles with resentment. I offered a few superstitions and beliefs I had learned over the years, ones Giles couldn't possibly have known. If a woman stopped to watch men building a house, it was bad luck and the work should be stopped permanently. Red-haired women, barefoot women, whistling women, and women dressed in red were all thought to bring bad luck to men who spied them on their way to work.

"I knew that," said Giles.

Francis said, "And in them times there was said to be good and bad days for doing things—"

But before he could tell us what the days were, Giles interjected in a dampening way, "Unlucky to cut one's nails on a Monday. Lucky to leave a cow out on Friday. Unlucky to marry on a Saturday. Friday lucky for removing furniture. Wednesday lucky for sowing potatoes."

I said, "If a hare crosssed the path of a pregnant woman, her child would be born with a harelip, and the only way to prevent that was by tearing the hem of her skirt or by catching the hare and tearing its ear. It was unlucky for a woman to cut a boy's hair or draw water from some holy wells, and if the gift of poetry descended to a woman—"

"It would stop with her and never be passed along to her children," said Giles. "Knew that as well."

I wanted to hit him.

Francis tipped his head toward me and said softly, "Come here, Rose. 'Twas also said that the stones of a ruined house should never be reused in the building of a new one. Now, when Bob Brown was fixing up your castle he used a lot of stones from ruined houses and castles around. That is not lucky."

A bright orange object flashed outside the window and caught my eye: it was Mamie Duffy hurrying past the pub and talking to herself.

Eamon the butcher said darkly from his corner, "It is not lucky, miss."

Though fundamentally at odds, religion and superstition served the same ordering, protecting purpose, and in Ireland the two seemed particularly intertwined.

Francis puffed on his cigarette and stared at me, waiting for an explanation of Bob Brown's heedless behavior, or perhaps trying to see if I was frightened.

"Nothing's happened so far," I said.

"What castle?" said Giles.

"Ballyportry," Francis said proudly. "And she's not frightened, in case you were wondering."

"I wasn't wondering," said Giles. "There's nothing to be afraid of. Only superstitious fools are afraid."

Jean O'Brien

J EAN O'BRIEN WAS STANDING at the bar in Grogan's Pub in
Dublin, shouting to me over the din of the crowd. We had been
introduced earlier that evening by a mutual friend. Grogan's
was dim, smoky, ugly, and popular among artists and writers; its walls
were covered with art done by regular patrons. But for the art, the
place reminded me of a skatehouse—all pocked paneling, vinyl-cov-
ered benches, and low-watt light bulbs. The pub was so crowded that
Jean and I, pinned against the oak bar, had no choice but to stay there
with our drinks.

Beside me at the bar sat Desmond Fennell, a white-haired critic
and columnist for the *Irish Times*. At the moment he was the center of
a heated debate over a pamphlet he had published criticizing the Irish
poet Seamus Heaney for selling out, for not making more political
statements in his poetry, for accepting the "patronage" of American
universities and the accolades of Helen Vendler, the American poetry
critic. I could hear Fennell shouting now around the stem of his pipe

to a very pretty, very young woman, "People who get cancer — it's psychosomatic; they bring it on themselves!" And behind me someone was shouting, "Helen Vendler is one of the great Jewish minds!" and another voice shouted in answer, "A marvelous feat when you consider she's Irish Catholic!" And Jean O'Brien was tapping me on the arm and shouting enthusiastically, "I've stood outside some queer old courthouses in my day! . . . Young women are going backwards in their attitudes!"

Jean's voice, though difficult to hear that night, was compelling; it was deep and full and had a rough but not unpleasant quality. Jean was slim and tall — I had to look upward slightly to meet her gaze. She had an expressive face and well-defined features, a long nose, a wide mouth. Her posture and mannerisms were decidedly feminine. The way she smoked made smoking look graceful, the cigarette an elegant accessory; she tipped her head back to exhale, steering the smoke away from me and straight up above her blond head in a thin blue stream. Her long, slender hand stirred the air as she spoke, then stopped to rest gently against her cheek as she waited for her point to sink in.

"And then I got visited by the Special Branch of the police," she was saying. "I live in Dartry, in middle-class suburbia. In Dartry, Rosemary, you're definitely not used to getting policemen at your door."

As Jean spoke, a pair of very thin, very pale arms snaked their way through the tiny space between us, reaching for two pints of Guinness on the bar and nearly tipping Jean's and my drinks over in the effort. I turned and found a shaven-headed, pale-faced waif wearing a huge pair of army boots and what looked like her grandmother's silk underslip. When she saw me peering at her she withdrew her arms in an apologetic hurry and said, "Jaysus, me eyes are bigger than me fuckin' reality!"

I handed the waif her pints and turned back to Jean. I had heard that she was a deeply political person who had involved herself in everything from protests on behalf of IRA hunger strikers to abortion rights. She told me she was an unwed mother, for which she had suffered silent opprobrium, and she had thought a great deal about the place of women in Irish society. At fourteen Jean had left school but later went back to get her leaving certificate, the Irish equivalent of a high school diploma. At thirty-seven she was, like many Dubliners, a poet.

She worked as an editorial assistant at *Poetry Ireland*, the country's largest poetry magazine. She was friendly and warm and knew an astonishing amount, not just about current Irish events but about the major political events of the last twenty years. I strained to hear what she was saying that night in Grogan's, but it was impossible to talk and so we arranged to meet at a later date.

⚎

IN A NEARLY EMPTY PUB at the end of Waterloo Road one early evening in August, Jean O'Brien resumed telling me the story of her unsanctioned pregnancy. I had no reason to suspect that the story would involve the IRA and its political arm, Sinn Fein. Jean told me she had become interested in the political turmoil in Northern Ireland in her early twenties, at the time the status of IRA prisoners was changed from political to criminal. Across the low table from me, she leaned back in her armchair and said, "The British prison policy got a lot of people involved in the northern issue, people who wouldn't normally have bothered their bum about something like that. These days a lot of people see the IRA as hooligans with a Mafia mentality: drug dealers and thugs. But at that time Irish society gave the IRA more support. People in the North still remembered 1969 and the Royal Ulster Constabulary burning down their streets. I had heard that IRA prisoners were political prior to 1976 but were suddenly not political after that, and that seemed wrong, so I got involved in a couple of small marches here in Dublin. And it was because of that that I got visited by the Special Branch of the police."

Jean had an earthy, vivacious way of storytelling. Dramatically and delightedly she re-created the lines of the principal players in her personal history, and she conveyed her meaning as much by gestures and facial expressions as by words. When I asked Jean how she felt when the police came to her door, she shrugged, tossed up her hands, rolled her eyes to the ceiling, mugged a worried face, and said, "Yeah, well, you know, I was sort of a bit, oh, you know, like, 'Never done anything like *this* before and, well, oh . . . ha-ha!'"

The sight of the policemen at her door did not have the deterring effect the police hoped it would have. Instead it made her indignant. She couldn't see what she had done wrong, or why the police had come to her door. She said, "It made me decide I was going to the very next march. I was working in a computer company at the time and was involved in women's groups. I had been interested in certain issues that had come up, like contraception and abortion, but this was the first time I was sticking up for the IRA."

When Jean began attending marches and meeting people in Sinn Fein, the situation in Northern Ireland was beginning to worsen. One of Jean's friends was a young journalist from Derry whose brother was "on the blanket," the term for Republican prisoners who refused to wear the uniforms of ordinary criminals and wrapped themselves in blankets instead. This was the beginning of the protests that eventually led to the highly publicized hunger strikes of the early eighties.

Jean said, "Every time I came out of a Sinn Fein meeting I'd come face to face with the police. They'd meet me at the bus stop and call out, 'Helloooo, Jean! Still living in Dartry?' And I'd shout back, all smiles, 'Why ask me that, fellas, when you already know? Ha-ha!' They wanted me to know they were watching me. They were calling to our house with more regularity now, and my father got a bit worried."

"Did he try to stop you?" I asked.

"No. And I admired him for this because he's very conservative. He asked me was I doing anything illegal, and I said, 'No, I'm not, Da,' and that was the only thing he ever asked me, which I admired him for, because a lot of people were being thrown out of their jobs and houses for Sinn Fein activity. A friend of mine had lost her job at the bank for being involved in the protests, and another friend lost her job with the Abbey Theatre for the same. The police were always asking me where I worked. My boss, though he didn't like my involvement, also didn't like the police telling him who he could employ or not employ. But he said to me, 'If I ever see you in one of those marches, Jean, you're sacked.' And the next minute my picture was in the *Irish Times* at a march. I had tried to avoid being photographed, because I wasn't too keen to lose my job over this. But I had also decided that if I had to lose my job, I had to lose my job."

By that time, March 1981, the Republican prisoners' protest had received international attention because of the hunger strikes led by Bobby Sands. Every day on O'Connell Bridge in Dublin there was a demonstration on Sands' behalf. For five months Jean marched on the bridge every day after work.

"Sometimes we marched to the British Embassy. It became a way of life. We thought, 'Any minute now it'll be okay, if you just march long enough and tell enough people.' You feel that if everyone knows, they'll put a stop to the unfairness. But of course life is not like that."

Jean paused to sip from her vodka and tonic and to light another cigarette. She smoked a great deal that evening, which she explained by saying, "I'm planning to quit tomorrow." She was dressed in a tight white dress with buttons down the front, a pink linen jacket, and pink high-heeled shoes. Her long nails were cherry red, and her hair, several shades of blond, fell below her shoulders. As she crossed her long bare legs and toyed with one of her gold earrings, she looked rather more like a hostess than a political activist. The only clue to Jean's toughness was a smattering of tiny white paint specks on her arms and watch face; that morning she had painted a room in her house.

"So where am I now?" she said. "Oh, yeah, the hunger strike election. During the hunger strikes this prisoner, Tony O'Hara, whose brother Patsy had died on hunger strike in May, was running for a seat in the Irish Parliament, so I decided I'd help out. I was never very fond of the Irish National Liberation Army, which he was part of, because they were very violent, but I would have campaigned for Jack the Ripper. Tony didn't get the seat anyway, and he was released from prison that September. I met him in September or October. He's my child's father."

I found it difficult to hide my surprise. Even I had heard of the O'Haras, an infamous militant Republican family. I said, "The father of your child is Tony O'Hara?"

Jean laughed. "Yeah. Finally the long-winded woman gets to the point."

"I wasn't impatient," I said. "I'm interested in the story."

Jean smiled wryly and pointed her cigarette at me. "And you'd better be, Rose, 'cause it's coming back later. So, anyway, when I got pregnant I didn't do the traditional Irish hiding thing. I was thirty-one years of age. I wasn't nineteen. I had never been married. You know we always say in Ireland—write this down, Rose, because it's the one thing we *always* say—if you went home and told your mother you were pregnant, she'd stick your head in the oven. No matter how sophisticated you think you are, you always feel that way. I remember when it dawned on me that I was pregnant, I thought, Oh, no! All that childhood fear came up, though my mother was dead. I told Tony, and he wanted to get married, but I didn't want to. At that stage we knew it was a mistake."

I asked Jean if she had ever had any doubt about having the child.

"Had I been under twenty-five I would have had an abortion. I'm thankful it never came to that. But at thirty or thirty-one what was I doing with the rest of my life? And I liked the idea. Now that was 1983 and the abortion referendum was on, and I was very involved in the meetings and the marches for the right to choose. I was up and down outside the Dail—the Irish Parliament—with my banner and my bump under my dress, which used to cause funny reactions with the SPUC crowd. I remember them coming up to the demonstrators and shouting, 'Murderers!' at everyone but me. They couldn't call me that, because I was pregnant. I was evidence that you don't necessarily choose to abort the child just because abortion is available. The right to choose is not always a negative, and a pregnant woman is not always against the right to abortion."

"But how did people react to you and your pregnancy in general?" I asked.

"There were people who definitely did not approve of my pregnancy. This is Ireland, no matter what. They weren't going to say it to my face, but there were people who thought I was too smart by half. They were thinking, 'There goes Jean O'Brien! Pregnant and not a bother on her!' Because I wasn't the typical nineteen, screaming and crying over it. I suppose I seemed a bit blasé to them."

I said, "But a lot of Dublin women would have been very self-conscious about being pregnant and unmarried, even at age thirty-one. Why weren't you?"

"It was the same thing that made me return to the Sinn Fein marches when the policemen called to my door and told me not to. I'm bloody-minded. A lot of Irish people are very bloody-minded. And I had no mother around. When my friends got into trouble they could be tough, but in the end they had Mammy around. I hadn't. My mother wouldn't have been happy about the pregnancy, but she wasn't madly conservative either. I remember when we were young, we were always hearing that our period was a gift from the Virgin Mary, and I went home and told my mother that, and my mother fell around the room laughing and said, 'Ridiculous.' She was fairly open.

She didn't sit around discussing sex, but neither did she sit around being negative about it. A lot of Irish women have received a huge negativity about their bodies."

"Was there sex education when you were in school?"

"There definitely was not. Absolutely not. You just copped on to what it was about. We had to figure it out for ourselves. I was already on the pill at nineteen."

"You chose that for yourself?"

"Yeah. At that stage in history the women's health clinics were moving addresses all the time, running away from the police. I remember going up to the door of a clinic once with my friend, hoping to get the pill, and this alarm went off and the two of us thought, Shite! We thought the alarm was to do with us, and we saw the story flashed across the evening papers: *Jean O'Brien caught in the act at clinic!* And I remember going into a chemist's another day to get this prescription filled, and the way the chemist intentionally roared out, 'MISS O'Brien, your contraceptive pills are ready!' If you had been faint-hearted, you would have given up. I had plenty of friends who were cool enough about those sorts of things. But I realize that a lot of them were probably more innocent than they pretended to be. I lived with a guy when I was nineteen in England. My father would have took a heart attack if he had found that out."

"What were you doing in England?"

"Oh, everyone goes to England. I had gone over with this chap. I knew a lot of women who had abortions there. Quite a lot, and that's back twenty years ago. We were the sixties generation. Even though Ireland was way the hell back in the doldrums, there were some of us who had taken on the sixties ethos."

"How did you know what that ethos was?"

"We read about it. We saw it in foreign film clips. There were a lot of women like me. They weren't prepared to be open about it because their mammy would kill them, but they were there. But even now you'd get some people who'd be absolutely shocked by the way we behaved. Take a trip out into the Irish countryside. Dark ages. But no matter what they tell you, it all goes on behind closed doors in the country too. It's just not spoken about."

I mentioned that I had read the report of the Tribunal of Inquiry into the "Kerry Babies" case, in which Joanne Hayes, distraught and unmarried, choked her own baby after giving birth to it in her mother's home. The Hayes family alleged that the police had conducted an unethical and abusive investigation and had invented "evidence" to be used against Joanne. Jean, along with thousands of other Irish citizens, had protested in defense of the young woman.

Jean nodded and said, "The justice who presided over that case told us that if we protested outside the court he'd have us all for contempt of court. I have stood outside a lot of courthouses for a lot of reasons and no judge ever said that to us. You see, when it came to a woman and woman's sexuality, suddenly it was contempt of court. There's only one sin in Ireland. Sex. It's to do with the religion and the suppression. It still exists. I mean, there was that little girl in Granard only a couple of years back who died giving birth to a baby in a grotto before the statue of the Blessed Virgin, and the baby died too. Did you hear about that?"

I had heard about it. Ann Lovett was a teenager whose pregnancy was utterly ignored—or, more accurately, stifled in a caul of secrecy—by her family, teachers, priest, and friends.

Jean added, "And there was another one in Blackrock whose baby died when its head hit the toilet, where she was having it. Those girls were dead scared to tell anyone. That little girl in Granard, it was absolutely disgraceful. Her family knew she was pregnant at fifteen years of age, and they let her go and have that baby in that grotto."

Jean grimaced into her drink, as though this sort of thing happened altogether too much here. "Who makes the laws?" she said indignantly. "Who has the power? The idea in most societies is that women are supposed to be the holders of the morals, which allows men off the hook. You see it in rape cases. The rapist says, 'But she was wearing a low-cut dress, Your Honor.' I do not know what the hell that has got to do with it. Does that mean the rapist should be treated like a moral imbecile? Like a child? That he is not responsible for his actions? The woman always has to be responsible."

I said, "But with your own pregnancy you decided that you wanted to take responsibility."

"Right. I didn't want to marry. None of my neighbors ever said anything to me, but I knew some of them didn't approve. That was partly because I wasn't in sackcloth and ashes. I looked like I was having far too good a time being pregnant. One neighbor of mine, an old woman who was the matriarch of the neighborhood, who had known my mother very well, came up to me and said, 'Well, Jean, I didn't know you had got married,' and I looked at her and thought, 'Come off it, missus!' This was a woman — no harm to her — who knew when the grass grew. She probably knew the night I conceived the baby. I remember thinking that if I didn't face her down, I was done for, that it would be the start of slings and arrows."

Jean laughed at this, stretched out her long arm and half-flicked, half-threw her cigarette ash deftly into the ashtray without leaning forward in her seat. The bangles on her wrist jangled up her arm. She puffed at her cigarette and laid her free hand flat against her chest.

"I just looked at the woman and said, 'I *didn't* get married, missus. I got *pregnant*.' And the woman backed off. She apologized. I never heard anything more about it after that. I've heard one or two of my neighbors referring to Patrick's father as my husband, and I wonder are they being polite to my father or are they comforting themselves. My father did suggest at the time that I might like to go to Australia. The logic of this fascinated me. I said to him, 'But I'd still be coming home with a child under me arm.' He seemed to think that if I had gone off and come back later, he could tell a story about how I had got married. Now, if the man had even thought about that for a sec- ond he'd have known it was a total load of rubbish. He knew the way I was. I would simply have said to people, 'No, I did not get married.' You hear people telling these ridiculous stories, and the truth always comes out in the end. It's much better to say, 'This is it, deal with it.' "

Jean had her baby in Dublin's Rotunda Hospital in 1983. More illegitimate children were born in the Rotunda than legitimate chil- dren that year.

"If I had been nineteen or twenty, I don't know how they'd have treated me in hospital. But when you're a grown woman, they don't make comments to you about not being married. And I wasn't poverty- stricken, which makes a difference in how people treat you. Ireland is a very class-ridden society. It's not that I'm madly middle class or wealthy, but you can tell the social differences in people. A couple of years back the Irish National Liberation Army kidnapped a dentist called John O'Grady and kept him for weeks and weeks and cut off his finger and all this business. The police decided that to get him back they were going to raid everyone. They raided trade unionists,

feminists—anyone they thought was left of center they raided, supposedly looking for John O'Grady. Why trade unionists would have
John O'Grady I have no idea. They raided forty thousand houses in
Dublin and they had only ten thousand warrants. I got a warrant. I'd
say it went by your address whether you got the politeness of a warrant
or not. If you lived in Finglas, they'd break your door down. It's not
fair. I was thankful during the prison demonstrations that I did not live
in Finglas, because I knew damn well they'd come and batter the door
down. I was glad I lived in Dartry, to be honest with you, but you can't
help thinking of those people who had it bad."

When Jean delivered her baby, Tony O'Hara's brother, Sean Seamus, was wanted by the police for kidnapping. Sean Seamus O'Hara
came to see Jean and the baby at the Rotunda and was arrested
there.

"I remember Tony was awfully distracted because his brother had
just been arrested. We were coming home from the Rotunda and
were stopped by the police."

"Were you worried for the baby?"

"I really was upset. The police were flashing the lights behind us,
but, sure, I was in a total dreamland having just come out of hospital
with no mammy to go home to, and I hadn't a clue what to do with
the new baby. I was going back to my father's house. We were all
standing there saying, What'll we do with this baby? So there was a
siren behind us, and I could hear it, but I'm in another world, and I
say, 'Oh, um, is that the police, Tone?' And, 'Ha-ha,' says Tony, 'yeah,
well, God, it might be, like.' Sure, they were *flashing* him like mad at
this stage to tell him to stop, and he was ignoring them totally. It
didn't dawn on me that he was ignoring them. When I realized he
was, I said, 'Look, Tony, no messing. I am not breast-feeding this
child down in Pearse Street."

Pearse Street was home to Dublin's police headquarters.

"I just couldn't handle Pearse Street. So they took Tony out of the
car and made him put his hands up on the top of the car. I was in the
back seat with the child, and the doors were locked. And this young
detective managed to make a total fool of himself by trying to open
the locked door. He was trying very casually, but his knuckles were
pure white. Obviously he had realized it was locked, but he wasn't
going to bring himself to ask me to unlock it. If he was playing dumb,

I was playing dumb. He was wrestling with the door like a fool, and the other detective looked in the window at me and said, Knock it off, there's a young baby in the back, which I thought was very civil of him."

"What happened to Tony?"

"They asked him a few questions and let him go again."

"With no explanation?"

"It's called harassment, Rosemary. They were always stopping Tony. They used always stop me if they saw me, because they knew who I was. During the O'Grady thing they came to my house with a warrant. Now they were no more looking for John O'Grady than my granny. They came in with four ugly machine guns on their shoulders and trotted around my garden looking for the kidnapped dentist."

"Was it your relationship with Tony O'Hara that made you suspect?"

"Any leftist. Any leftist on their books. Even if I hadn't been with Tony, they would have shown up at my house. I'd been in women's marches and antirape marches and that sort of thing."

"You were out in the streets marching during the abortion referendum."

"Yeah. Gettin' high blood pressure. It was nasty and frightening. I'm really scared of those SPUC people."

At this point in our conversation I heard a man's voice saying my name at the other end of the pub. I turned and saw a face I knew vaguely. The man seemed to be wandering through the pub looking for people he knew. I hadn't recognized him at first because he had dyed his hair raven black. I said hello to him, and after a minute of very small talk he moved on. When he was gone Jean said, "I think he was trying to pick you up, Rose."

I looked at her with interest. "No, he wasn't."

"Yes, he was. He certainly was. Take it from me. He was. Fat chance of it, but he certainly was trying."

"All he did was say hello," I said.

Jean raised her arm and flipped her hand violently at me, as though scattering confetti. "Will you cop on, Rose? He was hitting on you. Do they teach ye nothing in America?" She chided me in a good-natured way for my naiveté, and when she had instructed me to her satisfaction she returned to her story.

"I know quite a few single mothers in Dublin. After they get over the shock and horror of illegitimacy, the Irish like their babies, and that is probably our saving grace. I know some of the country girls can't go home again, but of the women I know in Dublin those children are the apple of the grandparents' eye. I said to my da, 'I'm sorry you're embarrassed in front of the neighbors, but this child will warm your heart. He's your flesh and blood, and what the hell are neighbors to you in the end?'"

"There are a lot of women who don't feel the way you do," I said.

"I know. It is a very sad thing. It's easy for me to talk, because my da is very easygoing—probably afraid of me, you know. But I read a thing a couple of years back about girls from the country who had not told their parents they'd had a baby and were living in dire poverty up in flats in Rathmines, which has one of the highest rates of single parenthood. They congregate there in horrible one-room flats and they go home at weekend, and their parents do not even know they have a child. They have kept the whole thing hidden. So, I read this interview with a couple of these women who were twenty-five and twenty-six, and one half of me said, 'Awful,' and the other half of me got very angry at those women for not standing up for their own children. I sound judgmental, but I do think there comes a time in your life where you must say 'This is my child and I accept it.' They're perpetuating the stigma themselves."

I said, "I sometimes think women are their own—"

"Worst enemies," Jean said before I could bring it out. "I know. And it sounds like I'm downing the women, but it's really the society they're in. Bring that child right in and say, 'That's your grandchild: deal with it.' Look what they're handing on to that kid. They're hiding it. I never want my child to grow up thinking there's anything odd about him because Tony and I weren't married. And I would hate for him to get this idea from other kids whose mothers have been hiding them and covering them up and giving them these hangups."

I said I thought there was great investment in Ireland in covering things up, and Jean leaned forward in her chair and said softly but forcefully, "That's right. That's right. Now, I'll tell you something. I believe my mother committed suicide. I believe she did. But I haven't had it confirmed."

I looked at Jean. "Wouldn't your father know the answer?"

"I don't know would he want to know. And I am left wondering did she do it by accident or not. My mother suffered from manic depression and took very high doses of tablets. So, there's always been the question whether she overdosed. The more I think of it the more I realize she must have killed herself."

"How old were you?"

"Fourteen. Old enough to take over the kids. And for years I believed my mother died of a heart attack. Okay, yeah, if you take enough tablets, you get a heart attack at the other end of it, right? My mother had been in and out of psychiatric hospitals for years. It took years for it to dawn on me that of course she killed herself. I often thought about saying it to my da. I certainly know that when she died, the doctor was called to the house, and all her tablets were thrown in the bin. I remember that, the shuffle to the bin very fast."

"How do you feel about that now?"

"In what sense?"

"Well, I suppose if you had known with any degree of certainty that your mother had killed herself, you might feel differently about it now. Maybe now it's just a mystery."

"As far as I'm concerned she killed herself. But when I was growing up, a lot of people wouldn't even say my mother was mentally ill. They'd say, 'Ah, sure, her nerves are at her.' You know that old Irish thing. Of course, they knew damn well she was mentally ill. And I used to go around and say out loud that my mother was as mad as a hatter. At least I was able to know she was as mad as a hatter and that this screaming maniac that we lived with who beat us up and did all these dreadful things, at least we knew why. It's very distressing to live with someone who's seriously ill. At least I knew, and that's why when people said, 'Ah, she wasn't well,' I'd say right out, 'She was mentally ill! She was mad!' I didn't mean that in a mean way, but just let's cut the crap. Let's talk about the truth. Children will do what they can to protect themselves from a parent who is being disruptive. I have a friend who says she always remembers her mother saying to her, 'Jean O'Brien's mother is dead. You've to be very very kind to her now when you meet her.' And up come I, boppin' up the road, and my friend whispers to me, 'Jean, I'm very sorry about your mother,' and says I, 'Sure, I'm not one bit sorry!' Obviously that was too simplistic, but I remember at the time my sister and I used to pray every single night that my mother would die. We used to actually pray for her death. And being Catholic at the time, of course when she died, we said, Shit! We thought we did it with the power of prayer. But it has left me with this idea that when things in life are really horrible, they will eventually go away. They did that time, didn't they? It has left me with a certain optimism."

Jean put out her cigarette and finished her drink, and when I asked her if she wanted another, she said, "'Course I want another. I'm Irish."

❊

As I WENT TO THE BAR to get Jean's drink I mulled over the notion that a mother's suicide might actually leave a daughter optimistic. The elderly bartender sat hunched over the bar doing a crossword puzzle. One of his index fingers was wrapped in a bloody gauze bandage. Without looking up from his puzzle he said, "Gimme the capital of Tahiti."

I had to confess I didn't know the capital of Tahiti. The bartender raised his head, grinning and showing a lot of broken teeth. "Then I guess you're no dumber nor no smarter than me," he said. He got up to get the drink, and when he handed it to me he winked and said, "Smile, can't you? And what are you two chatting about so gloomily over there? Tell your friend to cheer up. Two pretty girls have no reason to be serious."

When I returned to the table, Jean said, "My mother dealt us serious mistreatment. I remember walking around with my shoulders tensed up because we didn't know when we were going to get a belt to the back of the head. You didn't turn your back on my mother in a big hurry, because she'd just snap. One minute she'd be very nice, very pleasant, and the next minute she'd be beating the shit out of you. She created an atmosphere of terror."

These memories did not appear to disturb Jean unduly. It was clear that she had thought a great deal about what her mother's illness meant to her, and perhaps it was the attention she had given it in her mind that allowed her to speak with such ease. She spoke without bitterness or resentment.

"Looking back now as a woman with a child myself, I feel sorry for my mother. She could not cope. Having six children did not help her.

What on earth were they doing having six children? Catholic Ireland, how are you!"

Jean's mother had had three children, of whom Jean was the youngest, and seven years later she had three more. The last three were quite young when Jean's mother died, and Jean was left to rear them.

"I left school and brought the kids up. They were kept upstairs in a room in cots up to about three years of age. Mainly for their own safety. They were locked in this room, and we hated their guts, because with their arrival my mother started screaming, and we used to go and look at them like they were animals in the zoo. When I look back I see that we had no love to give them."

"Did your mother take care of them?"

"Not really, and they were taken away from her for certain periods and she was taken away from them at different periods. She quite badly beat them up and that. I was kept out of school a lot to do things like peel potatoes for the dinner, so I was with her a lot and probably saw a better side to her. She did have a great ability, which I'm hoping to do with my son, of allowing us to be ourselves. Now I know that sounds like a contradiction, because in between that she was beating us senseless. But she definitely didn't interfere in our lives in that sense. When you have a bad childhood, sometimes it gives you a bit of cop on, makes you stronger. It gives you the fatal flaw as well. I often feel the fatal flaw still sits in there, that wanting love, wanting that thing children desperately want from their parents.

"Out of six of us, only two of us have had children, and every one of us is over thirty years of age, and only two years ago did one of us get married, which is a very low rate. The Irish are not reproducing. There's an awful lot of alcoholism in Irish families. I was terrified when I had my son that I was going to do what my mother did, and in the beginning I did scream a lot. I look back and think it's a wonder Patrick has eardrums."

Reminded of her son, Jean mentioned the Children's Bill, which had recently been introduced to remove the bar of illegitimacy from children born out of wedlock.

"SPUC fought tooth and nail against the Children's Bill," Jean said. "They also objected to sex education in schools. I very much feel that SPUC have absolutely no interest in the fetus once it is born.

Their real interest is in control. They say they want to keep the family together; therefore they could not agree to putting illegitimate children on the same legal level with legitimate ones. SPUC have this huge concern for life, but what about the quality of life after birth? They have no concern for that. I think their purpose is just moral policing. They have this take-your-eye-off-the-women-and-they-murder-the-babies attitude."

"Does your son have the rights of any other child?" I asked.

"What rights *doesn't* he have? He's what's known now as a *non-marital* child." Jean laughed at the euphemism. "I like that one. As I said to the SPUC people when they came to my door one day preaching, '*He's* not illegitimate, *I'm* illegitimate, if legitimacy is the criterion we're using. They came to the door during the referendum. A man and a woman. The woman at least had a bit of sensitivity. I was about seven months pregnant, and the man starts saying to me, 'Do you know what a fetus looks like?' and the woman says to him, 'Ah well, now, I think she does, like.' I was polite but I did say to them, 'When this child is born in two months' time you are going to call it illegitimate. You and your organization are trying to keep this whole thing going, and it's you and people like you who stigmatize these children that we choose to have.'"

"How are your son's rights different from another child's?"

"Inheritance is still the main one. In Ireland it's a very gray area yet. They say there are up to seventy thousand new families in which one or both partners is still in a previous marriage that has not been annulled. Because there is no divorce in Ireland, people who have left a previous marriage and want to start a new family have no choice but to do so out of wedlock. Some of these people have got divorced in England or in other countries, but those divorces don't hold water here. They are still regarded here, in our typical way of doing things, as married, and they're taxed as married. But twenty years down the road the shit will hit the fan when one of them dies. Everyone is going around in a legal limbo, and everyone's ignoring it furiously and hoping that something will change. Some men now are adopting the children they have by a second woman, but others are refusing and asking why should I adopt my own child?"

"So if Tony O'Hara died, whom would his estate go to?"

"Not Patrick. Patrick cannot inherit it. Unless Tony willed it to him. It used to be that the illegitimate child could not even be included in a will, but now he can. I have a will, and although I possess nothing now I worded it so that anything I own at the time of my death belongs to my son.

"Inheritance is what the whole divorce referendum was about. They told the women of Ireland that their farms would be sold from under them if divorce became legal in Ireland. This debate went on for days on the radio. Older women would call up and say, 'Sure, 'twould be death to us if we had divorce. Anytime he went down to the pub and saw a young one sittin' there that he liked, that'd be the end of *us*.' And I thought, 'God, the confidence they have in their marriages!' They must know they're holding the husbands there by sheer dint of the fist and nothing else. They thought that if we had divorce, obviously the men were going to take off. Yet the interesting thing is that in places like England it's women who are instigating the divorces, not men. But people like SPUC scared the women of Ireland by telling them that the farms would be sold out from under them. Don't forget there are also— and this is an old fact—thousands of illegitimate children in their thirties, forties, and fifties already sitting out there in rural Ireland who might suddenly want to claim what's theirs, so they made the law inactive before 1980."

I said, "It's revealing that those women thought their husbands would leave them if divorce was legalized."

"Older women were always told that other women would be a threat to them. There was no sisterhood."

I had talked with a group of young women, students at Trinity College, who had told me unanimously and adamantly that they would never marry in Ireland because they would never be able to obtain a divorce here. I told Jean this, and she leaned back in her chair and looked at the ceiling and giggled infectiously and for a long time, gently hugging herself across the middle.

"Not only will they get *married* in Ireland," she said "they will get married in churches with big white weddings. It's all a lot of talk when they say they won't."

"They swore they wouldn't," I said.

"And I'm telling you they will. When push comes to shove, they'll have dirty big white weddings down in the churches. They have big church weddings and they haven't been to church for ten years before that, and they have no intention of going to church afterwards, and they do that because they are unable to step out of line. These are political women I'm talking about. I know the young women you talked to are feminists, and they're saying all that now, but give them ten years and you'll see. No. I'm telling you that they will walk up the aisle in white. You take their names and addresses and find out ten years from now whether they did. Marriages outside the Church are about two percent of the total. Oh, it's minuscule. They say, 'Sure, I only did it for form. Sure, I don't believe in it at all.' I knew this woman, a very radical woman. She was thirty and she put on a big fluffy white dress, which, God forgive me, if she was eighteen I'd be delighted, but I was left lookin' at her in the silly big dress. And then she says to me something like, 'Oh, you don't think I'd actually get my child baptized,' and I thought, 'Of course you'll get your child baptized.' She said she had the wedding so the relatives would give presents. I don't care what she did it for. She did it because she had an inability when it came to something big in her life to really step outside. I did not get my son baptized, but I had quite a bit of pressure over that. A lot of people disapproved of that, and they are all people who don't go to Mass themselves. They told me I was making things awkward for him. My father wouldn't push to have Patrick baptized, he knew he hadn't a chance. Out of six children, not one of us practices our religion."

"You know a lot," I said.

"I've been to a lot of meetings. There isn't anything happening now that gets me going, but there's still undercurrents happening over the contraceptives. It now looks as though they're going to allow the various health boards to decide where condoms can be sold. The government is washing their hands of the issue. They're giving up their responsibility."

"I see condoms for sale in the chemist shops."

"Oh, *they* are allowed to sell them now, but they weren't before. Don't forget, this is new. But, you see, only special outlets can sell condoms. They had a machine at Trinity that they had to bring home at the weekends because it used to be broken into. Not by people who wanted the condoms but by people who didn't want others to have condoms."

I asked Jean what she thought about the position of women in Ireland now.

She said, "When you look at these laws: no divorce, contraception only in certain places, no abortion, no information about abortion, it's very bad. And, as in the rest of the world, the women are still earning only sixty percent of what the men are earning. However you might feel about it on a daily basis, when you actually look at the laws it is very bad. It's very very difficult to get a sterilization except privately here. That's a big moral issue as well — women being sterilized. There's definitely a thing about women and control of women's bodies. Anything that comes up like that stops the conservatives dead.

"I really think that somewhere in the back of their heads men know damn well they've been dishing it out for years, and they're terrified that if they let go at all, it will all go with the wind. In a sense we are quite a matriarchal society. The woman is still a strong figure in the home. We live in a male-run society, but frankly I think the men are in terror of the women. The fear is that if women get control of their own bodies the society will break down, or that women will stop taking the shit that they've always taken. That's what I think."

A Seal for a Sister

FRANCIS MACNAMARA had shyly asked me if I would attend the Saturday evening Mass with him sometime, and though I rarely went to Mass, I found it difficult to turn down his invitation. I promised Francis I would go to Mass with him the first Saturday in December, and on the appointed evening I walked into the village to meet him. By six o'clock the evenings were completely dark now, and in the darkness of the Gort Road the headlights of oncoming cars were blinding. Each time a car passed, there were moments of utter blackness while my eyes tried to adjust, a darkness so profound it was deafening. But I knew this road by heart now. I knew when to expect the gravelly munching of cows from behind the hedges, the bovine sighs that were eerily human. I knew at which point the three vicious sheepdogs with their glow-in-the-dark fangs and their repulsive snarling would come leaping out of the darkness and hurl themselves against the iron gate that separated them from me. I knew when the low-hanging leaves of a chestnut tree would gently brush against my forehead. And I knew where to avoid the edge of the road and its patches of angry nettles. I knew that the weirdly radiating light in the middle of a dark field beyond the fork in the road was a heat lamp in a pumphouse. And I knew the mournful creaking noise just beyond Bridie O'Daly's farm was an arthritic oak tree. In the darkness these things, if you weren't expecting them, could have the same heart-stopping impact as the horrors in a haunted house. But I knew them all, and the puddles and the potholes and the ugly, sweetish smells of the various farms. I could even identify passing cars and tractors by their taillights and sometimes by the distinctive sound of the engine. The darkness that had once been so frightening had become a shield, a protective covering, and while most people who walked these roads at night carried a flashlight, I felt less vulnerable without one.

Just before the turn to the graveyard I heard footsteps approaching, and a woman's voice said, "Mary?"

I said, "No, it's not Mary."

An unfamiliar male voice said, "It's not Mary. It's only the Yank," and the footsteps passed by and retreated down the road.

I FOUND Francis sitting in front of the fire in Dillon's. Dressed in a jacket and tie, he looked younger than he had the day before and he seemed apprehensive. His gray hair was combed so carefully against his head it looked plastic, and the sandals he usually wore had been replaced by a brand-new pair of stiff lace-up shoes. He stared at the fire and said very little to me, though from time to time I caught him looking at me out of the corner of his eye. Michael was behind the bar, filling in for Francis, and the few men sitting at the bar kept turning around to look at Francis, sensing something different about him. Eamon the butcher was making himself sick with giggles, but it was always difficult to tell what was the source of his amusement and whether it was rooted in reality. From time to time Eamon shouted something that sounded like, "Hi, miss!" and waved at me, and I waved back at him and said, "Hi, Eamon," and eventually Francis turned to me and said in his wondering way, "You are a person who would talk to anyone."

As the church bells rang seven o'clock, Francis suggested we leave for Mass. Out on the lamplit street, solitary figures hurried through the brumous night toward the church, the men in woolen jackets and caps and the women with kerchiefs tied over their heads. The heavy air muffled the sound of footsteps and the ringing bells, and though many people were out that evening, the village seemed oddly quiet and still. Up and down the street the little windows glowed softly. Smoke idled from the chimneys in shadowy columns. Across the street from the church, a row of twenty men stood with their backs against a shop, smoking and waiting until the last possible minute to go in.

I followed Francis up a wooden staircase to the balcony at the right of the altar. Francis was uneasy in the church and chose to seat us in the back row, out of sight of the priest. I realized once we were seated that this balcony was full of men and that the opposite balcony was occupied entirely by women. I wondered whether this was a rule or the haphazard result of habit. This marked separation of the sexes was like a scale model of Irish society.

The church was old and humble and was lit by fluorescent globes that hung like moons from the ceiling. The pews were strict and straight. Francis tipped his head toward me and whispered, "See the woman across? That's Mick Pat's mother. She is a lovely person. One of the best. She worries herself sick over him."

Francis was speaking of Mick Pat Crown, a Corofin farmer famed for his courteous manners. Across and down on the left I could see Mad Mamie in her turban, sitting alone, and many other women whose faces were familiar. The older women whispered the rosary to themselves, lips moving, fingers knitting the beads. Young boys and old men lined up outside the confessional before the start of Mass.

In his homily the priest spoke of the shame of riches and reminded us that it was easier for a camel to pass through the eye of a needle than it was for a rich man to enter the kingdom of heaven. He spoke of the time he'd spent as a parish priest in Florida, how he had often visited two very sick men who were dying in a hospital in Miami. The rich man was lost and unhappy, but the poor man was ecstatic. That memory had never left him. "Take a lesson," he said.

The priest spoke in a pompous, mincing way and so slowly that the men around me seemed annoyed and impatient. They inspected their callused hands, their broken fingernails, the soles of their boots, the lottery tickets they'd stashed in their pockets, or they scanned the church bulletin, then rolled it up and drummed on their knees with it.

The altar boy was fat and yawning and red-haired, and at the consecration and the elevation of the chalices he rang the jangling little sacristy bell with a comical excess of verve.

AFTER MASS Francis suggested we visit Daly's Pub. Daly's was big and dark and cold; it had all the charm of a basement storeroom, and for all its colored lights and expensive linoleum it wasn't nearly as comfortable as Dillon's. It was popular nevertheless. As there was no dance that night, people sat against the walls in their overcoats and hats, older people who had just come in from Mass. They greeted each other by name and said little else. They seemed to be waiting for something new to happen. In Corofin I often had the feeling that people were waiting for something to happen, some unidentifiable thing that was just around the corner yet very far away. The men drank pints of Guinness and the women drank wine mixed with red ginger ale, and they were glad to be here looking at each other. They spent their days in glens and crags and bogs, in isolated and whitewashed cottages with crucifixes on the kitchen walls, a rooster strutting across the hood of the seventeen-year-old Ford parked in the yard, and a knock-kneed donkey tethered to an oak tree.

A toothless old woman in a blond overcoat sat near the fire with her forty-year-old son and her husband, a huge man with a huge, rubbery face like a Halloween mask. The woman had very red cheeks and wore a red woolen ski hat and rubber boots identical to her husband's. Strands of gray hair stuck out from under her hat like hay. She smoked and drank and laughed at everyone who came into the pub, not derisively but in a way that meant she was having fun, while her son sat stolidly beside her with his hands in his pockets.

I saw Francis assessing the room's appointments: the gas fire in the hearth with its arrangement of fake coals that looked real, the colored lights in the ceiling, the Scandinavian furniture from the fifties, the green linoleum. He turned to me and asked nervously, "Rose, do you fancy a pub like this?"

"Not at all," I said. Francis smiled sadly and looked around to see whether John Daly had overheard me.

John was a short, pudgy man with an elfin face and a big rear end. Everyone watched intently as he waddled across the room, put a box of light bulbs on a table, climbed up on a barstool, and began unscrewing a bulb in the ceiling. The toothless woman in the ski hat crowed, "Why would you be taking down the ones that's already up, John?" to which John replied, "So that I might be putting up the ones that's down, Bridget."

Bridget cackled uproariously at that, smacking her lips and rocking back and forth with one hand raised to hide her toothless mouth.

Francis commented on a man in a pea jacket, who he said was "on the drink" again, and vehemently he added that this was a man who shouldn't be given drink anywhere, ever. I wondered at this; so many people in Corofin appeared to fit that description. How could one tell the extent of another's drinking? Most of the drinking here looked severe. People wandered up and down Corofin's street going from one pub to the next. That was their entertainment on a Saturday night. That was it. They switched pubs hoping to see new faces, but there were no new faces. There were only the same old faces telling the same old stories, bearing the same old grudges, and harboring the same secret desires.

Francis was nervous and excited. He told me he rarely visited other pubs, as he was too busy with his own. He seemed out of his element and unsure how to behave. He ground his teeth and squinted at the room, and it was difficult to tell whether this was a sign of pleasure or of anxiety. He drank his alcohol-free beer without enthusiasm and looked longingly at the glass of Guinness he had bought for me. I tried to picture Francis drunk—he would probably be an amiable, quiet drunk who wept and confessed things.

We met a woman named Jacinta Rafferty, who looked younger than I but was eight years older. Jacinta had a cigarette stuck behind her ear and was drinking a pint of beer, which she brandished in the air as she talked. She told me she had been in Ballyportry Castle when she was nine years old with her mother and a friend, and when they were on the road going home she turned around and saw the figure of a priest standing in one of the upper windows. "A baldy-headed sort of a priest," she said. She said the image had never left her, and she wanted to see the castle again. I invited her out for a visit. She slapped her hands and said she would come out, though I knew from experience that she wouldn't. I had invited many people to come out to the castle, but aside from Eileen O'Shea and her husband and cousin not a single person had come. It wasn't simply that they feared the castle, but also that people here rarely invited anyone to visit in their homes. If they wanted to see their friends, they met them in the pub. My invitations made them uncomfortable. Paddy O'Brien had told me that men would hesitate to visit me because they wouldn't want to be seen going into a place where a single woman was living alone; people might talk.

When Jacinta left the pub, Francis said, "That girl is cracked, and everyone knows it. She was in Australia for years. She went there with a husband and came back without him. No one knows if he's dead or alive."

We left Daly's Pub and returned to Dillon's. Micky Nolan was there, and Mike Menahan, Ted Hogan, Sean Cahill, Eamon the butcher, Paddy O'Brien, Sean Waters, Denny Leary, Thomas Mac-Mahon, James Rohan, Joseph, the blond drunk who was interested in darts, Mick Pat Crown, and a gray-faced man I had never seen before, who wore pajamas and slippers and an overcoat and had a hospital ID bracelet clipped around his wrist. The pub smelled of sweat, and the windows were steamed over. Two women were seated at a table—an unusual sight in Dillon's—and Francis told me that one of them was Conor MacNamara's daughter Sile Breen. Sile was soft and big-eyed, and her smudged black eyeliner and slightly crooked teeth made her look sad.

Francis and I sat by the fire with Mick Pat Crown, and Michael MacNamara brought us drinks. Mick Pat was only forty-nine, but he appeared to be deep into his sixties. He had a lupine face that must once have been handsome but was now wrecked by cigarettes and alcohol. His hair was white, his eyes were watery, and his nose and cheeks looked abraded. The palms of his hands were orange with nicotine and so were the frayed cuffs of his shirt. One of Mick Pat's hands was considerably smaller than the other, the result of some childhood disease. I never saw him dressed in anything but a brown gabardine suit, a narrow tie, and a meticulously tailored brown tweed overcoat. He was the only man in Corofin who dressed this way regularly. Each Christmas he had a tailor in Kilfenora make him a suit, which he wore for the next year. Though his clothes were stained and worn, Mick Pat managed somehow to look elegant. Possibly it was his physique that gave him that distinction—he had the long, graceful body of a dancer—but more likely it was his manner, for he was certainly the most honest and gentlemanly farmer in Corofin. Whenever he saw me he shook my hand, welcomed me warmly, and asked about my health. He never referred to me as anything other than Miss. I often saw him bouncing down the middle of the Gort Road in his huge wooden-sided truck on his way to a cattle mart, and when he saw me he always waved with both hands.

Mick Pat had never married and still lived with his mother and an older brother on the Gort Road. He was said to own the best land in the area. Crown was a nickname—his real name was O'Dell—inherited from his father, who once sold rabbits for a crown, a coin in Ireland's previously British currency; his father's younger brother was known as Half-crown.

The Irish have a predilection for nicknaming people according to their own or their father's profession, natural phenomena associated with them, personal habits, physical attributes, and strengths or flaws of character. Children sometimes acquire the title of their father's profession or some article or tool related to it. A woman in a nearby village whose father had been a carpenter was known all her life as Mary Chisel; a man whose house was situated near a bridge was called Mickey the Bridge; another man whose father repaired bicycles for a living was referred to as Paddy Bike; a housekeeper for the parish priest was called Mary the P.P.; the village idiot, whose father was named Ruane, was known as Ruane's Fool; two of Conor MacNamara's sons were dubbed Brownie and Curly, in reference to their hair; and Bridie O'Daly's middle-aged son was called Butt because of the breadth of his rear end. In various places in Ireland I met or heard of people named the Horse, Sean the Cap, Foxy John, Fooleen Gorman, Twisty Slattery, Sean the Pony, Seamus the Wheel, Over He Went, the Mouth, the Hairpin, the Boot, the Whip, Pocked Hayes, Slow Molly, Bumpy Sull, and Bride of the Fork. One woman was known simply as Landlady. Some standard Irish surnames, too, were captivating in their descriptiveness: Lawless, Savage, Heckler, Hussey, Haggard, Hooligan, Looney, Mooney, Mullarkey, Barnacle, Hone, Crone, Boyle and Byrne (pronounced Bile and Born), Lynch, Greedy, Hickey, Horney, Moody, Flattery, Clarity, and Power.

Mick Pat Crown said, "Miss, may I say something? The people of Ireland one time were very backward. They were very backward. They had no money. Jesus, you have no way, if you haven't money."

Each time I met Mick Pat I was struck anew by his halting, repetitive, old-fashioned speech. He had a heavy accent and an odd monotone, a relentless emphasizing of every syllable, which gave his words the ring of a plaint. He always sounded worried and frightened, and his habit of repeating phrases made him seem slightly addled, as though his ideas were crossing and battling for space in his brain. Mick Pat was one of the heaviest drinkers in the village—by his own admission he began drinking at ten in the morning and continued all day and into the night—but because of his reputation as a gentleman he was never scorned or taken to task for this.

Mick Pat sucked on his cigarette, then put his hand, cigarette and all, into his coat pocket. "Can you go out above in the top of your castle, miss?" he asked. I nodded. "And what would you see from there?"

"Galway, if you were lucky."

Mick Pat made a sour face. "Jays, I would not like to be above on that. I would not like it. God, I would not like that."

"You wouldn't come out for a visit?"

"Ah, God, I would not like to be above in the top of that. Ah, no, I wouldn't. You would want to have no drink taken to be up in the top of that. How many steps in that castle?"

"Almost a hundred."

"And how many rooms?"

A wisp of smoke snaked out of Mick Pat's coat pocket and curled around his wrist.

"Ten," I said.

"And how many stories, like?"

"Five stories. Why don't you come out?"

"I will. I will. I will, miss. But, God, I will not. But Jays, miss, I will. But I won't, like. I wouldn't go up on the top of that at all. But your water out by the castle is the best water for miles."

He meant the stream outside my door.

"That water is a long way better than what you get in Lake Inchiquin. I've dranken it myself. It's miles ahead of the Inchiquin water. Kilnaboy water is good. Kilnaboy is good. Kilnaboy is good. But if you went to Kilfenora and drank the water that's coming up there, 'tis pure poison. Yours is the real spring water above in Ballyportry."

Mick Pat's hair fell forward over his forehead in spears, making him look disheveled and perplexed. He took a last wincing drag on the cigarette — now a flat, mothlike stub — and tossed it into the fire. Immediately he drew a crushed box of filterless Gold Flake cigarettes from his breast pocket, lit one, and began a story about how he had been cheated out of some money. Mick Pat held his glass in both hands between his knees and leaned forward as he spoke, looking into the glass as if into a very deep well. "Didn't I um . . . didn't I um . . . didn't I come down then to collect the check, and they wasn't still open inside in Gerry Murphy's."

A man with a wide face speckled with big cinnamon freckles sat down with Francis, Mick Pat, and me, and when he realized Mick Pat was telling a story he smiled skeptically. The pub was noisy, and because Mick Pat was difficult to hear, we sat with our heads pressed together in a tight circle, leaning forward in our chairs, our knees and drinks meeting in the middle of the huddle. Francis listened patiently. Mick Pat rambled, and it was hard to discern whether he knew where the story was going, but we continued to listen, if only because of the sheer urgency of the monologue.

"So, wait till I tell you. My brother the butcher, he bought three calfs above in Gerry Murphy's some time ago and never paid for them, and when I got my check from Gerry Murphy the next morning, Gerry Murphy had tooken off it the price of the three calfs my brother had bought. I got the check for my sheep with the price of my brother's three calfs tooken off it. I bought no calfs."

Francis said, "Wait a minute. Who was it bought the calves?"

" 'Twas my brother, I tell you. My own brother. And he never paid Gerry Murphy for the calfs. Gerry Murphy owed me money for some sheep I sold him, and he took the price of my brother's three calfs off the money he owed me for the sheep. Gerry Murphy put his hands in my pocket. That he shouldn't do."

Francis said, "I wouldn't accept that."

The freckled man said, "I wouldn't either," then winked at me to show how silly he thought this story was.

"Did you accept it, Mick Pat?" I asked.

"I did. I did. I did, miss."

"Why would you accept that?" I said.

"Because I don't like an argument. You'd get nowhere arguing, like."

I learned later that Mick Pat's preoccupation with money and drink was generally believed to have stemmed from an incident ten years before. Mick Pat had been deeply insulted by a man who had wrongly accused him of grazing cattle on land that wasn't his. The man had threatened him physically and had so insulted his famous integrity that Mick Pat struck him in the face, a thing no one had ever believed him capable of. The man's eye was slightly damaged. Mick Pat was sued for the assault and was forced to pay 16,000 pounds in damages, of which he had so far paid off only 11,000. Mick Pat Crown drank, it was said, because he was beset with worry.

Conor MacNamara came into the pub in a gray sweater, sweeping his long hair back with his fingers and smiling the happy smile that meant he had already drunk a great deal in some other pub. When Conor appeared, I sensed the mood in the pub stiffen slightly, but I was glad to see him, and he waved grandly to me. "Rose?" he called out. "How you going since?" He looked around the room. "How is *everyone* going since? What about a ghost story?"

Everyone in the crowded pub turned to look at Conor, all but Michael and Sile Breen, both of whom looked away from him.

Conor tapped his daughter on the shoulder and said in a tiny voice, "What a long face on Sile. What's wrong with Sile? Even the scarecrows wouldn't come to visit you, Sile Breen, with a face like that on you."

Sile puffed on her cigarette and blew smoke out the side of her mouth like a gangster's moll. She looked at her friend with a pained expression. When Conor persisted in tapping at her shoulder, Sile said, "Buzz off, Dada," and threatened him with the lighted end of her cigarette. Sile's friend, an indignant blond with a wristful of tinkling little bracelets, said, "Yes, Conor, buzz off, why don't you?"

Conor laughed and tugged on a hank of the friend's hair. Then he bought a pint of Guinness for me and banged it down on the table beside me. "Put that inside your blouse, Rose!" he said.

I thanked him.

"Thank yourself!" he barked. He settled into a chair and placed a pint of Guinness on each of the chair's arms. "Well, Rose, my little friend, what about a ghost story? Have you any Yankee ghost story to tell us?"

Without a trace of irony, Mick Pat said, "*I* could tell ye all a good one, but I wouldn't want to be talking about the dead."

Myself, I had heard a million ghost stories in my life and couldn't remember a single one. I was never able to suspend my disbelief long enough to take them in. I told Conor about the woman who had seen a priest in a window of Ballyportry Castle when she was a child, and Mick Pat Crown said nervously, "Sure, there was no one living in the castle at that time. I'd like to know who it was said that about a priest ghost."

" 'Twas only that Rafferty girl," said Francis, and everyone nodded knowingly.

The freckle-faced man said what I had heard countless times before: "There isn't a single person in this parish who would dare to stay out in that castle alone." All the faces turned toward me, waiting for my explanation. I felt mildly accused. I shrugged. I said, "I don't see anything to be afraid of. I don't feel afraid."

"And she's dead right!" shouted Conor. "And I guarantee everyone anyway there was no fuckin' priest in that window anyway. The priests never had the power to be ghosts. So that was all bullshit from the word go, so give us a better one than that, Rose!"

"I can't, Conor," I said. "I can't remember any ghost stories."

Conor squinted narrowly at me. "Well, I have a story," he said, and he wiggled his fingers before him, as if feeling the story in the air. "You know as you walk out to the castle there's a place with a lot of lovely flowers in it in springtime, at the T-junction where the road is going out to Cill Vaidaun cemetery. That's known as Lough Na Guna there."

Lough Na Guna sounded to me like "the Lake of the Dress." I wondered if Conor was pronouncing it right—his Irish was worse even than my own.

"Well, a fella was there one time—he crashed on his motorbike and died." Conor peered around at the attentive faces. Ominously he said, "Ye all know who I'm talking about. We all know who I'm talking about, so don't pretend that ye don't, and don't be lookin' at me like that. Well, something was supposed to have crossed that fella's path. Something terrible was supposed to have crossed him so that he got a fright and crashed the motorbike. Now, I don't want to scare anybody, but this only happened *a few years ago!*"

Conor seemed to be trying to persuade us that it was a ghost that crossed the man's path, that ghosts still existed and still interfered in our lives.

"Mick Pat," Conor said, "when that man got killed on the motorbike, how many years ago was that?"

" 'Twas five."

"Five," said Conor. "Not so long ago." Conor left the ghosts behind and moved on to a new subject. "Bob Brown had a cousin," he said, "who was visiting here from across in America one time. And she was very pretty, and one night when the pubs closed, Bob and the cousin and me went down to my house with two six-packs, and Bob's cousin was on my arm, and everyone thought the cousin was my girl-friend." Conor looked around the room and shouted gleefully, "Do not try to deny it! Ye all thought she was my girl! Well, anyway, when we got to my house didn't Michael the baby do his wee-wee down on top of her."

Conor hollered across the bar, "Michael, remember that? Of course you don't, you were only in the cradle then. But you did your wee-wee down on top of Bob's pretty cousin."

Everyone looked at Michael, who was washing glasses at the sink behind the bar. Michael did not look up.

As he made a move to throw his cigarette ash into the fireplace, Mick Pat spilled half of his drink on my shoe. He turned to me with a look of horror. "Miss," he said, "I am sorry. I'm sorry about that, miss. I am very sorry. I didn't mean to do that at all. I would not do a thing like that. I'm sorry, miss."

I tried to reassure Mick Pat that it was nothing, but he was heart-broken over what he had done. "I have more manners than that." He bent over and rubbed my shoe with the cuff of his shirtsleeve. When he sat up again, his face was pink with exertion and his eyes looked glassy and hot. "I would not do a thing like that. Especially not to a woman."

There was nothing abrupt or violent in Mick Pat's speech, nor in his mannerisms. He was inherently gentle. He said, "Miss, do you need a seat home to Ballyportry tonight? I'm driving out that way on my way home. I live on the road to Gort myself. I can give you a seat home, if you would like one."

I sensed Conor MacNamara watching Mick Pat with contempt or envy, and suddenly Conor shouted, "Rose! Would you like to have a baby by me?"

Had the shelf of bottles behind the bar come crashing to the stone floor, it would not have inspired a silence as dense as that which fol-lowed.

I sat back in my chair and lamely I said, "A baby?"

"Correct!" Conor cried. "A baby. And that baby would have a seal for a sister! Because I love sex. I *love* sex. I sleep with the seals in the ocean. I have sex six times per night."

Conor's hair kept falling into his eyes, and he kept tucking it delicately behind his ears with his forefingers. He bellowed and cranked his arms in the air. I half expected him to hit himself on the chest like an ape. The pint glasses on the arms of the chair jiggled and rattled with the motion of the chair. Conor gulped hurriedly from one glass, then from the other. Suddenly he grew coy and said in a little singsong voice, "If you played your cards right, Rose, you could become a very comfortable woman. Mick Pat Crown has a big farm and many acres of land. Or will you perhaps marry Francis? It is said you spend a lot of time in here a-chatting away with Francis my brother. Which will you marry? Or will you marry me? Will you walk home with me tonight?"

For several minutes Conor carried on in this provocative fashion, broadcasting his jealousy and his desire to walk me home. Three pool-playing teenagers emerged from the other room and stood in the doorway to listen, and all the smiling faces in the pub looked at once eager and worried. Eamon the butcher stared from his corner, and Paddy O'Brien looked disgusted. It was Paddy who was always cautioning me to avoid Conor MacNamara and all of Conor's children, calling them a bad and immoral lot. "Not a person in this village likes the MacNamaras," he had said.

"Our baby would have a seal for a sister!" Conor shouted again.

"And a donkey for a brother!" cried Mick Pat in excellent imitation of Conor's voice.

"You would learn more with me in two, three, four, five hours, Rose, than you would learn with anyone else," said Conor.

"What sort of things would I learn?"

The room seemed to flinch at my boldness.

"One heck of a hell more than you ever learned in your lifetime! I'm good, Rose. I'm very good."

Mick Pat said, "*You are a good mechanic, all right!*" and a burst of laughter followed. Mick Pat laughed loudest and with great pleasure at his own unexpected irony. His eyes turned to slits, and he grinned wolfishly into his beer.

Conor was hot-faced and frowning now. Angrily he said, "Well, you son of a bitch, Mick Pat! When was the last time you had a good cleaning out? When was the last time you had a good cleaning out of your pipes, Mick Pat? You never had sex in your life, you little bastard. You're a virgin. You are a virgin."

Mick Pat sat still in his seat. He looked at the floor, and his heavy gray hair fell forward boyishly on his high forehead. With his smaller hand he brushed his hair back, then laid the hand gently over his mouth; but for the nicotine stains, it was the hand of an adolescent boy. "I am not," he said. "I am not. I am not." But he spoke unconvincingly, as though trying to persuade his own doubtful soul. "I'm surprised at you, Conor MacNamara," he said. "What about the time, Conor, what about the time I went down to your garage with my truck and you told me, 'You have to push down hard on the clutch?'"

"Ha-ha!" Conor shouted gleefully, stomping his foot on the floor. "Give her the boot's what I said that time! Give her the boot, same as you would a woman!"

Mick Pat said, "Well, God, I wouldn't. You are a married man, Conor. I amn't. You had the experience which I haven't, you see. That's what counts, like."

Conor turned to me and said in a bullying way, "Well, what do you think of us now, Rose? Can you size us up at all now?"

I said nothing.

Conor snapped, "You have nothing to say, because you haven't got the guts! You haven't got the guts to tell me what you think of me. You haven't got the guts!"

Francis said, "For God's sake stop it, Conor."

Conor waved his arms at the entire room. "Ye *all* haven't got the guts to say! Ye have all not got the guts to say anything!"

The faces looked evasively at the floor and into their beer. I must have been staring at Conor, for he said in genuine apology, "I have put you too much to the point, Rose. I have come down too hard on you. You are a nice girl. Can I walk you home?"

"I'll be getting a ride from Mick Pat," I said.

"I would love to walk you home, Rose. I would love to walk you home. Mick Pat, are you taking that girl home?"

"I am," said Mick Pat with great determination.

Conor put on a babyish voice. "Well, if you take her home, Mick Pat, do you think she will make love to you?"

Mick Pat said, "Conor MacNamara, you do come out too strong, especially when women is present."

Conor began cursing in his heaping, pertinacious fashion, and again Mick Pat asked him to stop. The expression on Conor's face was at once furtive and distracted, stubborn and sad, condemned and defiant—the complex expression of a child who knows he has gone too far yet continues to lash out in an effort to cover his own abject sorrow. Conor tugged at the collar of his sweater, then swung suddenly onto the subject of Charles Haughey, the prime minister. "Know what Haughey done? He gave more than seventeen million pounds to fix up his fuckin' office. To have it done up. And we have a lovely river down here in the back of this pub—the river Fergus— and if we only got two million we could have that river cleaned up. And that dirty rotten cunt is spending that kind of money on an office. That's what kind of a bastard he is. The people of Ireland is starving. The people of Ireland is fucking starving. And that dirty rotten fuckin' cunt devoted that much money to an office!"

"Stop the cursing, Conor! Stop that cursing immediately," said Mick Pat. His hands were trembling; I thought he might leap out of his chair.

"Fuck off, ya lousy fucker!" shouted Conor.

Francis said, "Stop it, Conor."

Conor pointed a finger at Francis. "Virgin!" he cried. "You are another lousy virgin!"

Francis and Mick Pat stared at their hands. I wanted to defend them, but the room was so tense I knew it was better to remain silent. Finally Mick Pat straightened up in his seat and said, "All I know, Conor, is that you are not a man. I may not be married, but you had a lovely wife and you treated her badly. You went off to Africa and you never sent your wife home any money, and she would have starved with the hunger if it wasn't for Michael and Francis giving her money. You went off and you forgot about your wife, and she would have starved if it wasn't for Francis and Mike. A man would not do that!"

Mick Pat's lips trembled, and his hand shook with rage as he raised it at Conor. His face was scarlet. His voice broke, and he passed his hand over his face. He stood up. "You are not a man!" he shouted. "But I am a gentleman. Your wife was lovely. If I had that lovely wife, I would be nice to her. I would never do what you did. I could never do what you did."

Sile Breen grinned sickly and rolled her cigarette lighter back and forth across the table. Michael stood behind the bar watching, on the verge of tears. Conor looked pale. He hooked a finger inside the collar of his sweater and tugged at it as if it were choking him, and he stared into the fire. Halfheartedly he said, "Mick Pat, you don't know what you are talking about!"

Mick Pat put his face up to Conor's and hissed, "Everyone knows what I am talking about!"

The freckle-faced man took advantage of the moment to put his freckled hand on my knee and tell me that he would be happy to walk me home, that I wouldn't have to worry, that I would be safe with him. Francis, overhearing this, shot me a warning glance that said, *Do not under any circumstances go with him!*

Presently Mike Menahan came hurrying into the pub and called out excitedly, "The man with the peaked cap is on his way down!" which meant Sergeant Kavanagh would be here any moment to clear the pub out and to exact a fine from Francis if he felt inclined to, which he never did.

Francis stood up and said, "Thank you very much, everybody! Go home now, please!"

Francis followed Mick Pat and me to the door. "You'll be safe with Mick Pat," he said. "And Rose," he added, "I am very very sorry about this night."

We stepped out of the pub into a blinding rainstorm and a wind so vocal I couldn't hear my own footsteps on the street. As we walked past the church Mick Pat said loudly, "And I know what I say about him is the truth. He never sent his wife a penny."

Though he was very drunk, Mick Pat managed to fit the key into the door lock of his truck on the first try. He was breathless. He drove in first gear down the middle of the road. The truck whined, and the wipers squealed across the windshield. The overgrown hedges scrubbed at the sides of the truck. Mick Pat lit a cigarette and flung the still-lit match to the floor, onto a pile of old newspapers. He drove leaning forward, with the cigarette dangling from his lip and his forehead nearly touching the upper rim of the steering wheel. I could see the stubble on his chin shimmering in the little amber lights of the control panel. He would drop me off at the castle and then carry on the two miles to his mother's house, the house he had lived in all his life. I thought of Francis saying earlier that evening of Mick Pat's mother, "She worries herself sick over him."

"Conor MacNamara is not nice," Mick Pat was shouting over the whine of the engine, "and he does come out too strong when he has drink taken. But Francis his brother is nice. The nicest gentleman that ever walked in shoes. It is nice to be nice. And it don't cost you nothing."

With his droning shout and his simple sentences, Mick Pat sounded as though he were talking to a deaf person or a very young child, and in the semidarkness his voice was more uncertain and confused than ever. His words were steeped in loneliness, and as he spoke the cabin of the truck seemed to fill up with heartache.

When we reached the castle I jumped out of the truck and made my way across the field. The wind sucked at my hands and head and shoved my feet askew, and the sleety rain slashed at my face. In the soupy darkness I blundered face first into the hedge several times along the way. As I went up the muddy path toward the castle, I thought I saw the form of a little white dog darting across the path ahead of me, thought I heard its yipping bark. But the harder I strained to see the animal, the less certain I was that he was there at all. The cattle bellowed horribly in the field, and I could hear my big iron gates clanking and straining in their sockets under pressure from the wind.

I approached the gate with the same vague fear I always felt at night, never knowing what I might find within. I groped around for the padlock, unlocked it, shut the gate behind me, relocked it, and proceeded to the dark front door of the castle. I always locked the front door with a thick chain and padlock when I went out, and I was so familiar with this contraption that I needed no light to work it. That night my hand ran along the cold wet chain until it struck the padlock, and in an instant I knew that this padlock was not mine. After a moment of suffocating confusion I felt my face go slack with astonishment: someone had been here, had cut my lock, and had intentionally locked me out with this one.

I spun around to see what was behind me: nothing but the skeletal outline of the creaking, muttering gate and the dense shoulders of the outer wall and Mick Pat's faint taillights receding far off down the road. I wanted to hide but was too frightened to move. I was certain that someone or something terrible was standing around the corner of the castle, waiting to pounce. Or perhaps beyond the outer wall. Why else lock me out? I thought of the cap I had found in the court-yard, and I began to sweat so profusely my shirt was soaked through. The fear I felt was breathtaking. I took my coat off and stared dumbly at the gate. I would have to start moving. There was no way to get into the castle now. I would have to walk back into the village and get help, but I seemed unable to make my legs work. The wind screamed wretchedly through the crenelations at the top of the castle, and the gate clanked and the cattle howled. I pressed my back against the wooden door and thought I would die of hysteria. And then I glimpsed the ghostly figure of the little white dog again, bounding past the gate, and I thought, *That dog is with someone.* A minute later the little dog jumped between the bars of the gate and stood before me, still and staring, then raced off again, barking madly. I stepped forward in an utter daze. I unlocked the gate and went down the pathway to the road, tripping over my own leaden feet. I remember very little of my trip back to the village, except that I ran most of the way, and at one point I went sprawling and landed hands first in a patch of potent Irish nettles. Instantly my palms were aflame, and the pain traveled up my arms until even my face began to tingle. But I kept running.

❖

I WENT TO THE HOUSE of Davy Wren, the caretaker of the castle, an Englishman who had lived in the village for years and whom I rarely saw. I told Davy what had happened, and he gathered up some tools and threw on a jacket and drove me back out to the castle. When he saw the lock he whispered, "What the devil is this!" I held the flash-light while he tried to force the padlock with a stake and a sledgeham-mer. He pounded at the stake, muttering, "The swines!" At one point he missed the stake, and the sledge landed squarely on the knuckles of his left hand with a dull thud. He neither winced nor said anything, but kept hammering. Eventually the lock snapped and a piece of the chain came off in Davy's bloody hand. We pushed the door open and went in. Davy flipped on the light and held the broken chain up to it. The chain had clearly been cut. Davy said, "They cut it and pieced it back together with that lock, the clever swines."

I could hear the little white dog barking out in the field.

Davy and I searched all the rooms and closets and under the beds and behind doors. The search made him nervous. Like me, he was expecting to find something horrible around every corner. He opened a closet and jumped when he saw the outline of a man's jacket hanging on a hook, thinking it was a body. Oddly, nothing in the castle had been disturbed and nothing had been taken, and it was this that worried me more than anything. My camera sat on the dining room table where I had left it, and a radio and a potful of pound coins were untouched.

Davy stood in my kitchen and said, "They took nothing. That's the damnedest thing. I don't like to ask a lady personal questions, miss, or anything like that, but did you have any trouble when you were in Dublin, trouble with any person or man?"

Davy was in his early seventies, short, stocky, and white-haired. His faded jeans sat low on his hips, and he wore a blue ski jacket with a patch sewn onto the shoulder showing the silhouette of a naked woman in a saucy pose, the sort of image you'd see on the steel mudflaps of an eighteen-wheeler. Davy's question seemed to insinuate that this event might somehow be my own fault. I told him I had never had any trouble with anyone in Dublin and that I couldn't imagine who had done this or why.

"Me either," Davy said. "Nothing like this ever happened out here before. Except once somebody broke in and cooked some fish and sausages on the fire and drank some wine, and then they washed up all the dishes and put them neatly away and went off again."

Satisfied that I was alone in the castle, Davy went home, saying he'd return the next day with the police.

I covered the windows with my makeshift shutters and built a big fire and turned on all the lights. I sat up most of that night with my coat on and the fire poker in my hand. My hands, swollen and red from the nettles, had begun to go numb. I listened to the wind and the flitting bats and the rain crashing against the windowpanes with the force of a firehose, and I watched the dancing orange flames of the fire as they lit up the cap hanging from the antlers above the fireplace. Eventually I fell into a fitful sleep with my booted feet propped up on the table and the fire poker across my lap.

THE NEXT DAY was bright and bitter cold, and though the rain had stopped, the wind was so high I thought the windows at the top of the castle would blow in. Davy Wren returned to repair the chain on the door. When the job was done he came in carrying three bunches of grapes he had found growing in the circular gatehouse. They were beautiful grapes, small and violet and sweet, with jagged leaves the size of lily pads. Davy left, saying the police would be coming to visit me that afternoon.

Later I was sitting in the living room reading when I heard someone come in through the front door and hesitate out in the hallway. Presently the inner door opened and Sergeant Kavanagh appeared, looking dazed and amazed by the size of the room. When he realized I was there, he leapt back and cried out, "Oh!"

I invited him in. He stood in the middle of the room, looking around in wonder. He wore a navy blue uniform of heavy wool, a cap, a badge, and a walkie-talkie in a holster on a leather strap across his chest. The buttons of his jacket were fastened all the way up to his throat, making him look stiff as a toy soldier. He was clean and glowing, and his eyeglasses glinted in the rays of sunlight falling through the kitchen window. He had powdery pink cheeks, a long nose, and a lot of even white teeth. But the most striking thing about him was his exaggerated eyebrows, so black and heavy they looked fake. In fact, Sergeant Kavanagh's entire appearance suggested a Halloween costume.

He stood mute for a minute and finally said, "I was never in this castle before." He had a gentle way of speaking and a perpetually surprised look on his face. I told him what had happened the night before, and he listened attentively.

"Is the bank owed money by the owners of the castle?" he asked. I said I didn't think so. "Well, perhaps there's some dispute of ownership then?" I didn't think that was so either. "Well, then I can't puzzle it out at all, at all," he said, scratching his head and sitting down in one of the leather sling chairs to fill out his report. He asked me questions in a halting, hesitating voice, as though he was feeling slightly dizzy. Over and over he asked me about the padlock and chain; he seemed unable to keep the simple story straight in his mind. He sat forward in his chair with his knees together and his feet apart, hunched over his clipboard, fussily writing down everything I said and spelling the words out as he wrote them.

". . . found the l-o-c-k on the c-h-i-n," he muttered, and I watched as he scribbled with his pen. He paused to pull at his lip and squint at what he had written. "Chin? No, no. Ha-ha. That's not correct. I meant to write 'chain,' but I ha-ha wrote 'chin' instead." He chuckled delightedly at the mistake and scratched the word out. "It was the *a* I forgot!" he said. He reread what he had written, then stared into space, chewing on the pen, thinking, hemming, and hawing. I could see the clumsy fingers of his mind turning the pieces of this little puzzle over and over and failing to fit them together. I said, "Sergeant Kavanagh, perhaps you'd like me to write the report."

"Seeing where you are a writer by trade," he said, "that might be useful. You could correct my grammar."

I smiled and got up to take the clipboard from him. "How do you know I'm a writer?"

"Molly Cooney said!"

Molly Cooney was the postmistress. She was interested in acting. Every time I went into the post office she was poring over some play script and reciting the lines. She was a pretty, precise woman with an instant smile and a soft voice. She kept a picture of the sacred heart on the post office wall and an electric vigil lamp that glowed red above her head and that could be seen through the window at night, like an alarm light. She had asked me what Irish authors I liked to read, and she told me she was from Scariff, near Tuamgraney, where Edna O'Brien had grown up. Instead of being proud of O'Brien, she was bitter about her and scandalized by her work. She told me that her mother and Edna O'Brien's father had been in a hospital together and that O'Brien's father was always coming to her mother's room looking for bottles of Guinness. "Imagine it," she said, "my mother who never took a drink in her life! And Edna O'Brien simply went up and down the streets of that village and wrote down everything about everybody and put it in a book. You could pick out the people and who they were. Was that nice?"

I pointed out that James Joyce had done much the same thing, and Molly said indignantly, "That was different."

"How was it different?" I said.

"He was a writer!"

"Edna O'Brien is a writer," I said.

I gave Sergeant Kavanagh a cup of tea, which he sipped at noisily and gratefully. He ate bread with jam and butter and punctuated the silences in our conversation by saying, "Ho hum." When it was time for him to leave, he had great difficulty getting out of the low seat. The antenna of his walkie-talkie got caught on the arm of the chair and pulled him back into it again. He wrestled with the chair, then stood a moment, scratching his head and looking around him, tapping his shiny shoe nervously on the stone floor, and finally he said, "You know, Miss O'Mahoney, I would find it very lonely here."

PART

III

Annie MacNamara

THE SATURDAY NIGHT DANCE in Daly's Pub, which drew people to Corofin from the surrounding countryside, was one of the few opportunities the villagers had to talk with people they didn't ordinarily see. One Saturday night I stood at the dance with Sile MacNamara Breen, Conor's eldest daughter. The air in Daly's was blue with smoke, and steam dripped down the picture windows in rivulets, tracing a web upon the glass. There were many younger people in the pub that night, most of whom I had never seen before. Everyone held a glistening pint of beer or stout, and there was a feeling each time a glass was emptied that something important had been accomplished. The young women were shy, wore a lot of heavy makeup, and looked pale and unhealthy. The same old unlikely band performed in a corner of the pub: a fat accordionist in a white blouse and gray skirt, a teenage drummer, and a toothless guitarist with a handlebar mustache. They played waltzes and a faster version of the traditional Irish air. The old men danced together, and the young women danced together, and Mike Menahan danced crazily with himself in a flailing, stomping fashion.

Sile Breen drank wine and chain-smoked. Her husband stood behind her at the counter, and whenever Sile's glass was empty he brought her another drink, wordlessly, and returned to his place. His face was the color of raw salmon. He smoked a slender cigar. As I watched the people dancing I heard Sile saying beside me, "My mother drank in her later years. She started drinking at the change of life. We used to find the bottles everywhere all over the house, and we'd be giving out yards to her for it."

I looked at Sile's small oval face; she was in her late thirties but looked older.

"We didn't understand it," she continued. "Mama had a child every eleven months and was never well. I miss her. She was only sixty-two when she died. It was the drink that killed her. Dada's house is not the same without her. I feel I've no one to talk to now when I have troubles. You know the way my father drinks, like? Well, it's only recently he started drinking that way."

Sile had Conor's big laugh but none of his self-confidence. Her speaking manner was shy and uncertain, marked by a diffident smile, a habit of chewing her lower lip, and busy hands that touched her face compulsively as she talked—palming her cheek, plucking her eyebrows, or cupping her chin. She seemed to be trying to hide her face, as if from the naked light her own words threw at her. Sile told me she had had her first child, Monica, when she was sixteen years old and unmarried and that Monica, now nineteen, had just had a child of her own, also out of wedlock. "That's Monica," she said, pointing across the room at a pretty, sullen, wide-eyed girl with a cigarette and a pint of beer. "I'm a granny at thirty-eight. And you know my brother Michael? He has a daughter who's two years old. He's not married either. His girlfriend's only eighteen."

I smiled to hide my surprise. The illegitimate child was a transgression most people went to great lengths to hide. I pictured reticent Michael MacNamara behind the bar at Dillon's; it was hard to believe he was anyone's father.

Sile spoke urgently, as though these irregular facts pressed on her mind and she needed to release them. Casually she said, "Nuala, another of my sisters, is married to a half-caste."

Sile told me that Conor had trained her to mind his garage when she was only twelve years old. She had changed automobile tires, pumped gas, done tune-ups and oil changes, and replaced fan belts before she knew how to drive. She said the garage did a lot of business, but Conor was too soft on people, giving them too much credit and never getting paid for his work.

Conor was in Daly's that night, wearing a double-breasted suit jacket with wide lapels and white pin stripes. He wore huge black boots with the laces tied in a bow at the back of the ankle. When he saw me with Sile, Conor grabbed a young woman by the arm and dragged her over to us. Sile muttered, "Christ," when she saw him approaching.

"Rosie!" Conor exclaimed, "this is another of my daughters, Annie MacNamara Maher."

Annie was beautiful in a startling, mythological way. She was a modern Snow White, a delicate, heart-shaped face in a picture book. She had the high cheekbones and glimmering green eyes, the full red bow for a mouth, dark lashes and arching black brows, pale skin that blushed reflexively, a pointed chin, and black hair that fell in curls to her shoulders, hair so thick and glossy it looked unreal. Annie had Conor's plunging widow's peak. She also had Conor's barreling drunkenness.

"*You* are Rose," she said, smiling indulgently and wrapping an arm around me. She hugged me fast against herself. She was surprisingly strong for such a small woman. She pulled down on my arm, hiked herself onto her toes, and fitted her mouth to my ear. "Francis, my uncle, is a good man," she heaved, "and you are a good woman. And Francis is so lonely. And he really loves you, Rose. We *all* love you, Rose."

I looked carefully at Annie's shining, blinking face to see if she was kidding. I had neither met nor heard of this woman before. I was aware that people referred to me as Francis's girlfriend, that this was the way my conversations with Francis were perceived. A man and a woman couldn't spend so much time talking and not be united in the minds of the village, but I wondered what Francis himself thought. I wondered if he believed the rumor, or if he was encouraged by it. Francis liked to tell me about the house he owned at the bottom of the village, how nice it was, how he had put curtains in the windows, and how eventually he would give up the pub and move into that house. It was a big house, he said, the house he grew up in. Several members of the MacNamara family said they hadn't seen Francis so happy in years, and they said it with suggestion in their voices, as though it was somehow my doing. But I had done nothing except listen to him. Few people listened to Francis MacNamara, fewer listened to Mick Pat Crown, and no one ever listened to Mike Menahan. They were lonely. So was I. I found it easy to listen to them.

Annie widened her crafty eyes at me. "Francis!" she said with great significance.

Sile winced at Annie and said, "Jesus, Annie, leave off, will you? Rose, don't mind Annie. She only takes after Dada. She's half-steamed tonight."

Conor threw back his shoulders and frowned at Sile. "Speak for yourself!" he said.

Annie stepped closer to Sile and wagged one menacing finger in her face. "I take after nothing," she said.

Annie spoke in a slow, dramatic manner with regal diction and a half-British accent. She wore no makeup, in striking contrast to the other young women here, and no jewelry beyond a ruby engagement ring and a wedding band. She had a cigarette tucked behind her ear and was dressed in black jeans, a black beret, work boots like her father's, and an oily Barbour raincoat of forest green: terrorist attire. Despite her clothes, Annie had a sophistication far beyond that of the other women in the pub. I later learned that she had spent fourteen years in London, and that experience had stayed with her. She was as commanding as her aunt, Eileen O'Shea, and as tough as any man in the village. As we stood there that night she became enthralled by the ruby ring on her own finger. "Rose," she said, "do you think this ring is lovely?" She held the ring up for me to see.

"The ring is lovely," I said.

Annie flashed a brilliant smile at me and patted my face. "Ha-ha! A delightful way of speaking you have! Sile, my dear, did you hear her? 'The ring is lovely!' was how she said it!"

It was not how I had said it — Annie's imitation of my accent was simply a louder version of her own.

Annie caught my arm and narrowed her big eyes at me. "Francis loves you, Rose," she said; it sounded like a threat.

Conor said, "Francis MacNamara couldn't fight his way out of a paper sack!"

The band played a waltz, and Mick Pat Crown asked me to dance. Paddy O'Brien, the pock-faced man known as the Badger, sat at the bar looking as worried as ever. As I walked by him to get to the dance floor, Paddy said, "Rose, you're not with the MacNamaras tonight, are you?"

"Yes, I am," I said, though until then it hadn't occurred to me to make that distinction. Paddy seemed disappointed in me. I wanted to tell him that despite their unsavory reputation the MacNamaras had been most welcoming to me, that they were the only people in the village who had invited me to their homes and the only ones who had dared visit me in mine.

I danced three waltzes with Mick Pat Crown, and each time I put my hands in the wrong position he rearranged them good-naturedly. He pressed his bristly cheek to mine. I danced with Mike Menahan, Matty Keane, Cubby Ahearn—who crushed my fingers in his iron grip—and Micky Nolan. Toward the end of the night, when the band played the national anthem, Mick Pat Crown held one of my hands and Mike Menahan held the other, and I heard Mick Pat say to himself, "She might marry me yet!"

When I returned to talk with Sile, Annie, and Conor, Annie said to me, "Wait a minute now. Sile tells me you are living in the castle. How did you come by the key? Were you somebody to Bob Brown?"

Conor put his glass down on the bar. "She was a friend to him," he said importantly, wiping his hands on his lapels, "just like I was a friend to him."

Annie was beside herself with excitement. She raised her hands before her and peered at me. She wiggled her fingers and plucked absently at lint on my sweater, trying to think of a delicate way to phrase her next question. She had the sly, pointed grin of a fox. "Josie, darling," she said, getting my name wrong, "can I come out to the castle with you tonight?"

Annie was drunk, I didn't know her, and her volatility worried me. I didn't want to have to take care of her. The very idea of Annie hiking up the castle's spiral staircase made me uneasy. She sensed my hesitation and whined, "*Please*, Josie? I always wanted to see that castle. And I remember Bob Brown coming over to see my mother with his two big dogs. Once Bob carved my mother a manger for Christmas. He carved it himself. A baby's little cradle."

"It's cold in the castle," I said.

"I don't mind!" Annie said.

"And it's dark."

"Josie, I do not mind!"

"And sometimes there are bats there at night," I said.

Annie shrugged and threw up her arms. "A bat is nobody!"

"You won't be scared?"

Annie gave me a sudden breathtaking thump on the chest with the back of her hand. "Will you come off it, Jo! What would I be scared of, for Chrissake?"

Her insouciance, at least, was refreshing. And I had often felt that more people in the village should come and see the castle, for in some way it belonged to them. "Suit yourself," I said.

Annie hopped and clapped her hands. "Dada!" she cried, "I'll be going to the castle tonight with Josie!"

Conor straightened the big glasses on his nose and peered irritably through them at Annie. "Jesus, Annie, the girl's name is *Rosie*. Her feckin' name is *Rosie*. 'Tis not Josie and 'twill never *be* Josie."

❈

AN HOUR after closing time we spilled out of Daly's with Sergeant Kavanagh grinning behind us. Mick Pat Crown had offered to give me a ride home to the castle, but when he learned that Annie Maher was coming with me, his face soured and he refused to take her. He stuffed his hands deep into his coat pockets and insisted that Annie should be at home with her husband and children instead of wandering around Corofin so late at night and so far from home. Annie lived fifteen miles away in Ennistymon, where she and her husband owned a pub.

Mick Pat and Annie argued all the way up the street. Between piercing statements to Mick Pat, Annie whispered in my ear, "I have some hash we can smoke," and she slipped a ten-pound note into my pocket and directed me to buy a bottle of whiskey from Francis to bring to the castle. I told her I had a bottle at home, and that we didn't need to drink more anyway.

"We always need to drink more!" she said.

Mick Pat said, "You drink like a man, Annie MacNamara."

Patiently Annie said, "Stop worrying, Mick Pat, my love. The way the world is going, there are a lot greater things to worry about than me."

Mick Pat said, "But if you was interested in your family, Annie Maher, you would not be in Corofin this night."

"But I am *very* interested in my family, Mick Pat."

"You aren't," he said.

"I am, my love." Annie was speaking now in a reassuring and faintly disingenuous voice, as if to a frightened child.

"You're not," Mick Pat said.

"Will you go away out of that, Mick Pat, of course I am. My children do well in school. And I am running a business for them. I *work* for them."

Mick Pat Crown hated the idea of a young mother working. "Work away," he said. "Work away. I'll not ferry you out to Ballyportry this night. Isn't that good enough for you?"

Annie snapped. The softness in her voice was supplanted by a contemptuous, hard-edged sneer. "Shut up, coot. Will you for fuck's sake shut up? Jesus, the men in this world are always going after the women this way! Going after them and going after them, and there is not a minute's rest!"

With her tiny hands Annie snatched at the air in an eradicating fashion; it wasn't clear whether she was demonstrating what she would like to do to Mick Pat or expressing a feeling of claustrophobia.

Mick Pat stalked down the sidewalk ahead of us in a rickety, thin-legged way, tipped slightly forward over his knees. In the semidarkness the frayed cuffs of his shirt were like two bands of glowing light at the ends of his coat sleeves. "Miss," he said over his shoulder to me, "I am sorry. I cannot bring you home if Annie MacNamara is coming with you. I would never leave a lady behind, but Annie MacNamara is not a lady. I won't give you no seat, Annie MacNamara."

Annie gave me a jab with her elbow. "Will you *look* at this, Josie? Do you hear what this man is saying? This is an old man speaking to me this way. *Another* old man speaking this way." She slapped a street sign for effect. "This place is full of old men. This country is ruined with old men always getting on the women this way and pushing us down."

"No seat," said Mick Pat, and Annie laughed at him—real laughter that came from deep in her throat. "We will walk, then, Mick Pat, because I am afraid of you. I am really afraid of a man like you in this world."

The street was busy with people making their way home from the pubs, most of them old men. It was the street Annie had grown up on.

We passed the tiny house she grew up in, the house her father still lived in. Annie knew every inch of the street, and at thirty-six she was still on it, arguing about propriety with a man she had known all her life. Mick Pat Crown was like a difficult relative. He and Annie spoke to each other with familiarity and with the disdain that familiarity brings. In a little village like Corofin even the people who were not connected by blood and who were separated by generations had a connection that could not be broken. They were responsible for each other, they reflected each other, they were embarrassed by each other, and if one of them departed, they would miss each other.

"Do you hear him, Jo?"

"Yes, I do," I said, "and you're not going to change his mind, so forget it." I wanted Annie to relent. I hated to see Mick Pat angry, and I knew how difficult it was for Annie to be reprimanded and judged this way. I wanted to avoid this argument. It was easier to walk home.

"I'll give you no seat in my truck, Annie Maher."

"Stick your seat in your arse," Annie jeered.

Mick Pat turned to look at me. "Miss," he said softly, "I apologize for Annie."

I saw then that Mick Pat would never chastise me for associating with Annie MacNamara; as a foreigner I was beyond his rural purview. That was what he and the other villagers appreciated about me: I didn't have to obey their rules, didn't have to be watched or reined in. I could live alone in a creepy castle without annoying local sensibilities and without being termed mad or brash. Mick Pat had never asked me whether I had a husband or children. I had come from across the ocean and so was exempt from the question.

Annie took a swing at Mick Pat, missed, and fell against the dark window of a house, triggering the furious, high-pitched crowing of a little dog within. Her hair hung around her face like kelp. Her beret sat crooked on her head. "You do not apologize for me, Mick Pat," she snarled. "You are not my father!"

"Thank God for that," said Mick Pat.

Inside the house the little dog barked hysterically and jumped onto the wide inner sill, poking his head through the gap in the curtain. He bared his teeth and lunged at Annie. He danced and skittered like a puppet. He had a rat's face and the voice of an excitable old woman.

Annie studied the dog with a bemused expression. "There's your mother calling you, Mick Pat!" she cried. "'Tis your mother there calling out to you, you son of a bitch!" She hooted and slapped her thigh at her own imagination and hugged a lamppost. She grabbed my arm. Her crimson lips and even teeth shone wetly in the soft lamplight. "Ha-ha, Josie, my friend, did you hear what I said to that bastard?"

I had heard her, but Mick Pat hadn't; he was already standing by his truck across the street, fitting the key into the lock, the tip of his narrow tie licking at the door handle. He looked old and tired and lonely.

I steered Annie down the road toward the castle. In the darkness I could hear her booted feet flapping angrily on the pavement and her swinging arms zipping against the grain of her raincoat. She walked in a busy, hustling way and with a prodigal expenditure of energy; I could almost feel the heat she generated. She breathed in panting spurts, and her breath billowed out before her in ghostly white puffs. There were one or two lights on in the houses on the hill by the cemetery, but aside from those and the lights of the occasional passing car, the countryside and the clouded sky were very dark that night. I prayed Annie would not grow fearful, for there is no one more difficult than a frightened drunk. I talked cheerful nonsense to distract her, and she hooked her arm in mine and responded with morose nonsense of her own. Strangely, her breath smelled not of the whiskey she'd been drinking but of anise seed. She said, "Isn't it terrible the way they think? But, you know, I like Mick Pat. He is a nice man but a bastard sometimes."

A battered old car traveling in the direction of the castle passed us, then came to a screeching halt. A young woman leaned out the window and with a tinny shout offered us a lift. Annie put a steadying hand on my arm. "Shush, Josie. Say nothing now. Just say nothing. I shall handle this. You don't know these sort of people."

As we neared the car I recognized Annie's brother Willie at the wheel. The woman was Willie's girlfriend, Baba. She shouted, "Christ help us, 'tis Annie! Annie, where in the name of God do you think you're off to?"

With no idea who was talking to her, Annie gathered the folds of her raincoat about her with an imperious flourish and enunciated,

"Ballyportry Castle, please!" She skipped toward the car with one hand elegantly outstretched. When she realized whose car it was, she deflated and banged her hand down hard on the hood. "Ah, fuck me, 'tis only ye," she muttered. "Shove over, lads! We're hoppin' in."

Annie's accent fascinated me: it was British and slow when delivering a pronouncement and Irish and fast when vituperating. I noticed, too, that Annie liked to hit things.

We climbed into the back of the car; a baby carriage took up half the seat. Annie was wide-eyed and trembling with excitement. Willie complained about the weight of the car. "How many pints did you drink, Rose?" he said.

"Two."

"I'd say 'twas two barrels!" he cried.

Annie slapped Willie's head. "Shut up and drive, Willie. Josie is a good girl. Don't mind him, Jo, he's only taking the mickey out of you."

Willie turned his head, trying to see me in the dark, and Baba's arm swung out mechanically and struck him square in the chest. "You watch the road!" she commanded.

I had met Willie MacNamara once or twice in Crowley's Pub. He was plump and slow and had a japing, juvenile sense of humor. He had spent twelve years working in London, yet unlike Annie's, his accent and manner were unaltered. He had a marked stutter, and of all the MacNamara children I'd met, his accent was the heaviest—he said *care* for car and *trun* for thrown, and he spoke fast and with the snapping cadence of West Clare, the cadence of indignation. Willie was thirty-four years old but seemed twelve.

I invited Willie and Baba to come into the castle with us. Willie was thrilled with the invitation, but Baba sat still in her seat, staring through the windshield with her arms crossed over her chest. Her sweater was sheet-white in the dark car.

"Baba, don't you want to come in?" I asked.

Annie answered firmly, "Yes, she does, Josie. Baba is a lovely girl! Come along, Baba, my love."

There was a dire warning in Annie's voice for Baba.

Annie talked nonstop as we approached the castle. I couldn't hear myself think. "Annie," I said finally, "do you ever stop talking?"

"Ha-ha. Not really, Josie, my friend," she said.

"Not Josie," I said. "Rosie."

In a faintly suspicious tone Annie said, "So Dada said."

When we stepped into the living room and I switched on the light, Annie flung up her arms with joy and cried, "Ha-ha! This is the glory room!" Willie said, "You could have a massive big party here!" Baba said nothing but shrank back against the wooden door with her fists pushed into the pockets of her stirrup pants.

I added more fuel to the dying fire and urged everyone to sit down. Annie threw off her raincoat and plumped into a chair, saying, "Mind if I roll a joint, Josie darling?"

"I don't mind," I said.

Annie peered at me as I fanned the fire. "Do you understand what I am asking you, my friend?"

Her overweening caution amused me. "Maybe I don't," I said. "Can you explain it?"

The task of explaining delighted Annie. She raised her hands before her, and slowly and sweetly and with calm certitude, as if speaking to a skittish half-wit who might fly off the handle at any moment, she said, " 'Tis hash, you see. 'Tis a plant. 'Tis a little drug, like. I am sure it can be found in your country. You smoke it a bit, and then you begin to feel better about everything. Only 'tis not legal, so it is a risk that way. Will I show you a bit?"

"Please do," I said.

While Annie rooted in her coat pockets, Willie grinned sympathetically at me. I could hear him thinking, *Bumpkin!*

Annie brought forth a ceramic pillbox, removed its lid, and held the box up for my inspection. The three little lumps of hashish in the box were like crumbs of turf. Annie said, "So, you don't still mind?" She had the penetrating gaze of a sibyl.

"I don't mind," I said.

Annie got busy rolling her joint, and she and Willie drank big tumblers of Wild Turkey, while Baba drank orange juice. Annie looked around the room and said, "Wish my husband could see me here!"

Willie said, "I never had bourbon before," wiggling his heavy body forward in his chair so that he could hold his glass up to the candlelight and study the amber drink. He had a fat face, thin lips, a lot of tiny teeth, and an indolent grin. He sniffed at his glass, then tipped some of the liquid onto his tongue and said, "Ffft."

Baba sulked in her low-slung chair and stared at the gaseous orange and blue flames of the turf fire. She sat with her knees pressed together and her elbows drawn in tightly at her sides, as though she might sully her clothing if she touched anything. Every so often I caught her glancing around the room with a look of skeptical fascination. She grimaced at the height of the ceiling. "'Tis like a damn church," she whispered.

Baba was nineteen but looked twenty-eight. Her soft, plump face was floury with powder, and the scarlet lipstick she had applied to her lips in a generously uneven line transformed her mouth to a ghoulish wound. Against the red of her mouth and the true white of her face, her teeth were sawdust yellow. She had frizzy, weightless hair that hovered, ethereal as smoke, around her head—the firelight shone through it. Her bare ankles were as white as her sweater. I could see that Baba wanted to go home, and I tried to engage her. When I spoke, she glanced quizzically at me, scrutinizing my accent. Eventually she seemed to forget her anger. "I have two kids," she said with Sile Breen's matter-of-fact style of divulgence. "And Willie's the father. We're not married."

I said, "Oh?" and added them up in my head: Sile, Michael, Willie, Maeve, and Sile's daughter Monica—five MacNamaras so far who had had children before they were married. I couldn't tell whether they did this out of desperation, spite, or ignorance. Perhaps it was sheer defiance, perhaps they were all possessed of the same defiant streak, the unwillingness to conform, that separated Conor MacNamara from the rest of the villagers.

"The oldest baby is three," Baba said.

"And the other baby?" I said.

"Eight months."

Baba said she had gone to England during the first pregnancy because her family had disowned her. Her sisters, who lived in Corofin, hadn't talked to her since the first baby was born. Her brother, an assistant to Eamon the butcher, also wouldn't talk to her. I knew her brother; he was a flirt with meeting eyebrows who stood in an apron in the doorway of the butcher shop waving a bloody hand at young women who passed by and asking them lasciviously if they wanted a piece of meat.

"They can't stand it," Baba said.

"Can't stand what?" I said.

"Me."

I asked her why, and she frowned as though the answer should be obvious. "Because I made them look bad, of course."

"How did you make them look bad?"

With aggressive bluntness Baba said, "I screwed around with Willie—"

Willie's lip curled, and he snickered wickedly behind his glass of bourbon; the snickering made his fat body bounce. He said, "Har-har."

"—and that makes them look bad. Don't ask me why."

Annie, who had been removing tobacco from a cigarette in order to mix it with her hashish, paused to listen to Baba; her expression was serious and knowing. "They could not control you, Baba, my love. That is why, you see. And you were ungrateful to them, and disobedient. Tsk, tsk, mustn't be disobedient."

Baba stared bleakly at Annie.

Willie said he had been married before to a woman in London. "She got pregnant and I had to promise her feckin' father I'd marry her," he sneered. His first child was eleven years old now.

"Do you ever see that child?" I asked him.

"Nah. We're divorced. They're still in London."

"So you and Baba could marry," I said.

He said, "Baba won't marry me," and laughed his mirthless laugh.

Baba glared into the fire, and Willie stopped laughing and looked at her. "Baba has no faith in me," he said.

Annie sucked at her cigar-sized joint of tobacco studded with hashish. She smoked contentedly, her head enshrouded in a veil of blue smoke. She seemed to be summarizing the conversation in her mind.

Willie said, "Annie told me not to marry the girl in London, but I did it anyway and now I'm sorry I did."

"And wasn't I dead right?" Annie said, raising the big cigarette at Willie. "You should have listened to me, my love. That girl was only no good, and you were only too young anyway. You were only nineteen."

"You were right, Annie," Willie said agreeably.

I asked Willie what he did for work.

"Not much," Baba snapped.

Willie said, "I'm not working just now, but I do construction."

Annie said, "Not working is the national pastime. None of my lovely brothers work."

Willie said slyly, "Say, Annie, how about sharing that smoke?" and Baba stiffened perceptibly in her chair. She turned to look at Willie, and an icy wind seemed to sweep across from her side of the stone table. "You don't smoke that stuff, Willie," she said. "You know you don't smoke that. You are just acting the big man. Or maybe you do smoke it. Maybe when you're out with your friends you do smoke it. Admit it. You do, don't you. When you're out with Moynihan and Heaney and Rooney you do smoke that."

Baba's garish lips thickened and trembled. Her mocking, castigating voice was fired with perverse satisfaction. It seemed that something she had always suspected about Willie was now confirmed, and she was both vindicated and infuriated. She glared at him with the bitter expression of disgust and disrespect that accompanies betrayal. Her face was suddenly aged with disappointment, a disappointment somehow related to her children and her need to protect them. She had convinced herself that Willie was an irresponsible and deceitful father. Her soft, pale hand on the arm of the chair twitched with rage; if Willie were not twice her size she would have slapped his pudgy face. And Willie's surly expression seemed to say that if Baba dared slap him, he would return the slap with twice the force.

"That's right, Baba," he cried, "I do smoke it. All the time. Every minute your back is turned I am out smoking away! I smoke myself brainless!" Willie threw his head back and swallowed the rest of his bourbon in one gurgling gulp. His exposed throat was pale and fleshy, like the underbelly of a frog, and his big cheeks were mottled with patches of red. He gasped and grimaced at the sting of the bourbon and dragged his forearm viciously across his mouth.

Annie sat slouched in her chair with her feet up on the table, serenely watching this little drama, the corners of her mouth turned up in sage amusement. Smoke dribbled luxuriously from between her lips and floated up into her nostrils and hair. Her eyes blinked softly as she plucked bits of tobacco from her chin.

Unable to contain herself, Baba hurled a string of curses at Willie, who caught them and hurled them back. They struggled out of their chairs and screeched, and I thought that if he hit her, I would grab the fire poker and swing it at him.

But Annie beat me to it; she snatched up the poker and shouted, "Fight, ye devils!" laughing and brandishing the poker like a cutlass.

Willie shot Annie an impatient look and said, "Fuckin' Annie." He leaned across the table, wrested the poker from her, and flung it into the fireplace, where it rang sumptuously against an empty cauldron, startling us all into wide-eyed silence.

"We'll leave, then!" Willie said, as if in reply to the cauldron.

Tall Baba clacked across the stone floor in her high-heeled sandals. She clawed the heavy wooden door open and flew out into the darkness. Willie went after her, and I went after them both, with Annie cackling gaily after me, "Leave those two fools go, Josie, my friend!"

Out in the field at the side of the castle Baba was shouting "Asshole!" and "Cunt!" and other picturesque curses interspersed with threats to the effect that she would kill Willie and maim him in various creative ways and walk the eight miles home to Tubber, where she would lock the door against him for the remainder of his lifetime. I could just make out the faint flicker of Baba's bare ankles and her white sweater as she bounded across the hummocky field, arms flapping like the great wings of a bird. I saw her stagger wildly and fall and get up, then I saw her run directly into a hedge, and finally I heard her sandaled feet clapping a hasty retreat down the Gort Road. Baba's tightness and fear seemed to have disappeared with the advent of her anger.

Willie struggled to get his car started, and when finally he succeeded he roared off, wheels spinning in the mud, taillights burning like the eyes of a dragon.

As I made my way back into the castle I had a powerful feeling of *déjà vu*. The evening's familiar display had recalled an entire habit of existence, a vehement, mistrustful, precipitate way of relating that I had witnessed in Ireland but that I had also grown up with and was part of whether I liked it or not.

I found Annie sitting on the low table with her feet in the fireplace, dangerously close to the fire. She had wrapped a shawl around her shoulders and was playing with the sooty cooking crane, shifting the greasy pothook and banging on the kettle with the poker. Her glass of bourbon, which a minute before had been near empty, was full again to the brim; when she wasn't looking I poured most of it out and mixed the rest with water. Annie bent forward over her knees and peered under the kettle. Her beret slipped from her head and onto the ash-covered floor. I wondered what it would be like to see her long hair go up in a curly blaze.

"Christ, Josie," Annie shouted at the fire, "this fuckin' kettle has no bum! The bottom's burst clean out of it! How the hell do you boil any water?"

"I use the kettle on the stove," I said.

Annie sat up, looking baffled and baked. "What goddamn stove are you talkin' about now, Jo?" she said, sounding amazingly like her father.

I went to the kitchen end of the room and flipped on the lights. The stove was an enormous iron six-burner imported from Canada, an industrial stove of the sort found in a large restaurant. Above it hung a row of copper pots, knives, and cleavers. The undressed stones in the wall behind the stove were green with moss and looked as though they had just been pulled from a field. The deep embrasure of the window held a large wicker basket of handblown glass fishing floats, a brass clarion the length and shape of a musket, and an array of urns and ewers.

"That feckin' kitchen's like a goddamn play," Annie shouted from her seat on the table. "Look at them knifes! And what sort of a counter is that at all?"

The counter was black marble.

"Jesus, Bob did everything nice for himself, didn't he, Josie? And he was clever, too. He was an architect. Have a look at that window! 'Tis like a church."

I climbed into the window embrasure and pulled the wooden shutters—planks, really—across the dark windows. Since the castle had been broken into I was slightly more fearful of the dark. Annie saw me standing in the embrasure and said, "What are you up to now? Who's going to see us?"

"Anybody who wants to," I said.

"Will you for Jesus' sake cut it out, Jo? There's nobody out there." Annie lay back flat on the table, sprawling across a pile of newspapers and books, and stared at the ceiling. Her eyes and her mind roamed, registering everything, and she murmured a childlike list of what she saw. "Horns," she said dreamily of the antlers above the fireplace. "Spiders. Shadows. Fuckin' stones. Candles. The flag." Her voice was sleepy and soft; it seemed to emanate from the top of her head. "Dents. A loft. Boo! 'Tis like a boat upside down. A cap's on the horns." She turned her head to look at me. "Hey, Jo? Is that Bob Brown's cap?"

"No," I said. "I found it."

"Lucky you," said Annie enviously.

I urged Annie to take her own hat out of the fireplace and offered her a cup of tea, which she declined, preferring to stay with the bourbon. I made the tea anyway, put a mug of it down on the table beside her, and sat in a chair. When I told Annie in what style Willie and Baba had departed, she sat up and reoriented herself by staring methodically at the four walls with a blank look on her face, as though she had just sneezed. Then, dryly, she said, "Don't mind them two, my friend. They're both thick. 'Tis better that way. If they had any brains, they'd be dangerous."

Annie crossed her legs, swung her foot, and looked curiously around the room. "Bob Brown," she said wistfully. "How well I remember him. He was lovely, and he loved my mother. He used always be coming to our house, visiting her and bringing her gifts. They talked themselves blue in the face. It's weird they ended up two doors down from each other."

"Two doors down?"

"In the graveyard. Bob is buried two doors down from my mother. They were great friends. My poor mother. She's only dead a year. Where's your mother, Rose? Dead?"

The question surprised and scared me a little. "No, she's not dead," I said.

"But you've said nothing about her."

I hadn't had a chance to say anything about her.

Annie pulled a lock of her dark hair across her lips and stared incisively at me. "What's your mother like? Nice?"

Her keen gaze made me uncomfortable. This was the first time anyone in Corofin had asked me anything about myself, and I realized with a small shock that Annie herself was like my mother. When I said that, Annie looked pleased, then suddenly displeased, and without sarcasm or jest she said, "A drinker, you mean? My mother was a drinker.

Yes. All the time drunk. We'd be finding the bottles here and there. We'd be pouring them out, and she'd get more some way or another."

"Did your mother drink in the pubs?" I asked.

"Are you crazy? Women that age wouldn't drink in the pubs. The men always say they don't like the women in the pubs, because women would be fighting. I think it's too funny. Isn't it always the men fighting and arguing and having to be better than each other in the pubs? I don't know what men are talking about. Women are the peaceful ones. They keep the peace, like. But, Jesus, women can be shitty as well!"

Annie hung her head and laughed a long time at this. Her words reminded me of Molly Bloom saying, *itd be much better for the world to be governed by the women in it you wouldn't see women going and killing one another and slaughtering when do you ever see women rolling around drunk*, and adding in the same long breath, *we are a dreadful lot of bitches*.

Annie had picked up a pencil and was idly knotting a lock of her hair around it. She said, "My mother was not happy, you see. Too many kids, for one thing. Once she confessed to the priest that she didn't want to sleep with my father anymore because she didn't want another kid, and the priest roared at her to get out of the confessional and do what she was put on earth to do. 'Twas her job, he said. That's how they think. But that's not what they said to me. I had a child and they made me give him up because I wasn't married. They made me. I had other children. But that one, where is he? I'd like to know that. That is what I would like."

Annie spoke as though her words were nauseating her. From time to time her head tipped forward involuntarily. The pencil hung in her hair like a Christmas ornament. When she picked up the mug of tea, half of it slopped onto the floor. She remained silent for a moment, sipping the tea. "The tea is good, Josie, my friend. I'm sorry for what I said about the baby. Okay, my friend? I said something wrong. I'll not say it again."

Annie slid off the table and sat inside the fireplace. She pulled the blanket around her shoulders, and the fringe of it fell into the fire. I ordered her to move farther away from the flames. She obliged, crawling on her hands and knees.

"My husband loved me, too. Just like Francis loves you, Jo," she said, settling herself down again. When she pushed her hair back from her face, her hand left a heavy black smudge across her forehead. She was literally sitting in the ashes. The fire lit up half her face and threw the other half into deep shadow. She propped an elbow upon a cauldron.

I asked Annie why Francis had never married.

"Because Francis met nobody nice enough," she pouted. "If I weren't Francis's niece, I would marry Francis. I think Francis is lovely. Do you think so? He's got his own house down near the grotto. He's a millionaire. Francis is got a bunch more money than we can ever know about." She looked at me to see whether I was interested in Francis now. "Don't mind these people, all right, my friend? It's different from in America and other places. I don't know how to bring it out. They are good and they are bad. And Francis loves you."

"Francis is nice," I said. "But he doesn't love me."

Annie's head snapped up, and her two hands flew into the air and came down flat on the table with a loud slap—the uncontrolled gesture of a toddler. "Will you come on!" she gasped. "Francis is crazy about you!"

"He's twice my age."

Annie shook her fist at me. "Good! That is good! How old are you, anyway?"

"How old do you think I am?"

Annie's head fell forward, and she mumbled fiercely into her shirt-front, "Shut your lips! You're younger than me!"

"How old?"

"Twenty-two!"

I had to laugh. I knew I seemed twenty-two to these women who were mothers at age sixteen. "Thirty," I said.

Annie lifted her head and peered at me. "So what? So what? So what? You are six years younger than me."

"So what? So what? So what?" I said.

Annie laughed uproariously and sputtered, "Would you fuck off!" in the affectionate way only an Irish person can get away with. "I am thirty-six, Josie. I am thirty-six years old and my life is different than yours."

Annie's face had gone pale, and she seemed to be traveling back and forth between lucidity and stupor. She made noises in her throat like the sound of a creaking door. At one point I heard her saying sharply, "Will you stop that? I'm not frightening you! I'm not frightening you! Stop that! Of course I'm not frightening!" She was talking to someone who wasn't in the room.

"I had a child," she said. "What happened to him? I have three children. Four children. But don't say that." Annie enumerated her children on her nail-bitten fingers. "I have Johnny, which is fifteen years old. And I have Eddie, which is eight years old. And I have Caitlin, which is, let me see, eleven. And I have the last one." She looked down at the floor between her legs and murmured, "Don't say that. 'Tis wrong to say it. He was adopted."

"The last one was adopted?" I said.

"No! He was not adopted," Annie croaked. Her head wagged from side to side. "The first one. He is gone. He was the best one. I know he was the best one and he is gone. They tried to blame me. They still try to blame me. They make you try and forget, you see. That's what I hate. They make you feel that you are wrong because of what you did. And you are totally suppressed then. You don't know them people, Josie. Horrible people."

Annie paused to rummage in her coat pockets for cigarettes. She tussled with the coat, then gave up. "Jo? Will you have a recky in my coat for some fags? You can look in my coat pocket because you are my friend. No one else can look in my goddamn coat pocket. These fucking people." She looked at me. "I drink. 'Tis why I drink, Jo. Am I okay? Am I, my friend?"

Annie's face was twisted into a despairing grimace, and I realized she was not asking whether in that moment in the fireplace she was okay but whether she was, in general, an evil person or a good person. She seemed to be wondering whether she was damned or saved. She was tormented. She rocked back and forth in the ashes and pulled the blanket tighter around her, and in the faint firelight I could see that she was crying. She reached for her glass of bourbon and gulped the rest of it, as though it might save her life.

"Yes, you are, Annie," I said. "You're fine," and I suggested she might like to go to bed. She picked up the beret and pressed it to her eyes. "But I want to walk to the village and get some fags," she sobbed.

"It's three in the morning," I said. "Where would you get cigarettes now?"

"Francis! We can wake up Francis." Annie stopped crying and looked hopefully up at me. Her face was dirty, and her pale cheeks shone with tears. She smiled gladly at her plan. "Francis's got a fag machine in the pub, and he'd be delighted to see you!"

"Impossible, Annie," I said and went outside and locked the outer gate in case she got a notion to venture out on her own. I was afraid she would hurt herself before this night was through. I was sorry I had brought her here. Her drunkenness had caught up with her suddenly, and it was especially disconcerting that she seemed able to swerve in and out of it at will.

When I returned to the room Annie was hiccupping and shivering in the ashes. "I'm fine," she said. "Only we have no fags. But we don't need them. 'Tis bedtime. Where will I sleep?"

I put Annie in the lowest bedroom, so that in case she tried to go down the stairs in the middle of the night she wouldn't have far to fall. I said good night to her and went upstairs and climbed into my own bed, fully clothed. My head was spinning and my muscles ached. I felt depressed.

Fifteen minutes later Annie pushed my bedroom door open. I turned the light on. She was shivering and staring in her raincoat and beret and boots. In a tiny voice she said, "Josie. I'm frightened. Can I stay in here with you?" She wandered aimlessly through the room and banged her shins hard on a low table. "Ow. Jesus. I feel unwell," she said. She shuffled around to the other side of the huge bed with her arms held out to protect herself. She stood next to the bed, rubbing her shins and looking sheepishly at me. Her eyes were red. "Don't mind him, Jo," she said.

"Don't mind who?" I said.

"Him."

I pulled back the blankets. "Get in, Annie," I said.

Annie flopped down onto the bed, raincoat and all, and pulled the blankets up to her chin. "Thanks, my friend," she said. "You are good. In the morning we will have to get up and go back into the village and face all them people again. I don't want you to have to know some things."

"Take your boots off," I said.

Annie sprung up. "Sorry, Jo. I'm taking them off lickety-split. Francis loves you. And please love him." Annie flung the boots against the stone wall with astonishing force and deliberation and cackled at the noise they made and at the shower of crumbling mortar they loosened.

I wanted to snap, "Francis does not love me," but there is nothing more pointless than arguing with a drunk. I shut the light off, put my head on the pillow. Through the window I could see bright clots of stars—the sky had sharpened and cleared. A cow released a melancholy honk beyond the outer wall, and then there was blessed silence until Annie whispered with a mischievous giggle, "Can I ring my husband, Josie?"

I said nothing. I clamped my eyes shut. I could hear Annie's watch ticking on her wrist, near my head.

Annie bellowed gleefully into the darkness, "Oh, can I, Josephine?"

"I don't care, Annie," I said. I didn't care if Annie woke all of Ennistymon at that hour. The phone was next to the bed; Annie bashed around in the dark looking for it. She picked up the receiver, and I heard the buzz of the dial tone. "What is the damn number?" she murmured. She dialed a few wrong numbers and was hung up on by several people. She talked to herself and giggled and bounced on her side of the bed, and that went on for so long I was tempted to yank the telephone wire out of the wall. After a few more tries, Annie dropped the receiver into its cradle, flumped back into the bed, and blurted gleefully, "Ha-ha! I will never be in this situation again! I will never be in this Ballyportry situation again in my lifetime! Ha-ha! He won't believe me."

And then, as if we had not had enough adventure for one night, Annie MacNamara became thoroughly unhinged. She began to hallucinate. She dragged up a series of sentences that were only vaguely related. She sounded alternately like a woman witnessing a horror, a woman on fire, a woman amused, angry, and haunted, and a child frightened by a ghost. She spoke to Bob Brown, to her mother, her husband, her father, and someone named Michael. She muttered and moaned. She tossed so vigorously that eventually she rolled over to my side of the bed, whereupon she began scratching at my legs in the useless, weak-fingered way a baby claws at the wrapping on a gift. She pulled at my arm. She shouted, "Stop it, Michael!" I pushed her onto her side of the bed and she rolled back again. She snorted and roared. When I spoke sternly to her, she said with perfect sobriety, "I'm sorry, Rose. I'm sorry. I must be keeping you awake. I'm having trouble sleeping. Jesus, 'tis so quiet here you could hear the grass grow. I drank too much. What do you do for work?"

I told Annie I was a writer, and with the soaring sarcasm of the deeply drunk she cried, "Brilliant! So am I!"

The Scenic Route

Some of the lesbians I had met in J. J. Smythe's Pub in Dublin agreed to meet with me to talk about their lives in a way that would have been impossible in the pub. Mary O'Donell, a young woman I had talked with several times, offered her apartment on South Circular Road as a meeting place. The meeting was set for 8 o'clock on a Wednesday evening. Mary told me, "The door will be open, just walk in."

I arrived at Mary's basement apartment at 8:10. Not only was the door not open, there was no response when I knocked on it. The door was very thick and was elaborately carved in the manner of a Mexican casket; knocking on it was as effective as knocking on the trunk of a tree — the sound of the knock simply dissipated into the wood. I tapped on a windowpane, waited a few minutes, looked at the huge geraniums in the flower boxes and the motorcycle parked on the tiny patch of grass in front of the building, and tapped again. Eventually the door opened a crack, and Mary O'Donell's face appeared, pale and stupefied with sleep. "Oh, hiya," she said, opening the door wide. She was barefoot and dressed in a bathrobe. Sleep's posture had mashed her short hair flat against one side of her head and left a long red crease along one cheek. She looked so muddled and surprised I thought she was ill.

Mary explained that she had lain down when she got home from work and had fallen asleep. Like so many other Irish women, she seemed to have no awareness of the passage of time and no embarrassment at having forsaken her own plans. Oddly, in these situations it was I who was always embarrassed by my too literal interpretation of time.

Mary invited me in and, pointing to a director's chair, asked me to sit. The small living room was dark and close and smelled of cats. I could make out a large television and a sleek sound system whose long panel of lights glowed green. There was a futon for a couch and a few pieces of low, lightweight furniture that gave the place the feel of a temporary residence. Mary flopped down on the couch, gathering her robe around her. She stared into space and scribbled at her scalp with a fingernail. "I don't really know who's coming," she said. "Orla might have forgotten. I'll give her a ring. And maybe Carmel Byrne is coming, if she remembers. And Kate is coming a little later, if she didn't forget, and maybe Peg. We'll see."

She picked up the telephone and dialed Orla, and it was clear from Mary's half of the conversation—punctuated now and then with a vocal and infectious yawn—that Orla had forgotten. Mary said, "You remember, I told you about it at the weekend . . . The American . . . to talk . . . Well, I'm reminding you now, so get yourself something to eat and come down when you can."

Their casualness amazed and impressed me. I would have been unable to greet a visitor—a relative stranger, no less—clad only in a robe. What impressed me above all was the apparent absence of shame over their own breach; I felt certain that their approach to social engagements was the healthier one.

Mary dropped the receiver heavily into its cradle, went into the bedroom, flung off her robe, and talked to me from the bed, where she sat stark naked—her pale skin illuminated by a table lamp— yanking on her jeans.

Irish immodesty, too, surprised and impressed me. A few weeks earlier I had read a piece by William Styron in the *New York Times Book Review*, a recollection of a daylong visit he and Philip Roth had made to

Dublin some years before. Roth told Styron that he felt the Irish were an incredibly repressed people and that this was evident in the behavior of the girls. Styron wrote: "Just watch, he told me, give them a look and they'll raise their arms to hide their bosoms. I scoffed at this, trying to be ethnically correct, but actually he was right: the public modesty was extravagant, and we received not even furtive glances in return as we submitted these colleens to the glare of our X-ray eyes." This reminded me of a passage in John Gregory Dunne's book *Harp*, in which a miniskirted young Dublin woman whom Dunne was staring at from a taxi window shouted brazenly at him, "Take a good look! You won't see tits like this again in your lifetime!" When I considered these contradictory observations, it was difficult to decide which was more informative—the fact of these Olympian American writers showing up in Dublin to ogle the girls or the insights the writers claimed to offer about Ireland's psyche.

The Irish may be repressed, but they are not modest. I witnessed more nudity in Dublin than I have ever seen in Boston, Massachusetts. Along the six-mile stretch of shoreline from Sandymount Strand (where Leopold Bloom tried to sneak a peek up poor, unwitting Gerty MacDowell's dress) to Sandycove, I was forever seeing Irish women flinging off their cotton dresses and wading into the shallow waters of Dublin Bay in their bras and underwear or, better yet, in nothing at all. In Killiney and along the bay's Bull Wall were segregated bathing spots where men and women swam naked. I found it endlessly refreshing that in Dublin nudity was not reflexively linked to sexuality.

Mary O'Donell had left her front door ajar, and cars raced noisily by on South Circular Road not fifteen feet from us; it was like sitting at the edge of a highway. The evening sun was still high in the sky (at the same latitude as the Aleutian Islands, Dublin's midsummer nights are bright until after midnight), and people ambled by on the sidewalk, many of them dark-skinned. This was Portobello, Dublin's ethnic neighborhood, where Arabs, Pakistanis, Indians, Africans, and Asians lived side by side, and where shops traded exotic goods unheard of in most other parts of the city. We were not far from the one mosque in Ireland, a converted church with the words "Dublin Mosque" written across its front in Arabic, English, and, in what I thought was a gesture of great courtesy to their hosts, Irish Gaelic.

Muslims made up the majority of the foreign community in Dublin, but at the turn of the century Portobello had been so wholly a Jewish neighborhood that it was known as Little Jerusalem. The two remaining kosher grocers in Dublin and Leopold Bloom's fictive birthplace were only a few blocks from Mary O'Donell's apartment. For nearly a century, people who were not Irish had settled in Portobello, and it seemed no accident that the lesbians who would meet here tonight had also chosen to live in this area.

The roar of a city bus drowned out whatever Mary was saying to me from the bed. Mary spoke faster than anyone I had ever encountered, and that, combined with her soft, breathless Galway whisper, made her difficult to understand. I had to watch her mouth carefully to catch her words. From where I was sitting now I could follow her not at all. I saw her mouth moving, saw her gesturing with her hands, but understood nothing. I smiled and nodded at her as she fastened her bra.

Dressed in black and wearing a colorful African cap on her head, Mary finally came into the living room, turned on the overhead light, and brought out some glasses and a bottle of wine. We talked, and an hour later Orla O'Shaughnessy came through the door clutching a greasy paper of French fries. Orla was tall and thin. With her wrinkled silk blouse, leather vest, baggy jeans, boating sneakers, and purple gauze scarf wrapped around her neck, she looked like a cowgirl at rest. She said, "How'r'ye?" and sat on the futon licking her fingers. She slung one long leg across the other knee and held the bag of French fries out to me. Affably and without having been introduced, she said, "Chip, Rose?" She had a high, narrow forehead, a long chin, and a long, serious face that changed dramatically when she smiled, a wide, endearing smile that pushed her features upward and reduced her eyes to glistening slits. Smiling, Orla's face resembled the Greek mask of comedy. Her long blond hair pulled back in a loose ponytail was as heavy as a hemp rope.

Kate Gogarty arrived minutes after Orla. Kate was an eager, bright-eyed senior at Trinity College. She was shy and pretty and stood awkwardly with her feet apart and her fingers wedged into the pockets of her jeans. At the slightest provocation Kate's naturally rosy cheeks succumbed to a riotous crimson blush that spread to her throat, forehead, and ears. Her self-consciousness, her earnestness, her quick, uncertain movements, and her haircut combined to give her the effect of an adolescent boy. Kate sat down, and Mary propped her bare feet up on the coffee table and said in imitation of a newscaster, "What's it like being a lesbian in Ireland, Kate?"

With nervous sarcasm Kate answered, "It's great, Mary!" Orla dropped her bag of chips onto the table and flung her arms up in a wild gesture of victory and shouted, "Great, Mary! No problems! Millions of places to go! Millions of things to do! Freedom! And acceptance from the people! That's what I like about it!" Orla stomped her feet and collapsed over her knees, helpless with laughter. Then she sat up and rearranged the scarf on her neck and sighed, "Jesus, that'll be the day."

When I asked about the numbers of homosexuals in Ireland, Mary said, "We go by the Kinsey Report. They say one in ten people is homosexual. I used to think, Jesus, where are all the lesbians in this city? Why are they hiding? We have three and a half million people, fifty-two percent are women, and ten percent of that are lesbians: 182,000 lesbians in Ireland. But such a minuscule number of those women have come out, have even admitted to themselves they're gay. Whether I like a woman or not, I still have to admire her for coming out, for having the gumption in a place like this."

Orla said, "Never mind that there aren't many women coming out as lesbians, I mean there's so many that aren't even feminists. During the sixties women were proud to be feminists, now it's all undercover stuff. Women these days express their opinions by saying, 'I'm not a feminist, but . . .'"

Orla bemoaned the fact that there were so few places lesbians could go to sit and talk—only J. J. Smythe's Pub, the Parliament, and Ulysses, places not conducive to conversation. It seemed to me that the dearth of meeting places was directly related to the fact that so few women were openly gay in Dublin.

"But there are a *lot* of gay women," Orla said. "Thousands of women have used the Lesbian Line since I came out back in 1981. I think the reason more don't come out is that there *isn't* a friendly place to go."

Mary said that two women named Joanie and Ruth had started the lesbian pub at J. J. Smythe's fourteen years ago, and Orla said, "Ruth—the first lesbian in Ireland."

"Oh, Jesus, right," said Mary. "Remember that? Ruth went on 'The Late, Late Show' with Gay Byrne in 1981. She came out to her mother on national television. The first lesbian in Ireland."

"The first lesbian? What does that mean?" I said.

"It means you stand up in front of a fucking camera and announce to the unsuspecting people of Ireland that you're a lesbian before anyone else has the nerve to do the same."

Kate, who for no apparent reason was fitting the mouth of an empty wine glass over one of her scarlet ears, remarked that when the Irish writer Mary Dorsey was invited to talk on the radio about her lesbianism she couldn't find another lesbian "brave enough" to join her. I was reminded of an article the journalist Mary Holland had written in the *Irish Times*, a plea to Ireland's gay population to come out publicly to encourage greater public discussion of the subject of homosexuality and, ultimately, a change in the prevailing negative attitudes. When I mentioned the article, Mary said, "We need to know about famous gay people. It's positive role models for us. If you apply the statistics to Ireland, we should have twenty gay MP's in Parliament. But we've never heard of a single one. No one's public but David Norris."

I never saw homosexuals being physically open in Dublin, and at the risk of hearing the obvious I asked why. Orla raised her hand with the thumb and forefinger held an eighth of an inch apart and said, "Dublin is this small." She rearranged her fingers to form a circle, and holding the circle up to one eye, like the eyepiece of a telescope, she said, "People would *see* you, Rose, and remember you. It's so small that gays don't want to draw attention to themselves."

Mary, who worked as a temporary secretary, said, "There's a great threat that you'll have trouble in the workplace if people know you're gay. You don't want to put up with any more discrimination at work than you already have to. I worked in an office this week, and every day at lunchtime the subject turned to sex. I don't know how they do it. Male or female, it always ends up being about sex. When that happens I sit there. I say, Jesus, is sex all ye ever talk about?"

Orla said, "That's because the Irish think sex is shameful, something you don't talk about. But as soon as one person starts up a conversation about sex, everybody else flies into it. But it's always heterosexuals who do the talking."

Mary said, "The people I work with don't know I'm gay and they're not going to find out, either. I would never tell them what I do on the weekend. I wouldn't. I want to get another job after this one."

Mary said she had known she was a lesbian since she was a young child. "I totally denied it until I was about twenty or twenty-one," she said, "but when I was four I got a fascination for motorbikes. Maybe that's revealing. I remember wanting a motorbike from Santa Claus, and what I got was this bloody little scooter, you know the little thing you stand on and push with one foot. Jesus, I was so upset about it. When I was fifteen, I told my mother that as soon as I got the money saved up I was buying a motorbike, and she said, 'If you want to live in this house you won't!'"

Orla said she had had sexual feelings for women when she was eleven years old. "We'd be having a game of kiss chasing, like spin the bottle, and when I was eleven I had to kiss Sarah McInerney from down the road, and our next-door neighbor, Sean O'Neill, and when I kissed Sean I wasn't too keen on it, mind you, but when I kissed Sarah I thought, Oh, yes! Just this evening I was in the Parliament Pub having a beer and I saw a chap in there called Harry McInerney, who was Sarah McInerney's younger brother. So, if he's in the Parliament he's probably gay as well. Harry and I even went out with each other when we were about thirteen. He used to work in Roche's Stores and used to rob these clocks and boxes of chocolates for me. Finally I told him, 'Harry, I will have to break our relationship off, because you cannot be robbing clocks and boxes of chocolates for me,' but I knew even then that that wasn't the real reason."

"The real reason was you wanted to go out with his sister!" Kate blurted nervously, one arm draped across the top of her head, her grin half-hidden by the sleeve of her sweater.

Mary said, "Most of my friends accept the fact that I'm gay. And most of my family are fine about it. My da is fine. But my mother doesn't know and she's never going to know."

"Why not?"

"Let me put it this way, Rose: my mother discovered two years ago that my sister was living with her boyfriend in London, and as a result she wouldn't speak to my sister for the next six months, and she wouldn't see her for nearly a year and a half. That should explain why I wouldn't want to tell her a thing like this."

"It has to do with that generation," Orla said. "Anything you do—if you just live a normal life, if you just *live*, your parents get crazy. When your parents are over sixty years of age, and you're living in a flat in Dublin and working and having a boyfriend or whatever, it is always frowned upon. Definitely in Ireland. My parents are over sixty. No matter what their daughters do, it's always wrong. Or else they say"—here Orla raised her voice to a near-howl—"'You can do what you like in Dublin, but not in our house!'" Among rural people Dublin is considered Ireland's great port of iniquity.

Orla said, "I'd say in sixty percent of the cases, parents over that age feel that way. Unless you're married. If you're married, you're grand. You're off the list of things to worry about."

"But if you're single, you're still a child, no matter how old you are," Mary said.

"And in that case you're considered loose," said Orla. "My sister is thirty-eight now, hasn't been married, has had a lot of relationships with men, broken engagements and all the rest, and she gets a lot of shit from my mother, you know, 'Why aren't you married? Why don't you have somebody yet?' Everything is zoomed into heterosexual thoughts all the time in Ireland, because the family is the most important thing here. The family. The family. The family."

Orla said her mother seemed to have accepted her homosexuality, if begrudgingly. "I came out and fell in love just before Christmas that year," she said. "During Christmas there's a lot going on at home, shopping and putting up a tree, and my mother said, 'Why haven't you been around, Orla? You know we need you to help out at home.' So I told her I'd been with my friend. And she said, 'What friend? That Mary Kinnane?' And I said, 'Yes,' and she said, 'God, you'd think you were in *love* with that one! Positively in *love* with that one by the way you carry on!' And I said, 'That's right, Mum, I *am* in love with Mary.' Well, she went out of the room then. I didn't plan it at all. I always had an awful fear of telling her. And then when I came out and I fell in love, I felt so happy about it that I didn't give a shit anymore."

I asked the women why the Irish media referred only to male homosexuality and rarely to lesbianism.

Orla said, "Because lesbians are invisible in Ireland. In Ireland they just term you a spinster or left-on-the-shelf, or they say, 'Ah, sure, she always liked her book.' That's how they explain it."

"And they wonder how two women can have sex. They just can't work that one out," said Mary.

"And those puzzled people are the very ones who talk about all the 'filthy' things lesbians do. They're the people letting their imaginations run wild," said Kate.

The women laughed; they seemed to be enjoying the conversation. I realized I didn't have to ask many questions, for they knew what they wanted to talk about.

Peg Kennedy arrived wearing a navy pea jacket and skirt. She was forty-five, tall, and handsome in a rough way—she had the graceful physique of a quarterback. She had short, sandy hair, a flat mouth, and pretty eyes. Her demeanor was striking for its serenity. The first time I saw Peg, she was in a pub singing "Summertime" at the top of her voice. Another time I met her at a party, where she sat on the floor wedged between my armchair and the wall, hidden from the room in a childlike way. Peg wrote poetry, and at that party she had laid her head on the arm of my chair and recited one of her poems for me, a poem about an older woman she had seen on a street, dressed in a long coat down to her ankles. She imagined that the woman had never felt the touch of a man, that the only thing that had ever caressed her was the long coat. Peg had three teenage children and was the niece of one of Ireland's most famous writers.

Peg worked for a management consulting firm. I commented on the late hours she was working. "Well, I do love me work," she said, "but I'm a little distracted from it lately, so I have a lot of catching up to do." I asked her what was distracting her. Sheepishly she said, "I fell in love."

Mary said wryly, "Does your mother know?"

Peg looked up at the ceiling, as if for her mother. "She probably does. Her spirit might. I think she'd have a seizure if she realized I'm a lesbian on top of everything else."

Peg used her wide shoulders expressively as she spoke, lifting them or throwing them forward or backward at the appropriate moments. She gave her opinion of the 1983 abortion referendum. "When Family Solidarity were pushing the referendum, they were depleting the rights of the pregnant mother, which was my reason for opposing the change in the Constitution. The wording was so complicated that nobody in Ireland—on either side—knew what the hell they meant.

My estimation is that the people really didn't know what they were voting for. They got confused. They thought if you voted *not* to change the Constitution, that meant you were an abortionist. I'm quite against abortion myself, but I don't think it should be in the Constitution."

Orla said, "The point is whether you'll have the right to decide for yourself. That was the whole idea. Women here don't have a say about what they want to do. The referendum was telling women that in many ways they don't have a choice about their bodies *or* their futures in Ireland. A lot of women in Ireland don't have any choices."

Peg said defensively, "Why don't they? You can choose whether you want to have a child or not. You can have sexual intercourse or not have it. The real problem is that working-class women haven't a clue. Access to information on their rights, not just sexual, is not free to them. Our educational system doesn't show women what rights they do have. The working-class woman has always felt she absolutely had to have sexual intercourse with her husband if he wanted it, and that is still true today."

I asked whether in Ireland a man could get a separation from his wife on the grounds that she refused to have sexual intercourse with him.

"He could," Peg said quickly. "He could get a separation. But even with a legal separation you still can't get remarried. There is no divorce in Ireland. However, if my husband had looked for an annulment on the grounds that I am lesbian, he could have got it and then could have remarried. We've been married fourteen years, and we have joint custody of the children. My husband is an extraordinary man. He is gentle and caring towards me and has said he's actually pleased that I'm in love."

Orla said, "But generally speaking, in a case like yours, Peg, would the husband get custody of the children?"

"That would be very likely, if my lesbianism came up. We've only been legally separated since May. I wanted the separation because it was a lie for me to say I wanted to be in a heterosexual relationship."

For most of her life Peg had known that she preferred women to men, but she had only admitted her lesbianism to herself three years before and had come out just over a year ago. She said, "I left because I didn't want to live the way I was living. My children aren't living with me. They're very important to me, but my husband drew the line at having them living with me. The only time he lost his temper was over that. He said he would not allow the children to be brought up in an unnatural environment. He had a few drinks in him that time. I asked him what he meant. He practically said I was a pervert. I had spent years thinking I was a pervert, and now I know, finally, that I'm not, so it didn't matter to me when he said that. But I felt that he had given a lot to the children, he had taken care of them for years, so I consented."

Peg felt that most Irish people saw homosexuality as a perversion and that there were as many homophobics within the gay community as there were outside it. "I think a lot of homosexuals think their inclination is unnatural themselves," she said. "I think some of them actually think they are perverted. I'd say in America there's probably more general openness that allows a person to know she's gay."

Peg sat forward on her chair, jacket still buttoned tight, shoulders hunched forward, feet apart, hands tucked between her knees, looking at me as if for an answer.

I said that in the United States homosexuality was more visible, if only because there was a bigger community and a stronger lobby. There were many more places a gay person could go in America; one could watch gay television and theater, read gay novels, hear gay issues discussed on mainstream shows—homosexuality appeared in the media more often in the States. I said to Peg, "Your husband says he doesn't want his children brought up in an unnatural environment; I assume he means lesbian. Probably ninety percent of Americans would agree with your husband. But, on the other hand, there are places in America, like San Francisco, where women aren't necessarily thinking about hiding the fact that they're gay when they go to work. They may be thinking more about getting the right to adopt a child or to be legally married to another woman or to be artificially inseminated. Problems for gays there are at a more sophisticated level, while the problems here are still rather rudimentary."

Orla gave me an approving punch in the arm. "You're right there, Rose," she said. "Part of the problem here is that people really aren't aware of homosexuality. People sometimes don't realize they might have a brother who's gay—he's maybe played tennis with another man down the road for years, and it never dawned on anybody that he might be gay. A lot of the older generation don't think anybody is gay. They wouldn't hear of it."

"Homosexuality is just not mentioned here," Peg said.

I made the point that where there existed a heightened consciousness or a heightened visibility of homosexuality, there could also be a heightened homophobia. Americans, so conscious of homosexuality, always seemed to be clamoring to know who was gay and who wasn't.

"While here, out of pure naiveté, it's the very last thing they think of," said Peg.

"Artificially inseminated," Mary murmured, still thinking about those fortunate women in San Francisco. She picked absently at the crumbling cork to the wine bottle and said, "I love babies. I was thinking of having a child, and I had a father lined up — he's gay — and we were going to have artificial insemination. But my ex-lover couldn't see how two women could raise a child. She thought it would be wrong. I told her not to be so Irish, but actually I know only one lesbian in Dublin who has got artificial insemination."

Orla brought up the subject of sexual harassment. "If they did a survey in this area to find out how many women have been raped or sexually harassed, I think they'd be surprised at the numbers. From each woman you'd get at least three or four occasions of harassment," she said.

"It's annoying the way men comment on women when they're going down the street," Mary said.

I said that I often responded to such remarks by turning around and speaking to the men.

Orla said, "You *would* do that because you're American. Too many times Irish women carry on and say nothing. Irish women always put themselves down about it. That kind of aggression is very high in Dublin at the weekend."

Mary said, "Normally I ignore it in Dublin, because you don't know what's going to happen. It could turn nasty. I remember around the time of the abortion referendum I was trying to get my mother to vote — but sure, there was no fuckin' hope of *that* — but anyway I was in Galway, coming home from the pub one night, and there were some young fellas across the street shouting what they'd like to do to us, and I shouted across to them, 'You wouldn't fuckin' know *what* to do with us!' But that was in Galway. I wouldn't do the same in Dublin." She chewed on a thumbnail for a moment, then said darkly, "Knives have been known to have been pulled here." She looked at me. "New York, I suppose, would be another thing altogether."

New York was indeed another thing altogether when compared to Dublin. One of the things I loved best about Dublin was the feeling that I could walk in the streets at night without fearing the footsteps behind me. Of course there was crime in Dublin, including rape, murder, kidnapping, and drug dealing. But those were not usual incidents, and when they did occur they inspired the sort of disbelief and lingering heartsickness many Americans have become inured to. The bulk of Dublin's crime fitted into the category of purse-snatching, shoplifting, pickpocketing, fare-evading, and joy-riding, and although knowing that appeased horrified Dubliners not a bit, it had a liberating effect on me. More than once I had wandered down Kildare Street at three in the morning, delighted by my freedom. But when I told a Dublin friend that I thought Dubliners were fortunate to be subjected to so little crime, he chided me soundly. When I laughed at the overcautious people who warned me with a wagging finger not to venture out after dusk, my friend made it eminently clear that Dublin's little crimes were as serious to Dubliners as New York's big crimes were to New Yorkers. "No level of crime is fortunate," he said, putting me tidily in my place.

Peg said, "You see American women on holiday here, and you can spot them a mile away. Just the way they walk with their heads up, like they have a right to walk. Very self-confident people they seem."

I said, "I feel some hostility in Dublin toward my Americanness. Strangers on the street sometimes make fun of my accent or comment in a snide way on the fact that I'm American."

Orla said, "We know an American woman who's been here for years. She's from Georgia O'Keeffe's part of the country. Some friends and I used to live with this woman in a flat, and we were all branded as Yankees. All they had to hear was one American accent and it was, 'Yankees, the lot of 'em!' And then when they discovered we were lesbians it became, 'Jesus! Surrounded by a pack of Yankee lesbians!'"

Kate said, "Irish women are not just apathetic; they have a totally defeated mentality. They've lost everything."

"We're not assertive at all," Orla said.

I wondered if that defeated mentality couldn't be applied to the society as a whole, for I found Irish men to be unassertive also. My Irish friends seemed to want to avoid conflict at all costs, didn't like to show their anger, wouldn't dare ask their landlord to fix something that wasn't working. They were set on being polite, which I supposed was what gave them the reputation of being a lovely people, easy to get along with, welcoming, and simple.

"At home when I say my name is Mahoney it's often an occasion for a joke," I said. "People say, 'Irish! Cute!' and they fling an arm around my shoulders and say, 'I bet you love to drink and I bet you have a big family and I bet love to sing, and I bet you can spin a yarn, play the fiddle, dance a jig on the head of a pin.'"

The women clapped their hands and hooted with delight at this absurdity. I said, "It's as though an Irish name gives people license to be familiar with you."

Shy Kate, after a long period of intense listening, suddenly cried, "Right! And what they don't say is, 'I bet you love to drink because it's your only fucking chance for happiness. You've such a big family you've no time to yourself, you sing because you're going out of your mind, you dance a jig because you can't sit still because your goddamn nerves are at you all the time."

Orla said, "I don't like conflict at all. I hate aggression. I hate violence and rows and arguments."

I said, "But there's a difference between aggression and simply saying what you want or feel. It's possible to say what you want without getting angry. I have the impression that Irish people don't face the landlord because once they get started they may lose their temper, and they're afraid that if they open their mouths flames might come shooting out in place of words. They don't seem to have figured out how to ask for what they want."

Kate said, "I have to say I would have serious trouble asking my landlord for anything."

"Why?" I said. "You're paying him rent."

"Because it's ingrained in you that you must take what is given to you and you must be polite."

"How is that ingrained in you?"

Orla, Mary, and Peg said simultaneously, "Convent school."

"We were all brought up in convent schools," Orla explained. "And in the convent school the idea is: let other people go before you. Be polite. Erase yourself. It's not important what you want as an individual. Never put another person out of place. Never upset another person. Open doors for other people. If you're the last person let onto the bus, don't make a show about it, for it's God's will. Maybe it's just as well that you didn't get a seat on that bus. Offer it up to God. And when you have that beaten into you for so many years, you can't change it very easily. The entire context for women in Ireland is of the convent school. That's the way convent students are brought up, and there are thousands upon thousands like us."

"They tell you to love your neighbor as yourself," Kate said, "which gets twisted and perverted and becomes hate yourself. Hate yourself and love your neighbor! I'm not joking you! I'm like that. I'm a really typical case. I open doors for everybody. I'd toss my jacket in the mud to let some other one step across on it."

I told the women that I had noticed that if you bumped into an Irish woman and it was entirely your fault, she would spin around and say, "Excuse me! How clumsy of me!" And if you went into a shop and asked, "How much is that book?" the salesperson would invariably say, "Three pounds, is that all right?" as though asking permission to charge this much.

Kate said, "You're absolutely right, Rose. And it's not trivial. It's sad."

"It's something you have to fight for within yourself or you'll be apologizing all the time," said Mary.

"I have such a losing battle with that," said Kate. "I go over to Germany and go into the shops, and people push in front of me in the queue. That's one thing I am not able to do. It freaks me out. How does it happen in their heads that they should go before me? That's at the root of a lot of trouble for me. I shake from head to toe if I complain about a thing like that, so I don't complain."

Kate was visibly upset; I thought she would cry. She seemed to be experiencing deep discomfort over this conversation. As she spoke, her soul seemed to well forth into the room. She passed a hand over her hot face as if to clear her mind. "Oh," she said weakly, "I can't stop thinking about school. I know that in school things are a bit different from life, particularly in convent school, but I don't think it's unrepresentative that the only topic of conversation at break or at lunchtime in school was boys, the boys in the school across the road, or rock stars, or whatever."

Peg removed her jacket, folded it in her lap, and said quietly, "Ye are all talking about convent schools. Now, myself, I wasn't only in a convent school. I was in a convent. I was a nun."

An astonished silence followed, and we all turned to look at Peg. Mary said, "Peg, I didn't ever know that."

Peg nodded calmly. "And you're talking about how they taught you to deny yourself? I remember when it was being decided that myself and another woman who entered the convent together were to be sent off to college. I was the one with a mathematical background, and I was dying to do a science degree, and they knew that, but they wouldn't send me for that. They decided the other woman would do the science degree."

Mary stared at Peg. "And what had you to do, Peg?"

"Nothing. I was never sent to do anything for ages."

The loud laughter that followed this revelation surprised me; these women could see humor in something that struck me as only painful. Peg continued, "This was supposedly so that I would develop better. They told me I had too much pride. And when they were deciding what religious names to give us when we were to be received as postulants—"

Mary interrupted Peg again; her interest was fierce. "But why didn't ye use your own names, Peg?"

"Oh, God, Mary, cop yourself on," Peg said. "This was in the old times that I was a nun. It's not like now. Wait till you hear it. The night before we were to be received, they came around and asked the women what would they like to be called. They asked my friend Anna what would she like to be called, and she said, 'Sister Joseph.' In those days you could call yourself after any saint. Well, I was never asked what name I wanted. I knew they had asked Anna and the others, and I knew I wasn't going to be asked, and I knew it was because they didn't like me. They didn't like me because I was strong-minded and expressed my opinions. I remember thinking that the worst name they could give me would be my own name, for it would mean that I hadn't truly been accepted. My Christian name is Margaret, right? So the next day we were lying on the floor during the ceremony, and the reverend mother approached us and said, 'Right then, Sister Mary Joseph!' to this one, and 'Sister Mary Catherine!' to that one, and 'Sister Mary Immaculata!' to the next one, and then to me she said, 'Right then, Sister Mary Margaret!' and I thought to myself, Good Christ almighty, she must be joking! I was purple with rage. And then, after taking your name, you had to go around to the choir, and you bowed to them, and they bowed to you, and one of the little nuns in the choir was very funny, because I had told her that if they called me Sister Margaret, I'd die, and when I bowed to that one, she whispered, 'Sister Mary Margaret!' grinning from one ear to the next. I was glad she did that, because it made me laugh when I felt like crying."

Peg spoke in a measured, reassuring way, as though she had the mystery of her entire life solved in her mind, and there was a tremor of humor in her voice.

"As part of the ceremony you left the church and went out to the common room, and the reverend mother followed you out with a massive big scissors and went snip, snip, snip"—Peg made an aggressive cutting motion around her head—"and cut all our hair off. The reverend mother *attacked* my hair. She didn't attack Anna's or anyone else's. She just attacked mine. You'd think she was pruning a yew tree."

I realized then that Kate, Orla, Mary, and I had been listening to Peg with our hands held to our faces, and when Peg mentioned the haircut, Kate's hands fluttered up to her head. In a tone that suggested she was genuinely worried about Peg, Mary said, "Oh, Peg! I think you should have made a decision not to stay on after that! You were going to be victimized your whole way through!"

Peg smiled. "I remember how I said, 'Dreadful!' when I saw my hair in a mirror. I was Sinead O'Connor before Sinead was even born. I must have got a cold in my head, for the next day in church—and I was the tallest person there—I fainted. The nun who was behind me said, 'Good God, Margaret, when you fainted, all I could see was this big white mountain coming toward me.' "

I asked Peg how long she had been in the convent.

"Three years. It was all right. You didn't have to worry about where your next meal was coming from, you had no decisions to make, you got the best of food, and if you didn't want to express your opinion about something, you were in the perfect place. But if things annoyed you, as they often annoyed me, you were lost."

Mary lifted her hands toward Peg. "Oh, Peg, whatever made you join in the first place?"

Peg shrugged. "I wanted to help people. I wanted to go out and do things for people. I thought that this was the perfect vehicle for that. In retrospect I see I was also running away from my sexuality. So many of the nuns who are in there are there for that reason. You wouldn't believe it. No one would believe it. But I definitely did want to help people. I've always wanted that."

Orla said, "Did you go to a convent school as a child?"

"In 1959 I went to boarding school in a little village in County Kilkenny. As somebody told me before, I've gone the scenic route."

"The scenic route?" I said.

"Boarding school, where you realize you're a lesbian but don't have a name for it and don't know what's happening. I thought I was a pervert. I thought my feelings were unnatural."

"You didn't know that this was a way of being and that there were other people like you?"

"Not at all, Rose! I was living in the Irish countryside! I was barely in boarding school when I had my first crush on a female. I was thirteen. I can still see her. She'd brown eyes and auburn curly hair. She was gorgeous and thin and had very thin hands. Her name was Grainne. She was gorgeous, but she was involved with somebody else."

"Not another girl?" Mary said.

"Yeah. Another girl."

Orla said, "Come off it, Peg!"

"It's true. And they slept together. This was in school. They slept together, and according to one of the girls who was in the dormitory with them, there'd be unusual noises in the middle of the night coming from them. They were actually in a physical relationship. I was really very fond of that girl and was heartboken when she left. I had various little liaisons with other students, but I still kept saying to myself that I shouldn't be doing this, that this was not right. I couldn't understand the fascination that the rest had for boys, and I was roped along because everybody was doing it. Then for the last year of boarding school I decided I was going to stop all this perversion and I was going to be extremely holy, because I was going to be a nun, and I never looked left, right, or center at anybody for that year, and then I joined the convent, whereupon I promptly fell in love with another nun." Peg slapped her knee. "Ha-ha! So I left. I ran away from it and myself. I worked for a couple of years and tried very hard to be heterosexual, with the result that I would wake up in the morning and not know who the hell was in the bed beside me."

We were all leaning slightly forward now, the better to hear Peg's story. "What do you mean, Peg?" I said.

Peg's response was a loud laugh. She pointed a finger at me. "Rose," she boomed, "you're very innocent for an American!"

"Well, what?" I said. "You mean you slept around?"

Peg laughed again. "And you're also very Irish, Rose. That's your whole problem!"

The women laughed, and Orla seized my arm as a way of apologizing for this teasing.

Peg continued her saga. "That period is the real shame of my life. For about two years I was so determined that I was going to be heterosexual that I was wild. But I am one of the few people who has been rewarded for her sins; I had a son who is my pride and joy, and he was the result of my sleeping around and my promiscuous lifestyle. I was an umarried mother. Some years later I married. I didn't marry in a church as most people do here, especially out in the country. I got married in the Registry Office, the front room of the registrar's house in Rathdrum. I was thirty, which was quite old, and I was married for twelve years when I finally admitted to myself that this was all false."

"Was it difficult to be an unmarried mother?" I said.

Peg leaned away from me with a skeptical frown on her face. "Of course it was difficult! That didn't happen an awful lot here, or if it did you never heard about it. There were no unmarried mothers around. The organizations for unwed mothers hadn't been started at that time. But I survived. And here I am now. Living the way I want to. And I am very proud of it."

Kate said, "I wonder how many women must have done the same and stayed in the convent."

Peg said, "Lots. Around the country you'll find an awful lot of women who are getting trouble for their differentness, but it must be much more difficult for a working-class woman in Dublin. She cannot escape. She must have the children and wash and feed and clothe them. Men are also caught up in that. When I started working in Dublin, which meant that I commuted all the way from Arklow, Paddy, my husband, had to be the househusband, and it was difficult for him to do that in a rural town. He'd go down to the pub and talk about it to the men. He'd say, 'What oh what'll I give the kids for dinner?'"

Kate asked Peg whether she ever saw her husband now. "Every week," Peg said. "I talk to him when he brings the kids up to Dublin. He's a good friend. He's the best man in all Ireland. We have a laugh and a joke, and that's good for the children. My son is nineteen. He knows I'm gay, but the other two don't."

Inspired by Peg's tale, Mary said sheepishly, "I had a close call once. I got engaged. I talked myself into it." She stared silently at the greasy bag of chips on the table, conjuring the event of the engagement, and when that ghost passed through her, she shrugged and rubbed the African cap back and forth on her head as though rubbing away a pain and said cheerily, "Ha-ha! Oh, well!"

Mary told us about a friend of hers who became pregnant before she was married. "She and the boyfriend were going to marry eventually, but the pregnancy just happened too soon. The woman was literally packed up and sent off, was made to leave college and go off to London to have the baby at her brother's house. They were nineteen and twenty, and his father made him go over to London after the girl. Eventually, when they came back to Ireland, they got married. The mother arrived at the wedding at the last minute. There was no one but the bride and the groom and two witnesses, and when the mother arrived you'd think by the face on her that it was a funeral she was attending. This was 1979. We went out for a drink afterwards and we tried to get rid of the mother, because she was full of, 'Oh, how in the name of Jesus did I raise a daughter like this!' To this day that mother blames every worry she ever had on the daughter. She refuses to see the child and lies about his age to fix it properly with the date of the marriage. When my mother heard that story she said to me, 'Mary, if you ever do that to me, I'll kill you!' "

Peg said, "My son was about three months old when I finally told my mother about him, and she turned her back on me at that stage, and after that everything was blamed on me. She died three and a half years ago, and my sister told me on the day of her funeral that it was I that had killed her."

Mary's apartment seemed to grow very quiet; I could hear the faint static of the radio, tuned to no station, and the disconsolate voice of a little girl on the street shrieking, "Ma! Tell him to leave me alone!"

Poisoned Permission

Following eavan boland's directions, I made my way to her house in Dundrum, a suburb south of Dublin. Boland's street, quiet and orderly, was like any street in any American suburb: small, modern, semidetached houses, slender young birch and palm trees, Volvos and Toyotas gleaming in shrub-lined driveways.

As I walked up the street, a tinker woman and her two children approached me. The woman's thick-knuckled hand slipped from her son's dirty grip and presented itself to me, and in the velvety, ghost-like voice peculiar to Irish tinkers she said, "Change?"

I was surprised to see this woman here, for I had come to identify tinkers with noisy city street corners and muddy caravan camps set up in empty lots. In Dublin the tinkers' sole occupation was begging, but on a street like this there would probably be no one to beg from all day but me. I gave the woman a coin and moved on.

The day was cloudy and close. Powered by a faint breeze, stiff palm fronds scraped eerily along the asphalt with a creaking rattle. To the south, beyond the village of Ballinteer, lay the foothills of the

Dublin Mountains. Years before I had lived not far from here, and every day on my way home from school I watched these hills alternately glow and darken in the moody sunlight. The hills were a reminder that beyond Dublin's pale lay Ireland, a wild, rolling countryside.

Eavan Boland is one of Ireland's best-known poets and certainly the nation's best-known woman poet. Her work is an exploration of women's relationship to history, stories of women that have never been told in books, lives lived in a realm uninspected and unsung. She writes of these subjects with an assurance that bespeaks tradition and like company, although until recently the poetry of women in Ireland has been virtually nonexistent and Boland has been alone in her efforts. At the time she began writing, in the early sixties, Boland had no anchoring precedent. Of the start of her career she has written, "I believe . . . that when a woman poet begins to write she very soon becomes conscious of the silences which have preceded her, which still surround her. . . . There were no women poets, old or young, past or present, in my immediate environment."

One of the first things I learned in Ireland was how difficult it was for women writers to gain recognition. A week before my meeting with Eavan Boland I had talked with Ailbhe Smythe, the editor of Attic Press, Ireland's only women's press. If anyone was aware of the great constraints placed on women writers and their work it was Ailbhe Smythe. During our meeting Smythe echoed Boland's thoughts on the context of women's writing in Ireland. "I think the notion that women can actually say very political things in ways which women want to say them, I think there's a tremendous wariness about doing that—a fear that it won't be heard. Which is justified. It is not paranoia. There is a difficulty here in encouraging very political women to put themselves on the line and write."

I said to Smythe, "I know there's a feeling among the mostly male literary establishment here that there's a lowering of standards in women's writing. Is that true or is it not?"

She laughed and said, "Oh, that's classic! That's what that is! How do I know? We don't publish substandard writing. I mean if they see it that way, it's obviously somebody else who's doing it. I think what they mean is that women's writing is really very successful, it sells very well, therefore there's something wrong with it, because everybody knows that literary writing doesn't sell very well. It's a classic double thing. *A lowering of standards in women's writing!* I think that is a very dangerous and disgraceful thing to say, and it is also not at all unexpected. It is said generally, and there are also women who say it. Whether you're talking about culture, literature, visual arts, the business world, or education and the academic world, in a culture which is so desperately patriarchal and which is so shit-scared of women, a kind of double standard applies, and a doubly high expectation of women. Men would do anything to keep women at arm's length. I'm not going to sit here and say that Attic Press has never published a bad book. But what male publisher can honestly say that? They would never have to say it in the first place. They wouldn't get themselves into that situation. They wouldn't even be asked that question. You would not be going to a male publisher and saying, 'I have heard it said that the standard of the male writers in this country is really not very high.' They'd be outraged."

꧁

THAT EAVAN BOLAND has made her mark on the Irish literary landscape is a testament, not just to her great gifts as a poet but to her strength as a person who lives by her convictions.

The front door of Boland's house was open, and through it I could see a teenage girl sitting at a table toward the back of the house. At the sound of my knock the girl got up and came out, followed by a slightly younger girl. They were Boland's daughters, Sarah and Eavan, fifteen and twelve, respectively. They were pretty and slim and remarkably long-legged. They had big, embarrassed smiles and very long fair hair several shades away from copper. The younger girl wore braces on her teeth, and there was something sad in the eyes of the older girl, some teenage oppression. Their politeness, shyness, and exceptional good manners made me oddly uneasy; their behavior had the distinctly constrained quality of the rehearsed.

Eavan Boland came down the stairs dressed in a khaki skirt and conservative checked oxford shirt, the sort one might find at L. L. Bean's. On her pale unstockinged feet she wore the black penny loafers of a schoolgirl. She wore no makeup and little jewelry. The sleeves of her shirt were rolled above her elbows in the style of a country farmer. She looked prepared for hard work, prepared to dirty her hands. She had a pleasant face with high cheekbones, a small mouth, and very round, serious eyes. Her shoulder-length hair, with bangs cut across her fore-head, was flaming red and thick as a whisk broom. She had a slightly nervous, slightly breathless manner. She shook my hand firmly and told the girls to run along, and they scurried obediently up the stairs in a way that belonged to much younger children. The way Boland spoke to them struck me; it was purring, coaxing, soft-voiced, the kind of voice one might use to mask a terrible quarrel that has taken place only moments before. I was reminded of Boland's poem "Contingencies," in which women spoke to children "with a sweet mildness in front of company."

Boland opened a window, then motioned me into the armchair before it. I sat and felt a light breeze blow distractingly across the top of my head. As she went into the kitchen to get us coffee, I noticed she had an athletic walk—the slow, swaggering stride of a wrestler—but in this walk there was also an unmistakable and confounding fem-inine grace.

Boland's house was the modern sort the Irish call American, with a front door that opened directly into the living room rather than into a foyer or hallway. The furniture in the small living room was arranged in a haphazard fashion. A low coffee table in the middle of the room was so overloaded with trinkets and figurines, tiny carvings, painted eggs, a pocket watch, and other small, highly detailed artifacts that the table's surface was barely visible. When I managed—with difficulty—to focus on each discrete object I could see its beauty, but heaped together like this the initial effect was of rubble or the contents of a child's toy trunk. Another coffee table placed before the sofa was equally crowded with magnificent antique optical devices: a small brass microscope, tortoiseshell binoculars, two ancient telescopes, opera glasses. But again, so many beautiful things were piled together there that their beauty was obscured, and I found it difficult to distin-guish them at all. The tables left the impression of a householder in the process of cleaning out her attic and not knowing where to put things for the moment.

Boland returned from the kitchen and handed me a wide-bottomed mug shaped like a nuclear reactor. She sat in a chair across the room from me, and I realized after a moment that neither of us had any place to rest our mugs, for not only were the tables overloaded, they were all situated too far from the armchairs to be reached without getting up. Following Boland's lead, I put my mug on the floor by my feet. I wondered about the arrangement of furniture; it was as though the visitor was forewarned not to get too comfortable here or stay too long. Beneath Boland's loafers was a piece of carpet cut from the same carpet laid wall to wall, protecting the spot where her feet habitually rested.

Boland had agreed to allow me to tape our conversation and now, for want of a better place to put it, I laid my tape recorder on the floor and gave it a shove with my foot; it slid across the carpet and came to a stop midway between Boland and me. She lifted her hand toward me and said, "Oh, we'll do that. Don't worry, we'll do that in a bit. Hardly at this moment. You don't want to turn that on yet."

"I don't?"

"No. You can turn it on in two minutes."

I got up and turned the recorder off, worried that she was going to be difficult. But when I was seated again, Boland began, to my surprise, to talk with seductive candor. She talked enthusiastically about her friend Mary Robinson, Ireland's president. She talked about the poet Seamus Heaney, a man she liked and had known for years, but who many women felt had not done enough to rectify the invisibility women writers suffered in the Irish literary world. She talked about the anti-feminist book editor of the *Irish Times*. She talked about Edna O'Brien, Gore Vidal, Jacqueline Onassis, Helen Vendler, Sharon Olds, Louise Gluck, Adrienne Rich, Mary Gordon, and *The New Yorker* magazine. She had strong opinions about many subjects. From time to time her speech grew bright with vulgarity. She had a bristling intelligence and an elegant, adamant, urgent manner of speaking. Too, she had a way of heaping words and clauses so heavily upon each other that their meaning at times became obscured. I had to work to keep up with her, and it struck me how like the crowded coffee tables her speech pattern was.

I knew that Ireland's male literary establishment routinely attacked Eavan Boland for being too feminine and feminist, and that the feminist left attacked her for not being feminist enough. In the essay "The Woman Poet: Her Dilemma," Boland examined this trap, arguing that because they have no poetic precedent, women poets have been pressured to distort their emotions and experiences to make them acceptably "poetic." At the same time they face an equally dangerous pressure from separatist feminist thought, which urges them to reject the patriarchal poetic past and replace it with their own anger. In addition to these obstacles, Eavan Boland has often come under attack for her privileged background, for being too suburban a poet, too middle class, too domestic in her concerns.

When the preliminary conversation had run its course, I switched on my tape recorder and asked Boland how she perceived these obstacles. She sat with her hands on the arms of the chair in the spot where one's elbows usually rest, giving the impression that she was about to hoist herself out of the chair. She lifted her chin thoughtfully and said, "It troubles me that I probably have a profile which protected me. I have a first-class degree from Trinity College, which meant that literary editors initially might have found me more reliable for reviewing Restoration comedy, although of course I'm not nearly as reliable as the woman who's an actress or the woman who put the light on the stage. I'm not as illuminating to the reader, but nevertheless my profile makes me slightly more respectable. Then again I'm metropolitan. Living in a city and going to Trinity College allows you to make an oblique entry to areas of contact. And I came from a middle-class background, and that has made me an object of great suspicion. The other side of that is that I hear vicious remarks against women who come into the arts from working-class backgrounds. It seems to me that there is a class consciousness on the part of many of the people who perceive the arts, and that class consciousness does nobody any credit. There are a thousand things to say that are wrong with my poetry, but where I was born and the employ of my parents is not one of them."

I had heard that Eavan Boland's father was, in his day, the richest man in Ireland. I didn't ask her whether this was true, but it was clear that her family had been prominent. Her father was the first Irish ambassador to England, and in 1950, when she was five, the family moved to London. When she was twelve her father became the president of the United Nations, and the family moved to New York.

One of the arguments I had heard against Boland was that she could not possibly represent Irish women because she had not shared the experience of the majority of them. I mentioned this, and she smiled widely, as though she had heard it too often. With marked dis-

dain for the idea she said, "No poet has ever *represented* a people.
Poets represent themselves and the private obsessive world out of
which they make the poem. I make zero claims to do anything but
give the view I have of the time I live in, the obstructions I've found,
and the freedoms I've gained. And that is representative of nobody,
and if I had a mainstream background that connected me to the
majority of the people in any country I would find it extraordinarily
arrogant, dangerous, and inappropriate to claim that I represented
them. I'm not a politician, I'm a poet. Poets *subvert* representation.
They do not make a sort of stand on things. And to make them an
index of a community has never worked. Yeats is not representative
and is still being attacked in this country for his Anglo-Irish background. I want to be absolutely fair about this. I don't want to cheap-
en that argument or glamorize that argument or say I'm an individual
and I'm being falsely represented as someone who is not representative. Perhaps a country that has a bardic tradition has a hunger for the
representative poet, but the Irish community has an extremely disreputable history in its transactions with its artists. Its requirements
that the artist be representative kept James Joyce out of the bookshops in this country until 1969. You still couldn't get *Ulysses* in the
bookshops in the early sixties, and that is because they felt that this
man with his obscene view of the lived life in his time was not *representative* of the Irish people. The claims of the Irish people have usually been suspect, and they have led to the most draconian censorship
laws outside of the political tyranny."

※

AT A FORUM on censorship I had heard Maurice Earl, the manager of
one of Dublin's most popular bookstores, detailing the history of literary censorship in Ireland. Earl maintained that the Catholic Church,
which in mid-twentieth-century Ireland had tremendous social power,
wanted a state that would recognize health, education, welfare, and
morality as areas of Church rather than state jurisdiction. It was this
powerful Church presence that stifled Irish civil society. Chief among
the clergy's concerns was that books might contain challenges to
Church orthodoxy and authority. Writers were seen as harmful and
dangerous, and censorship was the most effective way of dealing with
the threat they posed. Among the Irish writers banned following the

establishment in 1922 of the Irish Free State were James Joyce, Sean O'Faolain, Sean O'Casey, Liam O'Flaherty, Oliver St. John Gogarty, Maura Laverty, George Bernard Shaw, Patrick Kavanagh, John McGahern, Brian Moore, Kate O'Brien, Walter Mackin, and Austin Clark. Foreign writers banned included Sherwood Anderson, Truman Capote, Joyce Cary, John Dos Passos, William Faulkner, F. Scott Fitzgerald, Anatole France, Sigmund Freud, Maxim Gorky, Graham Greene, Ernest Hemingway, Christopher Isherwood, Arthur Koestler, Norman Mailer, Thomas Mann, Somerset Maugham, Margaret Mead, Nicholas Montserrat, Alberto Moravia, George Orwell, Marcel Proust, Bertrand Russell, J. D. Salinger, Stephen Spender, John Steinbeck, H. G. Wells, and Thomas Wolfe.

(One of the first contributions to the debate over the Censorship Act came from W. B. Yeats, whose Protestant argument, placing private conscience above public authority, was rejected by the Catholic majority. Yeats had won the Nobel Prize for literature, yet in Catholic Ireland he was vilified. Maurice Earl remarked upon a commentary that appeared in the *Catholic Bulletin* after Yeats's death, which read: "A curious effort was made quite recently to impose the 'study' of the pointless outpourings of W. B. Yeats on all schools." The commentary dubbed the proposal "sinister" and instead recommended the study of "high grade prose literary material which will possibly constitute the study of a permanent Christian philosophy.")

Of course, the most obvious target of Irish literary censorship was sexual activity. Aristotle and Cato were banned in Ireland, not because of objections to the philosophy but because of objections to Greek sexual practices. (One result of the "antisexual crusade" of the Irish Catholic Church was that by 1952 only two out of five Irish men between the ages of thirty and thirty-four were married, the lowest proportion in the world; Ireland had the world's highest recorded age of marriage.)

But Ireland's putative sexual repression always puzzled me, for whenever I thought of rural Ireland I thought of a relatively uninhibited, notably irreverent people. I thought of the Irish villagers I had met who were forever making sexual allusions, who revealed their desires without undue shame, who arrived at midnight Mass (if they arrived at all) roaring drunk. I thought of people like Conor MacNamara and his family, and I had to question the stereotype.

According to Maurice Earl, the Irish attitude toward sex had once been the "standard, exuberant and uninhibited attitude found throughout peasant Europe." Earl cited the stories, drawn from the oral tradition, of two Munster peasants, which were published during the thirties in the folklore collection *The Tailor of Ansty*, edited by Eric Cross. The bawdiness of the stories was evidently so shocking that the local priest burned the book and forced the two guilty peasants to kneel and denounce their statements. During the Irish Senate's debate over the book, senators reportedly covered their ears to block out the lewd excerpts that were, of necessity, read aloud. According to Earl the advocates of censorship often claimed to be upholding traditional Irish values of purity. But it was *The Tailor of Ansty* and bawdy books like it that in fact showed traditional Irish attitudes. Earl said, "Oral Irish lore indicated that the puritanism of the twentieth century was in fact a new phenomenon."

BOLAND CROSSED her legs and bounced her loafered foot and said, "I understand that some of the skepticisms about me not being representative are because people do emerge as totems, because they are one of the few people who emerge, or something like that. One of the things I've always been careful to do is not to say what Irish women's poetry is. But I *have* made a point of saying what obstructs it. I've given a lot of workshops. I've lived in the male literary community. I know what goes on, and I am very clear about what is obstructive to the development and emergence and sustenance of the woman poet in this community."

"What?"

"Oh, there are several important obstructions. One goes back to what a society is. Nobody wants to look at this view because it is antithetical to the romantic perception of literature. Society has issued ugly, complicated societal permissions to people to be poets. Everybody wants to think that what Whistler said is true: 'No prince can depend on it, no cottage is safe from it.' 'Tisn't true. That's a Victorian notion of the artist. Look at one of the very painful and, to me, heartrending chapters of poetry in our time and for centuries: American black poetry. There have been some wonderful talents and some wonderful voices, and there have been enormous obstructions, enormous blindnesses, inabilities to include them, inabilities to realize that a society without that voice, a poetry without that voice, a critique without that voice is incomplete. But really, the first obstruction is the societal punishment. I've often quoted this, and I'm afraid I'm requoting it, but I was in a workshop ten years ago in a southeastern town, and a woman from a small town was in the workshop, and I spoke about something I believe to be true, which is that there's a very elusive difference between writing a poem and being a poet. You write the poem in a moment of feeling; you become the poet in a whole very complex set of transactions. And I said to this woman, 'Would you say of yourself, "I am a poet?"' and she said to me, 'If I said I was a poet in my town, people would think I didn't wash my windows.' And a whole sort of panorama opened of the expectations of her as a woman and the perceptions of the poet."

I told Boland that several months before, I had attended a public reading at a poetry festival in Galway. People of all ages and from all spheres of life came in off the street to read, and the reading went on all afternoon. I noticed that eight of ten poets were men, and without fail they were flamboyant, confident, proud, and delighted to be standing before an audience, while the women seemed shy, uncertain, and embarrassed, reading haltingly, with their pages of poetry held like shields before their faces. The women hurried off the stage when they were done, as if concerned that someone might recognize them. After the reading I spoke with a young woman, a student of journalism at University College Galway, who said, as many Irish women did, "I write poetry at home." When I asked why she hadn't read anything that day, she answered, "I'm only an amateur! I couldn't stand in front of people and read!" If an educated woman felt this way, I wondered how others less privileged and less affirmed must feel.

Boland nodded and covered her mouth with her hand as I spoke, listening with generous deference—she seemed to be struggling to mask her own desire to speak again. At times she shifted halfway around in her seat and threw one arm across the back of the chair with a sprawling, boyish physical ease. I asked her if the woman in her workshop had been able to make a distinction between the way she perceived herself and the way others perceived her. Was it that she was unable to say, "I am a poet," to others, or was she unable also to say it to herself?

Boland cupped her chin in her hand and peered at me. "Well, the outer censorships and the inner censorships are always very closely connected. The self-censorship in a person like a woman who doesn't say to herself, 'I am a poet,' comes from the fact that she feels she is presuming to say it. The young male poet very often doesn't feel he's presuming. One considers it a birthright and the other doesn't. That means that society has handed out the permission traditionally, by inheritance, by assumption, by gender stereotypes. It has handed out permission to the young male to say, I am a poet, and it's handed out a much more poisoned series of permissions to the woman, which are much more conditional, which force her to say, well, I can write a poem, but perhaps by doing so I am editing or constraining my other obligations. And that's the major obstruction, and it needs to be looked at. Of course, there are very important things in the poetry itself which require the poet to have the courage of her experience. To get that courage you have to have it partly by example, partly by obsession, and partly by relation to form. For many women who write poetry in this country it becomes a part of a secret life. They don't publish it, they don't send it out, they don't do it in public, and they keep it away from their families."

"Will that change?" I asked.

"I've had so many workshops with so many excellent women, and there has been such excellence in what they have done and there's been such achievement, but the actual distance from writing that poem to being that poet . . ." Boland paused for a long moment, indicating how great was the distance. "You can't enter the poetic discourse until you say, 'I am a poet,' and you've got to face the psychic pressure, which is enormous in the Irish poetic community. There is enormous psychic pressure, and therefore there is an enormous psychic investment in the power in that community and where it will shift to. Somebody like myself, who is perceived in different ways, is still very isolated within that community."

I found it difficult to fathom how one of the nation's best-known poets could feel herself isolated within its poetic community.

"Oh, I think I am. It's never easy to see things, but yes, I am."

"You're isolated within the community of women, or the community of men?"

"Within the community of men. I understand my relation to the women quite well. I am much more hurt by an attack from a woman than from a man. And I much more regret it but understand some-times where it's coming from. I have much less personal feeling about being attacked by men. I have been attacked by male writers since the day I began writing in this country. I have no feelings about it. I did have feelings about it, but I'm really very impersonal about it now. And I'm very adroit at recognizing languages of psychosexual domi-nation and resentment, when people can't recognize them them-selves. I don't hold it against them, but it's interesting to me. I brought out a book of poetry called *Nightfeed* in 1982. It was about the children when they were small. It was a very deliberate book. There was a very deliberate positioning of the lyric moment, where I thought the lyric moment was in the lived life as I saw it. And I knew perfectly well I was going up against two really formidable orthodox-ies; one was the romantic orthodoxy that you didn't write about this because it wasn't that important, and the other was the admirable feminist—or separatist—orthodoxy that would have argued that I was writing about oppressive conventions and thereby exalting them. And I knew very well what I was doing. And I knew what kind of response I would get. That was not really so much a difficulty, but what was very interesting was the language with which men spoke about that book. They almost never were able to say they liked the book, or they prefaced what they said by saying, 'My *wife* read it and liked it,' and what they finally were able to do was to indicate the con-tempt they had for the life that was presented in that book and begrudgingly accept the fact that it had come into poetry. And what was so fascinating to me was not how they responded to my poetry but that they walked out the door in the morning with that contempt in their minds, leaving the life their family lived with all its precious reality, intellectually distancing themselves. And that is, in a sense, a subsection being allowed to continue in society and in an intellectual discourse.

"Now, because of the great pressures in the intellectual communi-ty in the English language, and in the United States and increasingly in England and coming from the French—partly the French revi-sions of the viewpoint of women, the language of women—I have been able in a very small way to put considerable pressure on people, to remind people at certain moments that midnight has struck about all this, that the cheerful contempt that you could imply for women, their lives, their values, the cheerful way you could nominate the feminine community as the lesser one, that that's going. If you wish to hold a responsible position in the academy, you cannot come in happily trumpeting these views anymore. They are deeply disreputable views, they always were, but they are now seen to be what they are: very shabby sustenances of a power that never should have been there. So, in a sense, though I do feel isolated and exasperated at times, I know that those great shifts have taken place."

In her essay "Outside History" Boland points out that where women were once merely "the subjects and objects" of Irish poetry, they are now becoming the authors of it, and that in light of the way women have been used and portrayed in the poetry, this transition is a difficult one. She writes:

> The majority of Irish male poets depended on women as motifs in their poetry.... The women in their poems were often passive, decorative, raised to emblematic status.... To me these passive and simplified women seemed a corruption. Moreover the transaction they urged on the reader, to accept them as mere decoration, seemed to compound the corruption.... It seemed to me a species of human insult that at the end of all, in certain Irish poems, [women] should become elements of style rather than aspects of truth.

And further:

> A society, a nation, a literary heritage is always in danger of making up its communicable heritage from its visible elements. Women, as it happens, are not especially visible in Ireland.

I asked Boland how her work was received when she was first being recognized by the critics, who were — and still are — predominantly male.

"It was always mixed. To this day the response to my work has always been very mixed. I think I've come in for really personal, savage attacks, which as a reviewer I would never do. I just wouldn't get into that stuff. It's dangerous personal stuff. I think I have attracted very venomous personal attacks by male poets and male writers and male reviewers, which are very translucent. I have always got a lot of breaks too, so it's mixed. One time I think it was unmixed was in 1980 when I published a book called *In Her Own Image*, and then there was universal blame. Universal. No woman anywhere reviewed that book in this country, and there was a tremendous amount of very personal aggrievance by the male community."

At that moment the doorbell rang, and Boland got up to answer it. From where I sat I couldn't see who was at the door, but I could tell by the voice that it was a tinker woman. The woman was asking for money, saying, "I have a child." Boland said kindly, "Oh, let's see, love. I don't have much here," and I heard the woman thanking Boland for whatever it was she handed over.

In Boland's brief absence I noticed, on a table so crowded with photographs that I remember few of the faces, one particular picture; it was a candid shot of four men, one of whom looked like John F. Kennedy.

When the woman had gone and Boland was seated again, she said to me, "This is tinker country."

I asked her about the photograph. "Yes," she said, glancing at the photograph with a somewhat amused expression, "it's Kennedy and my father." She was silent for a moment, then said, "I hate that old photo. All those men in gray suits."

We both looked at the photograph, and then I asked her who was reading her poetry in Ireland.

"That's a very good question. I have no idea. It's difficult to say. I think—and I know every poet says this—I think I put a poem together differently from a lot of people. I'm very interested in the technical putting together of a poem. In the ongoing national controversy in which occasionally I enter as a pretext that never gets seen, nobody ever looks at that. Something comes up about the suburbs and women and background, you know. But a person like myself may well have two readerships, one for technique and one for theme. And in some ways I imagine that some younger poets would be reading me technically, that they would be able to get past the theme and look at it technically, which is not quite right. And I imagine that there are other people a little bit outside the poetic community, who because I touch on the themes of their lives buy these books."

"I meet a lot of working-class women who are very aware of you and appreciate your experience as expressed in the poetry."

"Yeah, well, you see they lived the life I live. There is actually no substantive difference between my life and their life. I may well have a machine they don't have, but I still bring my kids to school. We live the same life. That is what people who are so hung up on class don't see, that the life lived in a house in a community in this country is very widely experienced. I live the life of most women in this country who have children."

I asked Boland what sort of responses she got from her readers.

"It's very hard to put this," she said. "I live in a sort of small and constant circle of tension about responses. I'm one of the people that people have had difficulties with, and that is because I've written the Irish poem and put pressure on the Irish poem and haven't fitted into the main stereotype of the Irish poem, and that's been problematic for everybody everywhere."

I brought up the fact that in "Outside History" she refers to Ireland as having been her nation before it was actually her country. She said, "I believe that happened to Jewish people. Long before the state of Israel. I believe that actually is something that happens to the exiled expatriate. There's a point there when they pick up a static feeling of who they are in that text and context. My father came from a generation of diplomats, and this was a very difficult time, 1950. Ireland in 1948 had gone from being a member of the commonwealth to being a republic. For the first time, therefore, my father became an ambassador—you see, you can't be an ambassador of a dominion state of a country, only a high commissioner—and so I came to an awareness of Ireland through all kinds of oblique and odd things. I mean, there was a harp on the plates in the embassy in London."

Boland said the embassy was a bleak building, that London for that matter was a rather bleak place at the time. Her parents were not super-Irish patriots and had no particularly nationalistic language that could have influenced her; they had a very complicated view of Ireland and its relationship to England. They venerated Irish literature and were great admirers of Joyce and Yeats and others. Boland described her father, a graduate of Trinity College and Harvard University, as being cool and intelligent and profoundly anti-British, "though he didn't look it." She said, "My father told me much later that when he went to the 1947 Commonwealth Conference in London and argued with the commonwealth countries about the status that Ireland would have once she became a republic, he made the remark, 'I know that Australia and Canada wish to remain in the dominion, but there is not a house in Ireland which has not shuddered to the words "open in the name of the king."' And so that emotive language lay under the surface of a lot of the decorum which existed.

"The way that I picked up on Ireland was through very small hints, very small residues. My father had a very clear sense of the role of a small country and a very emotive sense — well hidden — of the remarkable history of that country in that century. I remember once standing beside him — which gives you an idea of the way a child picks something up — I was standing beside him when I was about six, maybe seven; King George VI had died, so my father went to present his credentials again, and I said to him, 'Well, did you meet the queen?' He said he had, and I said, 'Well, what did you think of her?' and he said, 'The queen and I haven't much in common.'" Boland looked at the ceiling and laughed. "I always remembered that remark. The sort of small musks and fragrances that you pick up as you go along. I think a childhood in another country is a complicated thing, but I definitely had a sense of a nation and I definitely knew I was Irish.

"I went to New York in 1956, at age twelve, and went to a Catholic school there. The Hungarian uprising had taken place, and some Catholic Hungarian exiles came to that school. And one day a girl sat down beside me and looked at me; she had no language, nothing, and I instantly knew she was a child without a country. I remember going home to my mother and telling her. Although she couldn't talk, I knew who the girl was and I knew my relation to her and I knew what I felt. Though it is not something that children are meant to sense in an exact way, I definitely knew what a nation was. And I knew which was mine."

As the hours of the afternoon increased Boland became more engaging and engaged. She was electric with ideas, and I felt strongly that it was in part her tremendous energy that had allowed her to maintain her beliefs in the face of the opposition and disrespect her own society had worked to defeat her with.

Halfway through our meeting Boland turned her attention to a cat that had come down the stairs, and in a voice suddenly filled with sweetness she called out, "Eavan! Bring Corky down, love!"

I had been here nearly three hours, and in that time I had heard not a sound from the two girls. It surprised me when young Eavan's voice answered immediately and sweetly and very clearly and calmly from the top of the stairs, "Okay"; it was as though she had spent the past three hours sitting on the top step waiting for this call.

Boland pointed to the cat and said warmly to me, "This cat had kittens. Unfortunately, three of the kittens died, but we have one left. And we have this cat's mother. Her mother is a magnificent beast who is in a tremendous sulk all of a sudden."

Suddenly I remembered hearing somewhere that Eavan Boland had lost one of her children—how or when or whether that was actually true I didn't know.

The two girls came down the stairs, Sarah carrying a tiny black kitten in her arms. Sarah came over to me and placed the kitten in my lap. Her mother watched carefully, smiling. Her tone and mood seemed to have changed. She clearly loved this kitten. The five-week-old kitten was mewling and milky-eyed. I asked the girls if they were going to keep him. They giggled and smiled their pretty smiles and said, "Yeah."

The kitten sniffed at a button on my jacket. "You must be glad about that," I said.

"Yeah." They nodded their heads at me. Again they seemed, in manner, younger than they were.

Boland said, "I wonder whether you shouldn't put him out in the garden," and Sarah said, "Okay."

When the girls had gone, I commented on their beautiful hair.

"Yes," Boland said. "They're great. They're going back to school soon."

I said, "Your girls are very polite. Very well mannered."

"Irish children often are," she said. "It's not that American young people aren't; I think actually that American young people are more forthcoming, but there's a much larger division between the adult and the child in this country than there is in America."

I commented on the sophisticated vocabulary of Irish children.

"Yes. The way people speak in this country is very interesting. I was looking at some program when Sarah was a little younger, and I said, 'Look at that!' and Sarah said, 'Now Mummy, I don't have your demented fascination with that.' That is so much an Irish remark. That interesting edge the Irish have of both exaggeration and extension. It's truly a common possession."

Boland went on to talk about the art of fiction writing. "Of all the worlds that seem to me to be under pressure—I mean poetry always comes and goes—but the new fiction writers are under pressure." She pointed at my tape recorder and said, "I'll tell you who, if you'll just turn that recorder off for a second."

Mna Na hEireann

O N A SATURDAY MORNING in December I stood on the bridge that passed over the river Fergus and led out of Corofin toward Ennis. I was hoping to thumb a ride to Ennis, where I would catch the bus to Dublin. The next morning I was to meet Mary Robinson, Ireland's president, at Aras an Uachtarain, the Irish equivalent of the White House. The day was rainy and windy. There were very few cars on the road that morning, and I was prepared to wait a long time for a lift. The riverbanks were carpeted with rooks and magpies, huge, hard-beaked birds who slinked through the grass with gliding, catlike movements, letting out sinister cries like warnings. An old black dog jogged down the road, jumped up onto the bridge's narrow stone wall, and trotted happily across it, his long pink tongue flapping, his teeth bright in his smile. When the dog reached the halfway point a sudden powerful gust of wind rushed over the bridge, and he lost his footing, tipped over the edge of the wall, and fell the nearly thirty feet into the river below. I ran to the wall and watched as the dog struggled to the riverbank; only his black head was visible in the swirling green water. He climbed out, shook himself off, and as though nothing untoward had happened, he began chasing cows through the field.

Presently a small blue car came rocketing over the bridge. I put out my thumb, and the car came to a wild screeching halt fifty yards down the road. I picked up my bag and ran after the car. The driver was a big, hot-faced woman in her mid-forties. I got into the car and asked her if she was going to Ennis.

"Where else would I be going on this road?" she snapped. She wrestled the stick shift into first gear and roared off down the road with such force that my head snapped back and the tires spun and sang on the wet pavement. I held onto the window lever and looked at the woman. Her face was heavy and angry, and her hands, fiercely gripping the steering wheel, were bloodless. She looked hung-over and slightly nauseated; her eyes were puffy and bloodshot. There was a bent cigarette tucked behind her ear, and the end of the cigarette was frayed like shredded wheat. She drove aggressively, stomping on the clutch and yanking the shift so hard I thought it might come off in her hand. We flew along the narrow, winding Ennis Road faster than I would dare travel on a four-lane highway.

"American," the woman muttered—a statement, not a question.

"Right," I said.

"You're on holiday." Another statement. I told the woman I'd been in Corofin for several months, and she glanced at me. "Then how is it I've never seen you before?"

I shrugged.

"Where you staying?" The woman spoke in a spitting, snapping, contemptuous way. Nervously keeping my eye on the road, I told her where I was staying.

"Oh, for Chrissake," she sneered, "not the *writer!*"

I nodded. She plucked a lipstick-stained tissue out of the sleeve of her sweater, swiped at the steamy windshield with it, then wiped her nose with it and flung the tissue to the floor near my feet. "I heard about you," she said with heavy skepticism. "What exactly would you be writing about?"

I didn't want to tell her.

"What would you be writing about?" She wanted an argument; I could see it in the slant of her eye and the way her jaw was set. She was angry about something and wanted to take it out on me.

"Ireland," I said.

"Ireland!" she howled. "What would *you* know about Ireland? You're American!"

"That's why I'm here," I said. "I'm learning about it."

"You think you can learn about a country in a few months?" she said in a tone that meant *You are a colossal idiot!*

"You can certainly learn something, yes."

"Bullshit."

I didn't want to protest too much, but the woman wasn't leaving me much choice. I had been studying Ireland for years, and my interest in the country was not a whim or a passing fancy. Though my spoken Irish wasn't very good, I had discovered that I knew as much Irish as many of the people I met here.

"It isn't bullshit," I said, trying not to sound overly defensive; she had control—or semicontrol—of the car, and I was entirely at her mercy. She rammed the accelerator to the floor. The little car's engine roared and whined, the door beside me rattled, and the wind screeched through a crack in the window. The woman was terrorizing me with great precision. I wanted to shout, *Stop the car!* but I couldn't bring myself to reveal my fear. We banged into potholes and sailed into the air over the frost heaves. We passed tractors and cars at the most dangerous points in the road. We sped around a sharp corner and I was thrown against the door. I put my seat belt on and said nothing and stared ahead through the windshield, certain that at any moment we'd go hurtling headlong into a herd of cattle crossing the road.

She said, "What I want to know is how a person who comes from someplace else can decide what should be said about Ireland. I want to know that. I really do. What the hell would an American know about Ireland? It steams me the way people think they can know something about Ireland and they never lived here. Did you see that thing in the paper? That French goddamn thing criticizing Ireland and saying Irish women were in the Dark Ages. 'Twas infuriating. I'd scratch the eyes of that bitch if I met her."

I had seen the article. An *Irish Times* reporter had discovered in the French magazine *Marie-Claire* a negative report on the status of Irish women and had written up a précis of the report. The French journalist had written, "Just two steps away from here, women are still living in the Middle Ages." The *Marie-Claire* article was a bleak portrait of a society where Catholic priests objecting to the use of condoms were allowed to announce on the radio that the AIDS virus was "smaller than the pores in a condom," where husbands beat their wives, and families of nine lived on a mere £160 per week, and where sex education was seen as "an incitement to debauchery." In short, Ireland was a society which, "by the voices of the Constitution and the Church, exerts an enormous pressure on women in order that they conform to an obsolete ideal of femininity and motherhood."

I had seen the report and had to acknowledge that much of it was true.

The woman driver's voice wobbled as we bounced along a rough patch in the road. "It takes nerve to come into a country and say things like that. France is not perfect. Let them talk about their own country. They're only laughing at us. There's nothing wrong with Ireland. We're fine, and we don't need smart-ass writers telling us what's wrong with us."

If she hadn't been preoccupied with driving, I am certain this woman would have tried to take a swing at me.

"Look what just happened in America with that judge and that liar of a woman that worked for him."

She was talking about Clarence Thomas and Anita Hill, news of whom had been all over the Irish newspapers.

"That woman lied. She exaggerated. Do you believe a man like that would do things like what she said? And if he did, why didn't she say so sooner? He's a judge. Who's she? And if he harassed her, she asked for it by not complaining. It's disgraceful what they dragged him through. And what about that Kennedy kid? Kennedy Smith. That's a lie too. Sure, he never raped her. She was only taking advantage. And what was she doing out with him at three in the morning? If he raped her, I'd say she nearly asked for it. It's a mess those women have got those men into. Ruined their careers. What's the complaint? Women obviously have a lot of power." She pointed a finger at me. "And *you* have a lot of nerve."

THE BUS TO DUBLIN was crowded and slow. The driver stopped along the way wherever he was asked to stop. Young children and elderly people with canes got off in the middle of nowhere and tromped away through the wet fields with their bags. The driver was cheerful and comical, singing and chatting and joking with the passengers. There was something familial about the way Irish officials dealt with the public; police, bus drivers, meter maids, shopkeepers, all acted with a familiarity and privilege usually reserved for the most intimate relationships. When bus drivers chided passengers for getting on the wrong bus, their voices were padded with remarkable affection. On this trip two very old women leaning on canes stood waiting for the bus in front of a news agency in Roscrea. The kerchiefs on their heads were yanked down to their eyes. They had tiny little faces and pointed noses and powerful plastic teeth that filled their mouths. They were holding onto a signpost for stability in the strong wind. The bus driver pulled up before them, opened the door with a slap, and shouted, "Girls! Hop aboard!"

The women giggled, hesitated, and giggled some more. "What time is the next bus?" they asked.

"Noon."

"What other times after that?"

"The times are posted on the window of the news agent!" the driver cried.

The women squinted up at him, baring the huge teeth. "The window of *what?*"

The driver shook his fist down at them. "Get on this bus this instant, or I'll give ye a belt with them canes!"

The two women tipped backward at the waist, hooting and cackling as though they had never in their lives heard anything so funny. Then the driver hopped off the bus and said amiably, "Here, I'll look in the window for ye."

❈

I LOVED the tiny back roads, the passing drivers who lifted their index fingers off the steering wheel in lazy greeting. I loved the rainbows and the glowing fields, the lakes and stone walls, the tinker ponies grazing along the edge of the road. We passed through places with names like Toomyvara, Moneygall, Borris in Ossory, Pike of Rush Hall, Kill, and Rathcoole. Villages, towns, farms, cows, churches, colorful shopfronts and pubs, huge oak trees, and children in school uniforms flashed past the window, revealing the sweet surface of the country with the vivid clarity of a slide show. What wasn't revealed was the 20 percent unemployment, the alcoholism, the 25,000 new college graduates competing for 2,500 jobs, the 30,000 people who had left Ireland each year during the late 1980s, the quarter of the Irish population living below the poverty level, and the 37 percent living on social welfare.

A very old woman got onto the bus and sat next to me. The tender blue bags under her eyes looked as though they were filled with ink. She had a letter in her hand, and after a while she said, without looking at me and as though we had been talking a long time together, "Turned out to be a fine day, and I'm dressed altogether wrong for it."

She told me she was from Wexford. "There are a lot of IRA's there. That much I know. The place is full of them." She looked cautiously around and whispered to me, "Kilkenny is full of the IRA too, if you want to know it."

I rarely heard people in the Republic talking about the IRA or mentioning the North at all. I asked the woman what the presence of the IRA in Wexford meant to her. "I'd better not say," she said. " 'Tis better not to be talking about such things as that. You never know who might hear you talking. But it's hard to get them to stop the violence. A man was shot in his bed only the other night in Belfast. I suppose it might be the work of the IRA. They say they want a united Ireland. But they don't. They only want to be hooligans. They're barbarians. What happened between England and Ireland happened a very long time ago, before we were born."

In a small village a Chinese woman got onto the bus, and the elderly woman said, "We have everything here now. Chinese. Japanese. Name it, we have it. The hospitals are full of black doctors. I would prefer a white doctor myself. The black ones are very rough. When they examine you, they're very rough. And they make their women walk behind them. If you ever saw me walking behind my husband, I'd put my boot in him straightaway, don't think I wouldn't. They make their women walk behind them. They call it religion, but 'tis not religion. 'Tis only sex. Men's dirty old needs. Men are all right, if you find a nice one, but men are queer."

The woman touched my arm with the back of her hand as she talked, and eventually she held onto my shirtsleeve, pinching it between her thumb and forefinger, as though testing the quality of the fabric. "Don't mind me asking, but are you traveling alone?"

"Yes, I am," I said.

"You are?" She seemed astonished. "Aren't you brave!"

"But you're traveling alone too," I said.

"'Course I am, but that's different."

"How is it different?"

"I'm Irish!"

　※

I SAT BACK in my seat and thought about what I would ask the president. It had been surprisingly easy to arrange this meeting with her. All year long I had been telling people that I wanted to meet the president, and the response was always, "No problem. Want me to call her up for you?" Finally I made the call myself and, as the people had said, it was no problem—she would be happy to meet me.

Mary Robinson's presence in Aras an Uachtarain still struck me as surreal. Never mind that she was a woman, the first to occupy the office of president in Ireland, but ideologically she was an extremely unlikely figure for the job.

The presidency, largely a ceremonial office and a symbolic representation of the state, held little power. The president could not speak publicly or travel outside the country without permission of the government and was not expected to give opinions on matters of policy. The office's only power was in calling elections, refusing to dissolve the Dail, and ensuring the constitutionality of laws. For years the presidency had been perceived as a reward for loyal political retirees appointed by the Fianna Fail government—a meaningless ghost of an office.

In 1990 the expected future president of Ireland was Brian Lenihan, the popular Fianna Fail Tanaiste, or deputy prime minister, and until Labour Party leader Dick Spring got other ideas, few people doubted Lenihan's uncontested nomination and appointment. Spring, however, saw the election as an opportunity to gauge the desire of the Irish people for changes in Irish society, or at least for a change in the office of president. He wanted someone progressive, someone young, someone dedicated to change, "a voice for the voiceless." He nominated Mary Robinson for the job.

Robinson was a famous liberal sore thumb in a very conservative society. She had attended finishing school in Paris, had received the highest academic honors at Trinity College, and had finished graduate school at Harvard with honors. A constitutional lawyer, she was the first Catholic ever elected to the Trinity College constituency and, at age twenty-five, the youngest woman ever elected to the Irish Senate. She was married to a Protestant, which in Ireland was considered by some to be tantamount to miscegenation. The focus of Robinson's legal work had been the defense of minority and oppressed elements in Irish society. She believed that constitutional rights were the foundation of society, and she acted upon her views that law did not belong in areas of private morality.

It was Robinson who introduced legislation to legalize contraception (ten years before the legislation was passed), and it was Robinson who introduced legislation for the removal of the divorce ban from the Constitution. In fact, Mary Robinson was responsible for many of the changes that had taken place in Irish law over the past two decades. She won rights for homosexuals, for illegitimate children, and for itinerants. She challenged sexual discrimination and won the right for women to sit on juries. She fought for the right to dispense information on abortion. She was a feminist and a human rights activist, and her fundamental goal was to ensure the rights of the individual, an unpopular purpose in Ireland.

With the support of Ireland's three smallest political groups — the Labour Party, the Worker's Party, and the Green Party — Robinson campaigned for the presidency by touring the country, making speeches, and meeting the country people. She projected an image of a new Ireland and a revivified presidency which, though lacking in executive power, might nevertheless empower others with its attentions. Robinson spoke of emigrants' rights, the environment, itinerants' rights, women's support groups, local self-development groups, and the Republic's relationship with the North. She supported a more pluralistic, more European, less bigoted, less pietistic Ireland, while at the same time emphasizing the importance of her role as Catholic mother and wife.

But as successful as Robinson's campaign was becoming, she had difficulty concealing the efforts she had made to subvert the patriarchal Catholic hierarchy. In one now infamous interview with *Hot Press* magazine, Ireland's *Rolling Stone*, Robinson voiced radical views that shocked not only the opposition but also her own campaigners. "The whole patriarchal, male-dominated presence of the Catholic Church is probably the worst aspect of all the establishment forces that have sought to do down women over the years," Robinson told

Hot Press. She also said she would support gay rights and, worse, when the interviewer asked Robinson if she would preside over the opening of a contraceptives stall at the Virgin Megastores (which had been prosecuted for illegally selling condoms), she said, "Yes. This is a very young country and I think it would be helpful to have a president that would be in touch with what young people are doing." She also said that the Irish government didn't "give a shit" about its emigrant population and, further, that if elected, she would confront the Taoiseach on the basis of having a superior democratic mandate. "As a president directly elected by the people of Ireland," she said, "I will have the most democratic job in the country. I'll be able to look Charlie Haughey in the eye and tell him to back off if necessary because I have been directly elected by the people as a whole and he hasn't."

Needless to say, the government took this badly. The Taoiseach commented that Robinson's attitude was "totally contrary to the spirit of the Constitution and a recipe for crisis that would affect the stability of our political institutions."

In the last two weeks of the political campaign, Brian Lenihan, Robinson's main opponent and the man who everyone believed would win the presidency, became embroiled in a political scandal that ultimately cost him the election. It was revealed that during 1982 Lenihan had, in order to protect the party and its Taoiseach, tried unethically to influence the president, Patrick Hillery, asking him not to call a general election, and that he had lied about having done this. When this news was leaked, the people reacted.

Robinson was elected by 52.8 percent of the population. My suspicion was that the *Hot Press* interview was probably the last time Mary Robinson had been able to speak out without curbing her views. Now that she was president, the beliefs she had fought for and professed were out of her reach. Many young Irish women I had talked with felt that while Robinson's election was a healthy sign for Ireland, Robinson herself was wasted in the office.

✠

THE MORNING of my meeting with Mary Robinson was cool and drizzly, the air heavy, the sky battleship gray. On my way to Phoenix Park I came upon a group of step dancers performing on an elevated platform in the middle of O'Connell Street: twelve adolescent girls in traditional costumes (stiffly spinning green silk skirts, white cotton blouses) stepping in unison through a fierce hornpipe. Their manner bordered on militaristic; their dance inspired the vicious thrill of a Memorial Day Parade. With every step they seemed to be saying, Watch this, and don't get in our way. They danced straight-backed, as though in casts from the waist up, arms held stiffly at their sides, the legs alone moving, and with the same paradox of delicate grace and thundering destruction displayed in the galloping of a horse. Their bodies rose and fell effortlessly, knees flexing, toes kicking at the air in a deceptively dainty fashion. I was struck, above all, by the dancers' faces, void of all expression but determination. The beauty of this dance lay in its contradiction: one half of the body was free, the other was not.

I moved on. I could feel the fine mist on my face. The toes of my shoes were wet from my walk through the park to the president's house. Michael Ferry, a tall, red-haired, big-eared guard, met me at the gate to Aras an Uachtarain. He pushed back the cap on his head and said, "Lovely morning."

I checked his face to see if he was kidding, though I should have known he wasn't. The Irish always thought this sort of day was beautiful. As long as there was no wind, the rain wasn't too hard, and the temperature wasn't too low, the day was beautiful.

"Are you *Vogue?*" Michael asked through the iron bars.

"Vogue?"

"The president has an interview this morning with *Vogue.* Would that be you?"

"Do I look like *Vogue?*" I said.

"I don't know," he said. "What is *Vogue?*"

I told him what *Vogue* was and that I wasn't it, and he opened the gate and brought me into the guardhouse to look at the list of people the president was to meet today, a list three pages long. At the top of it was my name, which I pointed out to Michael Ferry.

"Rosemary Mahoney," he said, peering at me. His face brightened perceptibly as the seconds passed. "Say," he said finally, "I know you. You were here before."

That was true. One day during the summer I had stood at the gate chatting in the rain with Michael about Aras an Uachtarain and

Phoenix Park. He had told me that the Aras used to be the hunting lodge of the British vice-regent. Michael was from Donegal, a pleasant man with the gawky, open-faced innocence of Barney Fife, Mayberry's deputy sheriff. I had told him then that I was hoping to see the president before the end of the year, and he had said agreeably, "If you're determined enough, you will, Rose."

"You got your meeting," he said now delightedly. "I never doubted you."

A feeble peat fire smoldered in the fireplace of the guardhouse; there was a black bicycle against the wall, a teapot on a table, and a slovenly armchair collapsing in a corner; the cozy room looked more like it belonged in a provincial cottage than at the entrance to a president's house. A car stopped outside the gatehouse, and the young woman driver rolled down her window, waved, and shouted through the open door, "Hiya, Michael! Chatting up the girls again?" When she had passed through the gate, Michael said, "She's a captain in the army and an assistant to the president."

"She's friendly," I said.

"She is indeed. With Mary in the house we see all kinds of friendly people now. Nobody ever used to come through these gates. But now there's people coming and going all the day long. All we ever saw before was men. Now it's all women. It's better. Mary is grand."

I said good-bye to Michael and walked down the long driveway toward the house, past long green lawns, a carriage house, horses and cows and a trio of black donkeys grazing behind a fence. I went over and patted one of the donkeys on the head, a tiny, knock-kneed baby with a swayback and thick bangs gracing his triangular forehead. His eyelashes were long and as fine as spiderwebs. I rubbed the donkey's forehead, and he chewed on the sleeve of my coat. As I proceeded toward the house he followed me.

The Georgian house was impressive, bigger and more imposing, I thought, than the White House. I went up a wide, shallow stairway to the front door. It was open, and through it I could see people putting up a Christmas tree in the hallway. A cheerful guard greeted me by name and shook my hand as though he had known me for years. He introduced me to several very relaxed security women in army uniforms, who looked delighted to see me.

The guard offered to show me the back garden while I waited for the president. In the garden I was taken with a stand of enormous conifers behind the house, taller and thicker than any trees I'd ever seen. I asked the guard what kind they were, and he smiled and said, " 'Tis one tree."

This seemed impossible, for it looked distinctly like six or seven trees planted close together. I went over to the trees for a closer look and discovered that the guard was right; there was only one trunk. "It's called *Wellingtonia gigantea*," he said.

On our way back into the house I looked up to the second floor and saw a tall light in one of the windows. I knew that this was the light the president had promised to keep in her kitchen window as a symbol of vigilance for all the emigrants, a conscious link to the 70 million people of Irish descent in the far corners of the world. The light was a bare bulb, tall and strange, roughly the shape of a television picture tube, and it glowed with a dense, opaque light. "Is that light incandescent?" I asked the guard.

"Excuse me," he said, "but I'm afraid I don't know what incandescent means."

※

BRIDE ROSNEY, a former schoolteacher who was now special adviser to the president, greeted me in the hallway of the Aras and brought me into an elaborately decorated, high-ceilinged drawing room that was like something out of a fairy tale—gold silk damask wallpaper, fish-eye mirrors, delicate plasterwork, chandeliers, and a fireplace packed with neat rows of peat bricks.

Rosney, the president's best friend and right-hand woman, looked like a schoolteacher dressed up for a special occasion. She was a big, soft woman with a beautifully soft voice and a schoolteacher's benign expression, but she was reported to be tough and strong-willed and determined. It was said that Mary Robinson took her advice without question. Rosney looked out of place in this room and there was something subversive and satisfying about that. We made small talk and sat in Louis Quatorze armchairs staring at each other and waiting for the president to come down. I could hear Mary Robinson's high-heeled footsteps banging back and forth across the floor overhead. She was twenty minutes late for our appointment. I pictured her combing her hair, putting on earrings, and flipping the kitchen light switch. It occurred to me that I didn't know how to address her. I asked Rosney. "President," came her sensible answer.

I had seen the president once before at a convention and had been struck by her unassuming presence. She looked like someone who lived down the street, a woman you'd see pushing a cart in a supermarket. As she spoke to a large audience of women, she looked surprised and embarrassed at her own position. Her clothes were beautiful, but she seemed uncomfortable in them, as though they were restricting her and weighing her down. She looked as if she would have preferred to show up in jeans and tennis shoes. It was well known that Robinson's aides had encouraged her to change her image from that of the slightly dowdy, absent-minded lawyer with a bad hairdo to a more glamorous, glittering picture befitting the nation's first citizen. The change had worked, chiefly because Robinson had a natural beauty and because the old self-conscious Mary was still faintly evident.

Presently a door opened and the president came into the room. I was immediately impressed with her height; she was nearly a head taller than I. She had an appealing, slightly crooked smile. She greeted me and sat on the couch with her hands folded in her lap. She looked attentively at me, her face displaying an intelligence and receptivity only half revealed in the photographs I had seen of her.

She was ready to listen to my questions, and I was struck by the idealism of her responses. She didn't seem to have much time for humor. I sensed that she took me as seriously as she would take the Taoiseach of Ireland, or anyone for that matter. Her words were delivered in a rapid-fire staccato with a brief pause between each word, the slightly anxious speech of a person thinking at twice the speed of her listener. Her mind traveled to the very end of the subject in question, exhausting all possibilities. It was not a conversational style but a series of tiny speeches delivered in the forceful manner of a person accustomed to presenting her point against tremendous objection, a person who expected to be challenged. She had few distracting physical gestures except for the way she held her hands palms up before her like a choirboy holding a hymnal and the way she nodded her head when listening.

One Irish journalist had commented that Robinson's election was, for Ireland, psychically comparable to the collapse of the Berlin Wall.

In her acceptance speech on November 9, 1990, she had said, "I was elected by men and women of all parties and none, by many with great moral courage who stepped out from the faded flags of the Civil War and voted for a new Ireland. And above all by the women of Ireland—Mna na hEireann—who instead of rocking the cradle rocked the system and who came out massively to make their mark on the ballot paper and on a new Ireland."

I asked Robinson to elaborate on what her election in 1990 had revealed about the desires and expectations of the Irish people. She held up her hands and said, "Well, there hadn't been a presidential election for seventeen years, so it was a different kind of election involving the whole country. Insofar as people were choosing an individual to represent the country, I think it showed there was a desire for some way of having issues or concerns represented which were outside the prescribed agenda of politics—things like the self-development of local groups, women's groups, and youth groups, and a concern about the emigrant issue, which wasn't policy but which was allowing a way of linking with the Irish abroad. What people said to me more often than anything else during the presidential campaign was, 'We want a president who will do us proud.' That's a very Irish expression—who will do us proud. I think it's a twofold thing: someone we can be proud of, but who will also represent things that we're proud of, so that we can have a more positive sense of ourselves. Because we don't have massive government resources in monetary terms, a lot of ordinary people in this country, apart from the job they do, give of themselves in some way to their local community, and I think it's a very good thing for this office to represent that by acknowledging it, by valuing it, by reinforcing it. But in order to do it you have to be in touch with it."

In her inauguration speech Robinson had expressed her belief that Ireland had something "strange and precious" to contribute to the changes taking place in Europe. I asked her what those qualities were.

"I wanted us to be more confident of our own role within the European community and in the world," she said. "Small doesn't mean insignificant. Small can be beautiful. We have a 150-year experience in Ireland of going from famine, deprivation, being colonized by a larger country, to an emerging independence and to reclaiming our own language and culture within that independence. Within the wider Europe we have a lot to offer. Part of what we can offer is the self-development and family-based participation and valuing what in other countries may have been either lost or changed but which we still have as a very inherent part of our culture."

I said, "But would it not be difficult, now that Ireland is becoming a member of Europe, to hold onto those things?"

"I don't think so. I mean it's arguable. It's very much a debate. I myself feel that because we were so uncertain of ourselves when we were first of all ruled by Britain, and then in this century when we achieved the Free State and then the independent republican status from 1937, we still lacked self-confidence as a nation. We still were defensive, ambivalent, self-deprecating. And I believe that it has been an enriching experience to have become part of a wider European continent; that's partly psychological. I think there has been an awareness that we have ourselves as strong a culture, that in many areas we can stand on equal terms. That has been good for the national psyche and for the sense of our identity."

I was reminded of something Ailbhe Smythe of Attic Press had said during my meeting with her—that there was no history of self-worth in Ireland. "Our history has told us," Smythe said, "that we're actually worth nothing at all and that if we want to make something of ourselves, we have to go abroad to do that, physically, economically, culturally, every way. There is also the notion of begrudgery. Anyone in Ireland who has achieved any degree of success finds that; anybody who has any kind of prominence, whether the prominence has been achieved here or elsewhere. On the whole, if success has been achieved elsewhere and you return to Ireland, it seems to be the case that you will be taken more seriously, but the more rooted in Ireland you remain, the more difficult it is to have people not simply value that success but tell you they value it. There is always, always a caveat. Mary Robinson's election is about not having to do that anymore."

I asked the president whether she thought her office could help change Ireland's postcolonial way of thinking, a mindset she herself had defined as "worrying uncertainty and self-deprecation."

She said, "I think that we're seeing a more positive sense of Irishness, and I'm talking about over the last five years, but increasingly. I notice it in small ways. I'm not in favor of flag waving particularly. But I notice that young children now when I go down the country wave the Irish flag with pride at me. Now, that would not really have been the case some years ago. I think there was a sort of defensiveness, a sort of running down of things Irish, a tendency to feel that we had to get imported goods because they were 'better' than Irish goods, that Irish crafts were somehow not particularly good. And it has partly been that standards have improved very significantly. I think we're in a very creative phase as a country, and also I think we've recognized that Ireland is not well known in European circles. They don't know much about our history, they don't know much about our culture, they don't know much about our sense of ourselves. They are amazed when told that we have a separate language. It's a kind of awareness that we have a lot to project, that it's about time we started doing it and doing it confidently. Also, we have a broader sense of what our Irishness is."

"I meet many young people who seem to have no interest in the Irish language and who actually know very little Irish, which surprises me. I know that Irish is important to you. Can your presidency increase awareness of and interest in the language?"

"Obviously the office is a modest one. It's not a policy office, and I wouldn't like to overstate what it can do or raise expectations that couldn't be fulfilled. I think that it helps that I'm fairly typical, that I grew up in the west of Ireland and so I have very good Irish. I then went to boarding school in Dublin, and Irish was boring and the nuns didn't like it, and then I spent a year in France and fell in love with French language and culture. Through my work as a lawyer, particularly in Europe, through my growing awareness of how Ireland was perceived and how we were perceiving ourselves and this whole question of identity, I began to value the Irish language incrementally more and more. When the presidential campaign started, in a way it was my opportunity to get back my fluency in Irish, and I saw it as a way of stimulating and symbolically reflecting its importance." She paused to sigh. "Irish was taught in such a way that it wasn't relevant to young Irish people. I think already it has become more relevant, and a great deal can be done to reinforce that relevance within the context of a Europe of cultural diversity. It's more interesting for people from outside Ireland to come and visit Ireland if we have our separate language and culture; that's what would interest a lot of Europeans."

In October 1990 Robinson became the first Irish president since

Eamon De Valera to travel to the United States. Brown University gave her an honorary degree, and in a speech delivered there she challenged a too-narrow interpretation of feminism that excluded women in the home. "Do we as women value the activities and concerns of so many women in homemaking and bringing up children?" she asked. "If we do not . . . how can we persuade society as a whole of their value and of the importance of ensuring that these activities are more evenly shared between parents and supported by society so that they do not oppress women or hinder the realization of their full potential?"

In Los Angeles Robinson addressed the World Affairs Council and spoke of the role that Ireland would play in the relationship between the United States and Europe. "The ties between Ireland and the United States are no longer those binding a desperate keeper to the hospitality and shelter of a great nation," she had said. "They are now bonds of common interest and contemporary friendship." While this was certainly true, disturbing numbers of Irish citizens were still emigrating to the United States, and many of them lived there illegally and under enormous psychological stress. I asked the president to comment on this particular reality of Irish life.

"I would have to say, representing in a broad sense the views of the people of Ireland, that it is enormously sad and a great tragedy for this country that so many of our very talented young people who have had a good educational base, who are potentially very adaptable, exactly the kind of modern people that we would like to harness here, are going. They don't want to go. And it is a terrible wrench for them and for their families, and it is an enormous sadness. What I was trying to say, though, is that the world has grown smaller. It's more cyclical now. I was talking in Los Angeles to heads of high-tech companies who have located in Ireland—they already had established plants here—and I was conscious that it's more now of a two-way process, and also the Irish who go now don't have to go forever. It's different from the Irish who went with no basic education. There are enormous problems of the illegal Irish in America, but I think the relationship is a different one and there is more mobility in it. There is more opportunity to make the point that for firms that are looking for a well-trained, adaptable work force, it's here in Ireland and can be employed here in Ireland. I think I was really trying to give a more rounded picture of the situation without denying—because we'll have it this Christmas when the young Irish come home for Christmas—the bitter scenes at the airport when they go back."

Rosney interrupted her to warn us that my time was almost up. Robinson nodded and said, "We are an island that has lost so many of its people, but that doesn't mean they've lost their Irishness. When I was in Chicago, and indeed in Boston and Los Angeles, I was profoundly moved not only by the way the Irish heritage has been cherished and maintained but has been enhanced. There was a quality of excellence in Irish song and dance and knowledge of literature. The American Committee of Irish Studies do phenomenal work of researching. Irish citizenship has always had that emigrant sense to it. It is what I try to do symbolically with the light in the window, I want to symbolically link with the extended Irish family."

"Can you comment on the effect that the presidency has had on you and your family?"

"Well, I'll comment first of all with something that I said recently at a network meeting here in Dublin. I don't mind at all being asked about the effect on my family, because it's extremely important to me, but I'm invariably asked it because I'm a woman president, and I wonder if the same question is asked of a man who's been elected president."

"Good point," I said.

She smiled her crooked smile and said, "It is a good point. It's a very important question, and it should be asked, but it should be asked of both men and women."

Having evaded answering the question, Robinson returned to the subject of Ireland's self-perception, which seemed to be her biggest concern. At times she sounded like the nation's psychotherapist. On Aras an Uachtarain she said, "It's a very good house to receive visitors from outside Ireland. I've had Tom Foley and various members of Congress here, and they are impressed in the right sense. It's a house that has been for more than two hundred and twenty years the head of state's residence in Ireland, so it's mirrored the history from the vice-regent to the governors general and now to the president of Ireland. It's a house that reflects what has happened on this island with an image that is grand in the right sense."

She turned to Bride Rosney. "I see you're looking at the clock."

"I'm always looking at the clock. I'm aware that Rosemary has one question about the North of Ireland that we might answer."

There were many more questions on my list, but since we were running out of time, this was clearly one that Rosney thought important for the president to answer. The development of a greater understanding between Northern Ireland and the Republic was one of Robinson's highest priorities. It was the exclusion of Unionist opinion in the drafting of the Anglo-Irish Agreement of 1985 that had inspired Robinson to resign from the Labour Party. Robinson was more conciliatory toward the North than any Irish politician had ever been.

Obediently I asked the question. "Can you measure the effect your gestures toward the North have had on the situation there, and what is the public response to your efforts in Ireland's relationship to the North?"

Robinson said, "In one way it's hard to measure, and maybe it's for others to measure, but it was something that I highlighted in my inauguration address and even before it. I wanted to say something that really hadn't been said explicitly by an elected representative person from this part of the island. I wanted to extend the hand of friendship and of love outside politics, to reinforce all the kinds of relationships and contacts which were there, which a lot of people were keeping very discreet because they were worried about political consequences, that any publicity might kill off the establishment of links and relationships and exchanges, and by saying it so publicly I wanted in fact to make a very positive statement about it and reinforce it by recognizing the amount of linkage that was already there. All I can say is I've been taken aback by the response. We've had numerous groups from Northern Ireland here. We've had more than a group a week which is either cross-community or cross-border. We've had women from the Shankill and the Falls sitting here. We've had politicians, we've had cultural groups, we've had bus workers. I think that has its own significance. I've had numerous invitations to visit Northern Ireland, and I'm hoping to be able to take them up. It's a complex matter. It requires that it be something done in consultation not just with one but with two governments, and I'm aware that it's necessary to be patient about it."

"I can hear the next group arriving," said Rosney. "I was going to suggest to Rosemary that she might like to join the next group, a Wexford women's group. She might like to see your interaction with them."

We moved into the next room, where the women from Wexford had gathered. When Robinson entered the room they applauded her roundly and flocked around her, murmuring, "She's lovely! Ah, sure, isn't she lovely?"

As I stood nearby taking notes, Bride Rosney came over and stood beside me. "You use the same notebooks I use," she said cheerfully. She was drinking tea and eating a cookie, and there were cookie crumbs in the corners of her mouth. She was natural and casual and entirely likable. She invited me to stay longer. I saw my opportunity to ask Rosney if the president wasn't muzzled in this office. Rosney laughed. "Not really. She has a lot of power. She gets noticed. When she goes to visit a women's group in Galway, their place gets freshly painted. Wherever she goes, people are inspired to improve things. She is as effective now as she was in the courts."

We drank tea from china cups decorated with gold harps. The women asked Robinson about her life and the house, and Robinson told them that when she and her family first entered the house they were awed by it, and her young son had turned to her and asked, "Why are we whispering?"

❖

As ROBINSON talked to the women, I realized that when I left here I would be returning to Corofin for the last time before leaving Ireland for good, and I was inordinately pleased that I finally had something to brag about to Conor MacNamara.

Corofin

THE EVENING BEFORE I left Corofin I stopped by Conor Mac-Namara's house to look at a photograph he wanted to give me as a going-away gift, a photograph of his boat in Bally-vaughan. When I knocked on his door, Annie Maher answered it. I was surprised to see her there, for I knew Annie rarely came to Corofin. Her coat was disheveled and misbuttoned, her beret was askew on her head, and she was weeping drunkenly. Again.

"Jo, darling!" she sobbed, throwing her arms heavily around me. "Thank God you are here! I am after having a domestic dispute with my husband! Come immediately in! Come, come!"

I stepped through the doorway of the tiny, very old house into a narrow room with a plaster ceiling so low I could have reached up and touched it.

Annie dabbed at her puffy red eyes with the backs of her wrists and steered me toward the couch. "Siddown, Jo," she sniffled. Her face was streaked with tears. "Aidan, my husband, is cruel and abusive."

Annie's brothers Brownie and Curly were sitting in armchairs around an electric fire. The room was rather dark, lit only by a lamp on the windowsill and the glow of the electric fire, but I could make out some of the photographs on the walls, and a piano, a child's bicycle propped against a chest of drawers, and three ancient TV sets Conor had repaired. The ceiling and the wooden floor were slanted and warped; in fact, the entire house looked roughly constructed, as though it had been built freehand, without measures or levels or plumb lines. But there was something beautiful about the place too; it was warm and cozy, and every object looked beloved and pleasantly aged. The smell of baking bread came from the kitchen at the back of the house.

Brownie was rolling a joint on the arm of his chair. "It was your own fault, Annie," he said without looking up from his project. "You provoked him. I don't blame him for giving out to you. You had no dinner made for your kids."

Annie flopped down beside me on the couch and wailed, "But there was a good reason for that!" She looked pleadingly at me, as though I should defend her to her brother.

Curly said, "You and your husband shouldn't argue like that in front of your children, Annie."

Brownie stopped what he was doing and peered at his brother. Bitterly he said, "Didn't *our* parents argue in front of *us?* They never cared what we heard in this house. Weren't they always roaring at each other in front of us? They never cared what we heard. They never cared about that, did they?"

"It's bad for children," said Curly.

Brownie said, "It wasn't bad for *us.*"

"Was it not?" Curly snorted.

Brownie and Curly were in their late twenties. They were handsome and slender and drunk, and they both wore heavy black work boots, laces untied.

Annie said, "Aidan is mean to me. He expects too much."

Brownie said, "Never mind her, Rose. It's only the drink talking. Jesus, never mind her. She's an alcoholic anyway."

Curly said, "We're all alcoholics."

"I am an alcoholic. That's right," said Annie. "And who can blame me? You don't blame me, do you, Josie?"

"No, Annie," I said.

"'Course you don't. You are a woman and you understand. And our mother is dead and so is yours, Jo, so I know you understand."

"My mother is not dead, Annie," I said. "My mother is living."
Annie's desire to erase my mother fascinated and disturbed me.

"Not dead?" Annie peered at me with new interest. "She Irish?"

"Yes, she is."

"When's she coming back, then?"

From the serious, expectant way Annie asked the question I understood that she meant not when was my mother coming back for a visit, but when was my mother coming back to Ireland, where she belonged.

"My mother is American," I said.

Annie gave me an accusatory look. "You said Irish."

"But she was born in America."

"Her parents were Irish?"

"Yes, they were."

"Then your mother is Irish."

"She's both."

Annie clawed the beret from her head and stomped her foot on the crooked floor. "She's *Irish!* I have kids who were born in London and they are not English, I can tell you that right now, Jo. So let's get that straight. If your mother's alive, she's Irish!"

I told Annie that my mother's parents had made America their home; they had made their life there. Annie responded by swinging the beret slowly around on her finger, yawning and sighing loudly, nodding her head, and rolling her eyes at me in a stagy depiction of boredom. "I know, I know," she sighed, "famine, poverty, things were better in America, 'the people of Ireland is starving!' and all that blubbering historical bullshit. I don't blame them. I do not blame them. I did it myself. I went to England. But it's different now. I didn't stay there. To be honest with you, I hated England. The English look down on the Irish. They say we're ignorant and uneducated, but it's them who have their head up their arse. They call us stupid because they are frightened, you see."

"Frightened of what?" I said.

"They're worried that we're smarter than them. They say we're violent. IRA and all that. But they know better. That's an excuse for looking down their nose at us. Tell me, Jo, have you seen one single piece of violence since you've been in Ireland?"

I thought about that and had to confess I hadn't seen any violence of any kind here. I had seen scores of emotional arguments, shouting matches, verbal duels, but as for violence, I had never seen so much as a fistfight. At the same time the Irish newspapers and television carried daily reports of new violence in the North, funeral processions sprayed with gunfire, taxi drivers shot dead in their cars, hospitals bombed, Ulster Defense Regiment barracks bombed, IRA men shot in their beds, wives on both sides kidnapped, Royal Ulster Constabulary headquarters bombed. The news was so common that it had become unremarkable, and people gave it the same attention they gave advertisements: they heard the words and saw the images but didn't consciously take them in. I rarely heard people in the Republic of Ireland commenting on the violence in the North. It was like a war taking place in a distant land.

"You haven't seen any violence because there isn't any," Annie insisted. "We are a peaceful people."

"That's not what I would have said a minute ago when your husband was here," Brownie said, lighting the joint and passing it to Curly.

Annie hurled her beret at her brother and hit him in the face. "You shut up, Brownie MacNamara."

Curly passed me the joint, and I waved it on to Annie. I looked around the room and tried to imagine thirteen children growing up here together. "How old is this house?" I asked.

"Older than me, I guess," said Annie. "Dada built it all by himself. Would you believe that, Jo?"

⠿

LATER I FOUND Conor MacNamara holding forth in Dillon's Pub. "I flew a plane one time," I heard him saying as I stepped through the door. "They were making a documentary film about County Clare, and they shot some of it from this plane, and I went up in that plane with them. A little, little plane it was, with propellers, but we flew all over the county and we went down over the Cliffs of Moher and down so low over the sea that the wing of the plane touched the water. Like this . . ."

Conor flew his hand in a swooping motion over the table before him and dragged one finger across its surface.

"We were very free that day," he continued, grinning and flashing his hands before him. "We could have picked up a rake of bombs and flown right up to Belfast with them, or over to London and bombed the shite out of the queen. But, no, never mind any of that sort of fighting chat just now. Anyway, there was this funeral beneath us in Galway Bay that day; they were scattering the ashes of a fisherman there, and all the fishermen were in their boats, jawing on the short-wave."

It was late, and the crowd in the pub had dwindled to Eamon the butcher, Conor, Mick Pat Crown, Francis behind the bar, and James Rohan. Rohan, a plump, red-haired young man in a white suit, had just been to the funeral of his best friend's mother. He was drunk and afraid to go home, afraid that his wife would "get into an aggravation" with him for his drunkenness and for not coming home hours before to help with their new baby.

Conor carried on. "And when 'twas time to land at the airport, we came in on the tail of this massive big jet airliner, and we almost crashed because we got stuck in the backwind of it. They never should have let us land behind that plane. I had to take the controls of the plane then, and we was halfway between zig and zag with the situation, bouncing up and down and tossing here and there so hard I could hear my own liver rattling in its socket. A plane taking off and landing is like a goose taking off and landing. I have a small bit of experience with geese, you see."

Conor was standing now, and in a sudden burst of exuberance he grabbed the metal pole that went from floor to ceiling in front of the bar and swung himself around on it, like a boy in a playground. He went on to talk about celestial navigation, the North Star, and the inventor of the compass, who was Irish. The other men listened, looking neither interested nor bored but as though Conor Mac-Namara simply weren't there. Occasionally James Rohan made a lack-adaisical attempt to contradict Conor.

Francis came out from behind the bar and put a glass of Guinness in front of me, saying, "There, Rose." This meant the drink was on him. Francis was very quiet that night. He had waved sadly to me when I first came in, but he hadn't spoken to me.

"There are nine things that you should take with you when you go on a boat," said Conor loudly. "Matches, a torch, life preserver, anchor, water, a torch, a flare, um . . . a life preserver . . ."

"You said life preserver already," Rohan said wearily.

"Um, a flare, and well, I forget the rest of the things, but there are nine of them that you should never live without."

Mick Pat Crown picked a glowing coal out of the fire with the tongs and lifted it to his face to light his cigarette, at the same time pouring beer deftly from a bottle into his glass. He talked around the cigarette about a man he knew who had the job of helping ewes deliver their lambs. The man was so good at the job and so devoted to it that he actually had had the last two fingers of his hand and part of the palm surgically removed so that he would have less trouble fitting his hand into the sheep and pulling the lamb out.

"Mick Pat," I said, "I don't believe that."

Mick Pat flung the hot coal back into the fire, dropped the tongs on the floor, and made the sign of the cross on the lapel of his overcoat. " 'Tis the God's truth, miss."

I still didn't believe it, but the other men in the pub confirmed that it was true. "And 'tis bringin' that fella in a heap of money, too," Conor said, delicately curling his white hair behind his ears. "And that reminds me, do ye remember that time them two fellas was in Connolly's Pub comparing the size of their penises?"

I saw Francis wince at this. He turned away from the room and began wiping glasses.

Earlier that day Francis had finally come out to see Ballyportry Castle. He had walked out from the village with Michael, his nephew, carrying a bottle of wine and a glass Guiness mug, and the somber way he presented them to me made them seem more like a viaticum than a gift. In the castle Francis took a tape measure out of his pocket and measured the size of every room, every fireplace, every window and door. He commented on the tiniest details of the place, and at one point he stood in the middle of the main hall with a worried look on his face and whispered to himself, " 'Tis weird."

I brought Francis and Michael to the top of the castle so they could look out across the land. As we stood in the cool breeze I felt there was something very familiar about the land and the light here, a familiarity that satisfied something childlike and deep in me. The land had been altered tremendously by human hands — all those gray-white walls made of stones pulled from the fields, all those hedges and whitewashed cottages, fences and barns, roads twisting and winding like snakes, the churches and rectories, the pubs and shops. And still it was wild. To the north there were the bog and the lakes, and Mullaghmore Mountain and the Burren, and to the south the rolling, flowing green fields, russet hedges, and stone walls, hundreds of snowy sheep racing up a hillside, and the sky full of cumulonimbus clouds like smoke from an atomic explosion.

When we were seated by the fire, Francis said to Michael with genuine puzzlement in his voice, "Rose is like an Irish girl, isn't she, Michael? You're not like a foreigner, Rose. But, no, that's not right either, for even an Irish girl would never talk to me about regular things like you do. Even an Irish girl would be bored of me."

Francis looked at me, trying to figure out how I was different from the girls he knew. "And you wouldn't be afraid here, even after someone broke in, would you?"

"Not afraid enough to leave," I said.

Francis said, "I couldn't really see why a person like yourself would come to a village like this," and after a long silence he added, "But you like it here, don't you, Rose?"

✺

"THEY TOOK OUT their penises and put them up on a barstool and measured them," Conor was saying now. "And one of them's penis was fifteen inches long, the biggest penis in County Clare, and he never used it until he was six years married! Big strong fella he was. He could pick up a huge bag of cement with his teeth."

James Rohan said, "And remember Jack Gurley could pick up two barrels of Guinness in each hand?"

Mick Pat said, "And Martin Gleason carried an anvil all the way from the garage to the grotto."

Conor began to tell a joke that involved a pretty zebra on a visit to a farm. The zebra went around the farm asking each animal what his job was. The dog told her it was his job to guard the farm; the hen told her it was her job to lay the eggs; the cow's job was to give milk; the cat's job was to catch mice; the pig's job was to get fat. When the zebra asked the stallion what his job was, the stallion answered, "Throw off them pajamas, darling, and I'll show you what me job is!"

Conor roared and roared at his own joke, slapping his thighs and sticking his fingers behind his glasses to wipe the tears of delight from his eyes. James Rohan sighed and pulled off his red woolen necktie and said in a tone of drunken exasperation, "Ah, Jesus, we're a sorry pack of fools, aren't we? You must think that about us, Rose. You must really think that."

Conor snatched the necktie out of Rohan's hand. "She does not think that, ya pup!" he snapped, winding the necktie loosely around his own neck. "Rose loves us. You *love* us, don't you, Rosie?"

Coming out from behind the bar with two more pints of Guinness for Conor and Mick Pat, Francis said softly, "Well, she might not love us, Conor, but she'll come back, and when she comes back, we'll be here."

Afterword

SINCE DECEMBER 1991, when I left Ireland, several things have happened there that are worth noting in the context of this book.

In early December 1992, Ireland had a three-part referendum on abortion. The electorate, by a two to one margin, voted down the main part of the referendum, which would have allowed for abortion in the Republic of Ireland under certain extreme circumstances—particularly in cases where the life, as distinct from the health, of the mother was threatened. It is important to note that pro-choice elements voted *against* this proposed change in the Constitution because they felt it did not go far enough toward relaxing the law. (The referendum stated specifically that the possibility of a pregnant woman committing suicide as a result of her pregnancy was not enough of a risk to warrant an abortion; this was a direct reference to the case of the fourteen-year-old girl who was finally permitted to travel to England for an abortion chiefly because she had threatened suicide if forced to carry the pregnancy to term.)

The reaction to this particular clause in the 1992 referendum was not surprising. What *was* surprising, however, was that in the same election 62 percent of the electorate voted in favor of allowing women to travel abroad for an abortion and 60 percent voted in favor of allowing abortion information to be distributed within the Republic. This was a marked change in the attitudes of the Irish electorate.

The December election also revealed changes in the general political climate in Ireland. Fianna Fail, then the parliamentary party, lost its majority for the first time in nearly twelve years, and there was an extraordinary demonstration of support for the decidedly more liberal Labour Party, the party that had put Mary Robinson up as a candidate during the presidential election of 1990. The number of women in the Irish government increased from 13 to 20 (although women are still only 12 percent of the 166 members of Parliament), and the first black member of Parliament was elected.

Recent polls show that most Irish people now favor some form of legal divorce. After the revelation in the spring of 1992 that Ireland's best-known bishop, Eamonn Casey, had fathered a child, 68 percent of the people said that they didn't care whether their priests were celibate or not. It is generally agreed that the Casey affair has done much to undermine the great moral authority the Catholic Church has enjoyed in Ireland.

It seems, then, no mere coincidence that the Irish singer Sinead O'Connor destroyed a photograph of Pope John Paul II in a live appearance on American television in the autumn of 1992. In a subsequent interview with *Time* magazine O'Connor voiced her views about the Church's influence on the Irish people. She said, "In Ireland we see our people are manifesting the highest incidence in Europe of child abuse. This is a direct result of the fact that they're not in contact with their history as Irish people and the fact that in the schools, the priests have been beating the shit out of children for years and sexually abusing them. This is the example that's been set for the people of Ireland. They have been controlled by the Church, the very people who authorized what was done to them, who gave permission for what was done to them." About destroying the photograph of the pope, O'Connor said, "I wanted to do it for Ireland because they [the Church] have done a terrible thing to us. They've made it so that Irish people can't seem to stand up for their own identity without it in some way being associated with the IRA, and I want to create another avenue for expression."

The reality in Ireland now is that things are changing. The birth rate—still the highest in Europe—is declining, more people are using contraception than ever before, and the number of births out of wedlock has risen from one in sixty ten years ago to one in ten. The results of the recent election and the responses to various social and political events demonstrate that the people of Ireland are indeed seeking a more liberal course for their society.

R.M.

JANUARY 1993